The Freshwater Fisherman's Bible

The Freshwater Fisherman's Bible

Third Edition

VLAD EVANOFF

Illustrated by the author

Doubleday

New York London Toronto Sydney Auckland

PUBLISHED BY DOUBLEDAY
a division of Bantam Doubleday Dell Publishing Group, Inc.
666 Fifth Avenue, New York, New York 10103

DOUBLEDAY and the portrayal of an anchor
with a dolphin are trademarks of Doubleday,
a division of Bantam Doubleday Dell
Publishing Group, Inc.

LIBRARY OF CONGRESS CATALOGING-IN-PUBLICATION DATA

Evanoff, Vlad.
  The freshwater fisherman's bible.
  Includes bibliographical references.
  1. Fishing. 2. Fishing—North America.
I. Title.
SH441.E856   1990   799.1′1′097   90–3192

ISBN 0-385-26223-X

BOOK DESIGN BY PATRICE FODERO

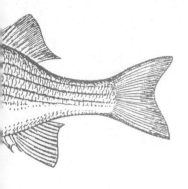

Contents

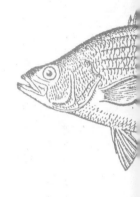

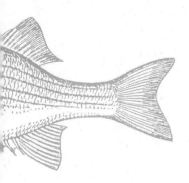

Chapter 1

Basic Freshwater Fishing Outfits

Many young anglers start fishing with a makeshift pole cut from a sapling or with a bamboo pole bought in their local hardware or tackle store. These bamboo poles, which run from 10 to 20 feet in length, are popular with hundreds of thousands of young and even adult anglers. Others prefer the more durable telescopic glass rods that can be extended to 20 feet. Both bamboo and glass rods, with several feet of line tied on the end, are suitable for still-fishing or even for casting lures or baits. Of course, these simple rods have certain disadvantages, the most important being their limited casting distance, and many anglers turn to more sophisticated tackle—a spinning, spincasting, baitcasting, or flycasting outfit. These enable an angler to cast farther and fish deeper; they also work lures better and offer more sport. In recent years, there have been many advances in rod design and materials. There is also a wide choice in lengths, actions, and handles. Many rods today are designed for specific fish, lures, and methods of fishing.

Fiberglass rods are being gradually replaced by graphite rods, which are lighter, stronger, and more sensitive. They are still more ex-

pensive than fiberglass rods, but prices have come down in recent years. Rods made from boron appeared on the market, but they proved expensive and heavy, and many rod makers discontinued using this material. The new forms of graphite with a higher modulus produce more powerful rods without adding weight or thickness.

Spinning Tackle

The spinning rod and reel is the most popular outfit today and is used by most freshwater anglers. The many different spinning outfits available enable an angler to handle almost any kind of freshwater fish. To simplify matters, we can divide freshwater spinning outfits into four groups: ultralight, light, medium, and heavy.

The ultralight rod ranges from about 4 to 6 feet in length. With this rod, you use an ultralight spinning reel filled with line testing from 2 to 4 pounds. The whole outfit—rod, reel, and line—weighs only a few ounces and is a pleasure to use. The ultralight spinning

1

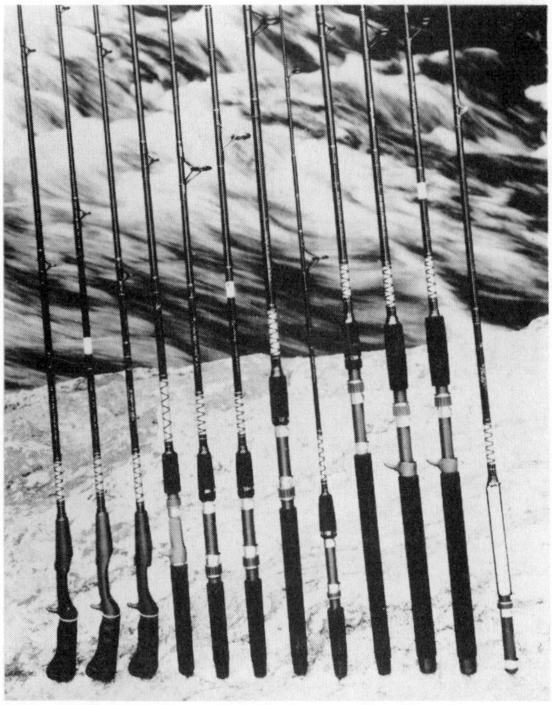

A sampling of the variety of specialized rods available to the modern angler. All are from the Eagle Claw Black Eagle graphite series. From left: three offset-handled rods designed to accept baitcasting or spincasting reels. Next, straight-handled rods for spinning or trolling. Last, a fly rod.

outfit is best for small fish, small waters, and lures weighing from 5⁄16 to 1⁄4 ounce. It is often a deadly outfit for wary game fish, such as trout and bass, in low, clear, heavily fished waters. And you can't find a better outfit for seeking the smaller panfish. However, for the freshwater angler who can afford only one spinning outfit, the ultralight rod is not the best one to get. It limits your fishing to small fish in open waters and to short casts with very small, light lures.

The light freshwater spinning outfit is more practical for fishing in most rivers and lakes. The rods, which range from 5 to 7 feet in length, are best for casting lures weighing from 1⁄8 to 1⁄2 ounce. You can use them with most freshwater spinning reels, but the smaller, lighter models will balance the rod better. Lines testing 4 or 6 pounds are usually used with a light spinning outfit.

The medium freshwater spinning rod is about 5½ to 7 feet in length. It has a stiffer action, especially at the butt end, and has the backbone to cast heavier lures long distances and to handle bigger fish. Lures from 3⁄8 to 1 ounce can be cast with this outfit. This includes most of the spinning lures made and most of the baitcasting lures that are too heavy to use with lighter spinning rods. This rod can be used with most spinning reels, and with lines testing from 6 to 10 pounds. The medium-weight spinning rod and reel is the nearest thing to an all-round outfit for freshwater fishing. It can be used for big trout, bass, walleyes, pickerel, small pike, steelhead, small catfish and carp. Yet it is still light enough for most panfish. If you can afford only one rod and reel outfit for freshwater fishing, the medium spinning outfit is the one to get.

Heavy freshwater spinning rods range from 6 to 9 feet in length. The shorter rods in this class may be cast with one hand, but the longer ones are cast with two hands. Many of these rods are made especially for handling big freshwater fish. But other rods in this class are really saltwater models. These heavy spinning rods should be used with big freshwater and small saltwater spinning reels, with lines testing anywhere from 10 to 25 pounds. They handle lures and sinkers weighing from about ½ ounce to 2 ounces.

Heavy spinning rods can be used for big black bass and for steelhead, salmon, lake trout, pike, muskellunge, big carp, sturgeon, gar, big catfish, and striped bass. They are most suited for big fish, big waters, strong currents, deep rivers, and for fishing in areas where there are weeds, logs, sunken trees, or rocks. They are made to cast heavy lures long distances and for fishing on the bottom with bait and heavy sinkers. Heavy spinning rods are also used for trolling but are not as suitable for this purpose as baitcasting or trolling rods with revolving-spool reels.

Open-faced fixed-spool spinning reels have been greatly improved since they were first introduced after World War II. Today you'll

Open-faced spinning reels are available in many sizes for all kinds of fishing. These are Browning Midas reels.

This is a closed-faced spincasting reel made by Johnson Fishing, Inc.

find a matching spinning reel for any rod and for almost every kind of freshwater fishing, and with so many special features available that it is difficult for a beginner to choose the reel he needs. For most fishing, choose a reel with a skirted spool, a smooth-working bail and roller guide, an antireverse mechanism, a smooth drag, and a gear ratio of around 4:1. Higher gear ratios make it possible to reel in lures faster.

Spincasting Tackle

Spincasting reels are popular with kids, beginners, and those who do not fish too often. These reels are similar to open-faced spinning reels in that their spools are stationary, but spools are covered rather than exposed. Most spincasting reels are mounted above the rod, but some are made to hang under the rod. In order to cast with them, you simply push a button or depress a lever, then release it to send the lure out to the target.

Spincasting reels are popular because they are almost foolproof, quite accurate, fast, and very easy to use. They also prevent coils of line from slipping off the reel—a problem with

open-faced spinning reels. All the working parts are inside the reel and are protected from dirt and sand. And with the new, improved models available, even expert anglers use the spincasters under certain conditions and especially when fishing at night.

Spincasting reels are now made in various sizes to handle lines testing anywhere from 4 to 20 pounds. The reels usually come prespooled with lines testing 6, 8, or 10 pounds. The average reel will hold anywhere from 80 to 150 yards of line. This is enough for most kinds of freshwater fishing for small or medium-sized fish.

The rods used with spincasting reels are similar to baitcasting rods, if the reel is mounted on *top* of the rod. For spincasting reels mounted *under* the rod, you can use regular spinning rods designed for open-faced reels.

If you are buying a first outfit for a youngster or even for yourself, you can't go wrong with a spincasting reel with a rod to match. For all-round fishing, get a medium-weight rod and a reel holding 8- or 10-pound-test line. This is suitable for many freshwater fish. With such an outfit, you can go out on any water and in a short time learn how to cast a lure or bait a sufficient distance. With regular practice, you will be able to cast accurately, too.

Baitcasting Tackle

Baitcasting rods and reels are used for many kinds of freshwater fishing. These rods can be divided into three classes: light, medium, and heavy. The light baitcasting rod runs from about 5 to 6 feet in length and has a limber action for casting light lures from ¼ to ½ ounce. It is used with a small baitcasting reel filled with 6- to 10-pound-test line. A light baitcasting rod is adequate for small or medium-sized fish such as trout, bass, pickerel, and panfish. It is used mostly in open waters with no vegetation or obstructions.

Medium baitcasting rods run from 5½ to 6½ feet in length and cast lures from ½ to ⅝ ounce. Since most baitcasting lures weigh around ⅝ ounce, the medium baitcasting rod is ideal for handling such lures. The baitcasting reel for this rod is filled with line testing from 10 to 17 pounds. This rod makes a good all-round outfit for catching bass, walleyes, big trout, carp, catfish, and the smaller pike and muskies.

Heavy baitcasting rods range from about 5½ to 7 feet in length and are made with enough backbone to cast heavy lures and manipulate them in the water. Many of these rods handle lures ranging from ⅝ to 2 ounces. The larger baitcasting reels used with this rod can be filled with lines testing from 15 to 25 pounds. This rod is best for fishing for larger game fish such as big black bass, steelhead, salmon, lake trout, striped bass, pike, and muskies. It can also be used for bottom fishing with fairly heavy sinkers for big catfish and carp, or some of the fish mentioned above. In addition to being a good trolling rod for many freshwater fish, the heavy baitcasting rod is also the most practical for fishing in strong currents, or in lakes or rivers filled with obstructions.

Baitcasting rods have either straight or off-set, pistol-type grips. Long, heavy rods have a long handle for casting with two hands.

The trend in recent years has been toward more functional, or specialized, rods suited for certain types of fishing or lures. There are rods made for flipping, jigging, or topwater fishing, for crankbaits, plastic worms, or spinnerbaits. And other special rods are made for fishing for crappies, walleyes, steelhead, muskies, salmon, or striped bass. The trend is also toward longer spinning and baitcasting rods—from 6 to 8 feet—for many kinds of fishing. And many anglers are using the so-called European rods, which are spinning rods up to 10 or even 12 feet long. These rods have a fast, limber tip, but the rest of the rod has plenty of backbone to handle fairly heavy lures or baits and fight big fish.

There have been many innovations and advances in baitcasting reels. Today these reels come with such features as magnetic cast controls, quick-changing drags and gear ratios, extra high-speed retrieves, and even minicomputers that let you know the distance you cast, how deep you are fishing, the rate of retrieve, and other data.

However, the main features to look for in a baitcasting reel are a free-spooling device, a smooth drag, a good antibacklash mechanism, and a lightweight body. Modern baitcasting reels are easier to cast with than older models, but they still require more skill and practice to use efficiently than do spinning or spincasting reels. If you're a young angler or beginner, you would do better to buy a spinning or spincasting reel with rod to match. Later on, if you feel you need a baitcasting outfit you can get one.

The modern baitcasting reel, such as this Shimano Bantam Super Speedmaster, has many features for easier casting.

Fishing Lines

When choosing a fishing line, expert anglers take into consideration such things as strength, or pound test; diameter; stretch; stiffness or limpness; visibility; color; and abrasion resistance. They choose a line to match a particular rod and reel, the lures they'll use, and the kind of fishing they plan to do.

For most reels, nylon or other monofilament and the newer copolymer and cofilament lines are best. When choosing such a line for a bait-casting reel, make sure that it is limp. Some anglers prefer braided Dacron lines for their baitcasting reels because they are limp and easier to cast. Lead-core lines and wire lines are used for deep trolling. You can't go wrong buying a top-quality line such as Trilene, TriMax, Stren, Prime, or Plion made by such companies as Berkley, DuPont, or Cortland.

Fly-Fishing Tackle

Many freshwater anglers feel that for the most sport and thrills, you can't beat a fly-fishing outfit. If you plan to do any trout or Atlantic salmon fishing, a fly rod is recommended. It is also being used more and more for such fish as bass, shad, steelhead, panfish, and even pike and striped bass.

Fly rods are available in various lengths, weights, and actions. Generally, the smaller the fish and the smaller the waters, the shorter and lighter the rod. For bigger fish and bigger waters, the longer and heavier the rod. Also, for casting big flies long distances or against strong winds, the heavier and longer rods are best. Not too long ago, very short rods of 6 feet or a bit longer were used by many anglers, but today the trend is toward longer rods.

Fly rods are now available in ultralight models from 6½ to 8 feet long and weighing only about 1½ to 2 ounces. Such rods are used with very light (No. 2 or 3) fly lines. The shorter rods in this class are used for fishing small streams for small trout where casts are

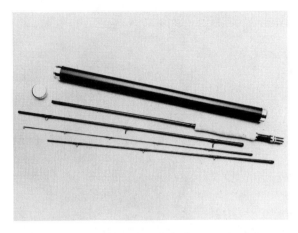

Fly rods come in different lengths, actions, and weights to suit the fish and the water. This rod is a Browning.

short. They also provide good sport when fishing for panfish.

Light fly rods come in lengths from 7½ to 9 feet to match No. 4 or 5 fly lines. Such rods are ideal for most trout fishing on small and medium-sized streams.

Medium-weight fly rods are made in lengths from 8 to 10 feet for use with No. 6 or 7 fly lines. Such rods can handle most of the flies, streamers, and small bugs used for trout, bass, pickerel, shad, landlocked salmon, and big panfish. If you can buy only one fly rod, this is the one to get.

Heavy fly rods range from 8½ to 12 feet in length and accept No. 8, 9, or 10 fly lines. Such rods are powerful and are used to make long casts on big waters for large freshwater fish. They are the best rods for casting big, bulky streamers, bucktails, and bass bugs. These rods are often used for Atlantic salmon, steelhead, coho and chinook salmon, pike, big bass, and striped bass in fresh water. They can also be used for fly fishing in salt water.

Fly reels to match these rods come in a wide variety of sizes and weights, and with good adjustable drags for fighting big fish that make long runs. Automatic fly reels that retrieve the fly line quickly and easily are preferred by a few anglers. But automatic fly reels are heavier, have less line capacity, and are not suitable

Fly reels are made in many different sizes for all kinds of fly rods and freshwater fishing. This is a Cortland single-action reel.

Fly lines are available in many weights and tapers to match all fly rods and most kinds of fishing.

for fighting big fish, so most expert anglers use a single-action fly reel. If you are going after big fish such as Atlantic salmon, coho or chinook salmon, steelhead, or striped bass, get a big single-action fly reel that can hold the fly line with anywhere from 100 to 200 yards of backing line.

The fly line you use with your fly rod will depend on the kind of fishing you will do. Today, lines come in so many sizes, weights, and colors, with different tapers and designs, that it can be very confusing to the beginner. Actually, you don't need many different fly lines. You can fish most waters and match most fishing conditions with only two or three. And you only need one reel to hold one line and extra spools to hold the others.

For casting dry flies, a double-tapered floating fly line is best. It tapers to a slim tip, enabling you to present a fly delicately without frightening the fish. Such a line is ideal for fishing small streams where long casts are not needed. A weight-forward line is tapered on the end and has a heavy thick section, then tapers again to a small-diameter level line. It comes in different sinking speeds—slow sinking, fast sinking, or extra-fast sinking—choice depending on the current and the depth being fished. A weight-forward line is a good all-

round fly line for fishing with nymphs, wet flies, and streamers. It can also be used to cast tiny bugs, spoons, spinners, jigs, and natural baits. This line can be used on most streams for most fish and on big rivers and lakes where long casts may be needed. There are also special fly lines made for casting big bugs, streamers, and lures long distances. They are called bass-bug fly lines, shooting-taper fly lines, and saltwater-taper fly lines.

A fly line should match the fly rod you are using. Most tackle manufacturers list the correct weight of the line to be used with their rods. Or ask your tackle dealer to recommend a fly line of the correct weight for a particular fly rod.

Many fishing tackle manufacturers today make special rods and reels for heavy-duty fishing, for such fish as coho and chinook salmon, lake trout, and striped bass. These are usually designed for deep trolling with or without downriggers. They are similar to rods and reels used for light saltwater fishing. In fact, many freshwater anglers buy saltwater rods and reels for such trolling. Other anglers buy light saltwater casting rods and reels for making long casts to big fish. Such saltwater trolling and casting rods are suitable for salmon,

Special heavy-duty reels are made for freshwater fishing. This Penn Graphite 320 GTi level-wind reel is rugged enough to handle lake trout, salmon, and striped bass.

lake trout, big catfish, sturgeon, and striped bass.

Before you buy any of the tackle described in this chapter, you should decide where you plan to fish most of the time and what kind of fish you expect to catch. Often you can obtain advice from a fishing-expert friend as to the best fishing outfit for your area. Most tackle dealers can also recommend a suitable outfit, if you tell them where you plan to fish, or you can write for the catalogs of tackle manufacturers, which will give you a lot of information about their rods and reels and the fishing these are designed for.

Many tackle companies also put together special kits containing rod, reel, and line that are balanced to work together. When you buy a rod and reel, avoid cheap models. They won't perform well or last long.

Freshwater anglers also need various accessories: boots or waders, vest or jacket, hat, fly boxes, tackle boxes, landing net or gaff, fish stringer or creel, bait bucket, knife, pliers, oil, reel grease, sunglasses, and insect repellent. And, of course, there are various kinds of fishing lures, baits, hooks, sinkers, rigs, and leaders, which will be covered in the following chapters.

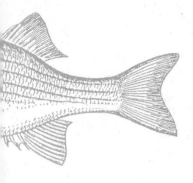

Chapter 2

Fishing Lures

Today, when an angler walks into a well-stocked fishing tackle store and examines the many lures on the racks, he often scratches his head in bewilderment. He may wonder which lures to buy or which lures are best for a certain fish. This chapter will discuss the wide variety of lures available to the modern angler. In the chapters on specific fish, we'll refer again to those lures and explain how best to fish them.

Most lures are designed to look like something good to eat from a fish's standpoint. They try to represent an insect, worm, crayfish, frog, minnow, small fish, or other creature that fish feed on. In recent years, more and more so-called natural lures have been created to represent the real thing as closely as possible. But other lures look like nothing on this earth and often come in gaudy colors; yet they catch plenty of fish. Whether fish mistake them for food or strike them out of curiosity or anger is not definitely known.

An expert angler who knows fish habits will often catch more and bigger fish on artificial lures than most anglers who use only natural baits. Such an angler knows when to use each lure for a certain kind of fish, which tackle to use with that lure, which water and depth it is designed for, and how to manipulate it to provoke a fish to strike. Today, most expert anglers carry a good assortment of lures to meet most fishing conditions.

Spinners

Spinners have been popular and effective lures for many years. A spinner has a straight wire shaft with a U-shaped clevis that holds a blade that rotates when the lure is moved through the water. The blade may be round, oval, long and narrow, or kidney-shaped. The shape of the blade determines how fast it turns and the angle at which it rotates. Blades come in different sizes, weights, and finishes. A silver, nickel, or chrome finish is the most popular, but gold, copper, brass, and painted finishes are also effective.

Spinners may be weighted for casting or trolling in deep water. There may be one, two, or as many as six or eight blades in tandem,

Spinners

and single, double, or treble hooks. Hooks may be dressed with feathers, hair, rubber, or plastic skirts, plastic worms, grubs, minnows, or other attractors. Some spinners are fished with natural baits.

For casting, the French type of spinner such as the Mepps is widely used. It has a short wire shaft and is weighted. It has a heavier blade than most spinners.

Weight-forward spinners have a keel-shaped weight in front of the blade. A single or treble hook behind the blade is dressed with hair, feathers, a plastic grub, or some kind of natural bait. Weight-forward spinners can be cast or trolled for many freshwater game fish, but are especially popular for trolling deep for walleyes.

Spinners come in a variety of sizes and weights, from less than 1 inch to several inches and from under ⅟₁₆ ounce to 1 ounce or more.

Small ones are used for panfish, trout, and small bass; the bigger ones for walleyes, pike, muskies, salmon, and lake trout.

Spinnerbaits

Another popular and highly effective lure is the spinnerbait. Instead of having a blade on a straight shaft, it has two V-shaped wire arms that resemble an open safety pin. The upper arm holds the spinner blades while the lower one has a lead head with a skirted hook. There can be one or two blades on the upper arm. Blades on spinnerbaits are similar to those on straight-line spinners. The hook usually is dressed with a skirt of feathers, hair, vinyl, live rubber, tinsel, Mylar, marabou, or plastic. Some spinnerbaits come without skirted hooks; instead, you can add pork rind, a plastic

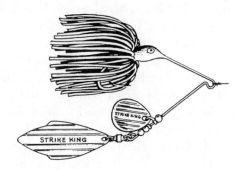

Spinnerbaits

worm or curlytail grub, plastic minnow, or natural bait.

Spinnerbaits are widely used for largemouth bass but will also take many other game fish. They come in weedless models and are highly effective when retrieved on or near the surface in heavy cover, but they can be fished at almost any depth.

Buzzbaits

Another lure that is similar to a spinner or spinnerbait is the buzzbait. Instead of using a regular spinner blade as an attractor, it has a propeller-type blade with two or three wings. There are two basic types of buzzbaits. One has a straight shaft similar to a regular spinner. The other has two wire arms; a short, straight upper arm to hold the propeller and a longer lower arm with a weight and hook on the end.

Buzzbaits come in different sizes and weights, and with different types of skirts. Some have weed guards.

Buzzbaits are used mostly for largemouth bass in heavy cover. They create a disturbance on top of the water that attracts bass from a distance. They also "buzz" or make a gurgling sound on top of the water, and fish may hear the lure before they see it. Buzzbaits are also good lures for pickerel, pike, and muskies. They work best in calm, shallow water during the spring and summer.

Spoons

Most anglers are familiar with the lures called spoons because that is what they originally looked like—a spoon with the handle cut off. But today spoons come in a wide variety of sizes, shapes, weights, materials, and finishes. They are usually stamped out of brass, copper, stainless steel, or other metal and are either polished, plated, or painted. The majority are silver, but gold, brass, copper, and painted spoons are also widely used. They can be painted or sprayed almost every color in the rainbow.

Most spoons are oval shaped and dished, but others are shaped like an S or curved in the front or rear. Other spoons are thick, heavy, and straight or slab shaped with little or no curve. These are used for making long casts or for vertical jigging. Some spoons have different outlines or shapes, many of them designed to imitate a minnow or small fish. Spoons have a wobbling or swaying or darting action with a lot of flash, which is attractive to many freshwater game fish.

Most spoons have a free-swinging hook or a fixed hook attached to the body. They may have a single, double, or treble hook on the end. The hooks may be plain or they may have feathers or hair tied around them. Some single-hooked spoons also have weed guards. These are often used with pork rind, pork chunk, or a pork frog, or with a plastic worm or curlytail grub on the hook.

Buzzbaits

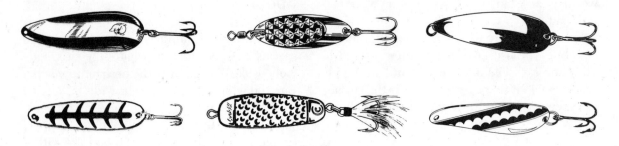

Spoons

Small spoons are used for panfish, trout, and small bass. Medium-weight spoons are good all-round lures for casting and trolling for such fish as big trout, bass, walleyes, pickerel, steelhead, small pike and muskies. The larger and heavier spoons are used for casting and trolling for big fish such as lake trout, pike, muskies, striped bass, and salmon. These are the standard spoons, but there are also special trolling spoons, often called flutter spoons, which may be up to 4 or 5 inches long but weigh only a fraction of an ounce. They have ultrathin bodies and are used for slow, deep trolling. They have a fluttering action that appeals to lake trout and salmon.

Plugs

Plugs are widely used for many freshwater fish. Made of balsa wood, hardwoods, or plastic, plugs have single, double, or treble hooks attached either singly or in series. They come in a wide variety of sizes, shapes, colors, weights, and actions. Plugs are designed to be fished on the surface or to dive underwater and travel at various depths; still others sink and swim at any depth an angler chooses. Plugs are made to imitate minnows, small fish, frogs, crayfish, mice, small birds, and other creatures.

Poppers and Chuggers.

Poppers and chuggers are surface plugs with a slanted, concave head, which, when jerked through the water, produces a popping or chugging sound. When reeled slowly, they create a wake or ripple. The commotion attracts fish from a distance. These plugs work best in shallow water near lily pads, weedlines, stumps, or other cover near shore. But they

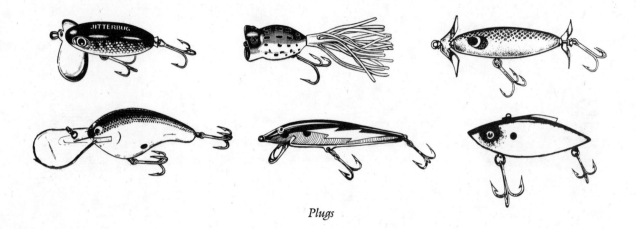

Plugs

can also be used when fish are feeding on shad minnows or other small fish in deep water. They are used for largemouth and smallmouth bass, white bass, striped bass, pike, and pickerel.

Propeller Plugs.

These surface plugs are also called sputter plugs. They have torpedo-shaped bodies with one or two small propellers on the ends. When reeled and jerked, they throw a small spray and look like a crippled minnow. Or they can be reeled slowly to create a wake. Either way, they attract bass, pickerel, pike, muskies, and striped bass.

Stickbaits.

These surface plugs look like cigars. Also called nodders, they have no built-in action and must be worked or activated by the angler to make them look alive. An erratic, swaying, side-to-side action, often called "walking the dog," is produced by rapidly moving the rod up and down. These plugs work best in fairly shallow water but will take largemouth bass and striped bass in deep water.

Crawlers and Gurglers.

These are surface plugs with extra-large lips or face plates or flapping wings that create a big commotion on the water. Because of this, they are good lures to use at night for largemouth bass. They will also catch pike and muskies.

Minnow Plugs.

These are light, slim plugs with small lips, designed to look and act like a minnow. Originally they were made of balsa wood and many still are, but now some are plastic. They have a lively swimming action that appeals to many fish. Most are shallow-running plugs, but some are designed to run deep. Floating minnow plugs can also be used on the surface if reeled very slowly and twitched at regular intervals to make them look like a crippled minnow struggling on top. They come in different sizes and are effective for big panfish, big trout, bass, walleyes, pickerel, pike, muskies, salmon, steelhead, and striped bass.

Crankbaits.

In recent years, crankbaits have become popular for many freshwater fish. These plugs are deep-divers or deep-runners. They usually have a short, thick, fat body and a big lip. They are usually reeled fairly fast and have a snappy wiggle that fish can't seem to resist. The size and angle of the big lip determines the depth at which the plug travels. Some are shallow-running, going down only 2 to 4 feet; others are designed to run as deep as 20 feet or more. Crankbaits can also be reeled slowly, and those that float can even be twitched on the surface, but they are basically underwater lures that are cast and reeled fairly fast to cover as much water as possible. Originally designed for largemouth bass, they can also be used for smallmouths, walleyes, pike, muskies, striped bass, lake trout, and salmon. The smaller ones will catch big panfish and trout.

Trolling Plugs.

Designed many years ago to catch Pacific salmon in salt water, these lures are now being used for salmon and other species in fresh water. These are big plugs with the head slanted at about a 45-degree angle. They usually come with two big treble hooks. Some trolling plugs have curved bodies with big lips. Trolling plugs come in different sizes and run at different depths, depending on how much line you have out and the speed of the boat. Without added weights, they usually don't go much below 30 feet. For deeper trolling, they are fished with weights, wire lines, planers, or on outriggers. Besides salmon, trolling plugs will also catch big bass, walleyes, pike, muskies, lake trout, and striped bass.

Trolling Plugs

Vibrating Plugs and Lures.

These are often called rattle plugs or sonic lures because they produce a high-frequency sound that attracts fish from a distance, especially in roiled or murky water. They usually have flat, oval bodies and often have fins to make them look like minnows or small fish. The fishing line is attached to an eye on the head or back. Some of these plugs have a hollow chamber filled with metal shot to produce a rattle. Other sound-producing lures are made of metal and look more like a spoon than a plug. And still others have a small body or a regular plug body and a small spinner attached to the rear. Most of these rattling or vibrating lures are made to sink and can be retrieved at various depths. They can be used for largemouth and smallmouth bass, walleyes, pike, and striped bass.

Jerkbaits.

These are the big boys of the plug world. Usually made of wood, they have wide heads and long, tapering bodies. Some of them also have metal tails. They have anywhere from two to four treble hooks along the body and may weigh up to 3 ounces or more. So it takes a heavy rod to cast and work them properly. They are called jerkbaits because after you cast them, they float with the head pointed down. Then they are jerked quickly so that they dive well below the surface, rise, are jerked again, rise, and so on during the entire retrieve. It is tiring, but the action simulates a crippled fish, which appeals to muskies. Although jerkbaits are used mostly for muskellunge, they can also be fished on the surface for pike and striped bass when these fish are feeding on top.

Jigs

Jigs were used by saltwater anglers long before freshwater anglers became aware of their deadly fish-catching qualities. But now the jig has become very popular for freshwater fishing and is considered one of the most versatile, all-round lures. A jig is simply a heavy metal head, usually formed of lead, with a hook molded into it. They are often called leadheads and come in different shapes and sizes, usually

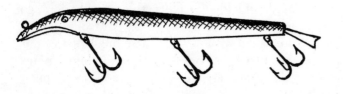

Jerk Baits

Jigs

with a dressing or skirt of hair, feathers, nylon, rubber, or plastic around the hook. Some jigs have no dressing or skirt. These can be fished with pork rind, pork chunk, pork frog, plastic worms, plastic minnows, or plastic curlytail grubs on the hook. Or you can add a live minnow, leech, or nightcrawler. Jigs may be plated with nickel or chrome or painted the same color as the skirt.

Jigs can be cast and retrieved, trolled, or jerked up and down vertically. Because the eye to which the fishing line is attached is on top of the lead head, jigs always ride with the hook facing up. This makes them highly effective for bouncing bottom where other lures would hang up. And because jigs sink fast, they perform well in fast currents when you want to get down deep to fish that are lying on or near the bottom. But jigs can also be retrieved at various depths—even just below the surface

when fish are schooling and chasing baitfish—by reeling or trolling fast. Jigs come in different sizes for almost every fish from panfish up to big pike and muskies. They are especially effective for largemouth bass and smallmouth bass, walleyes, and striped bass, but they will also catch trout and even catfish.

Plastic Worms

Most bass anglers agree that the plastic worm is one of the deadliest and most effective lures ever created. The plastic worm is a very versatile lure which can be fished in many ways at all depths and speeds—it can be cast, trolled, jigged, or just allowed to sink naturally. Plastic worms can be fished throughout the year. And since a plastic worm doesn't cost too much, it is often fished in heavy cover,

Plastic Worms

where there is the danger of hang-ups. If a plastic worm does get hung up and you lose it, you just reach for another one and continue fishing. More bass are caught day in and day out on plastic worms than on any other single lure or bait.

Plastic worms come in different sizes, from 2 inches up to 14 inches long. Most expert anglers like to carry worms from 4 to 8 inches long. They may also have a few worms going up to 12 inches to use in heavy cover for big bass. A 7-inch worm is a good all-round size to fish in most bass waters.

Early plastic worms were hard and designed to sink. Today, most bass anglers prefer soft floating worms since they have better action and feel more natural to a fish. Also, it's easier to set a hook that is buried in a soft worm. Soft floating worms rise above the bottom when fished with weights on the leader. A floating worm can be retrieved on the surface to create a wake like a surface lure's.

When it comes to colors, you'll find a wide variety of plastic worms to choose from. Most bass anglers like purple, grape, black, blue, and red worms, but yellow, green, and brown worms are also good at times. Two-toned worms with dark backs and light bellies, such as the shad type, are also highly effective. Other worms have dark bodies and lighter colored tails. Fluorescent "firetail" worms are widely used. Plastic worms also come impregnated with various flavors or scents that are supposed to attract fish. You can also buy different scents to dab on the worm.

There are special hooks made for rigging plastic worms. The size of the worm hook you use will depend on the size of the worm and the size of the fish you expect to catch. No.

1/0 or 2/0 hooks are used for small worms, No. 3/0 or 4/0 hooks are used for medium-sized worms, and No. 5/0 or 6/0 hooks for the biggest worms, used for going after big fish. You also need sliding bullet sinkers for rigging plastic worms for many fishing situations. These run from 1/8 ounce for shallow water up to 1/2 ounce or more for deep water.

There are many ways to rig plastic worms for varying fishing conditions and the fish being sought. When fishing in heavy cover or near the bottom, the barb of the hook is buried inside the worm. Other rigs employ a weight about 2 feet in front of the worm to take it down to the bottom but allow the worm to float high above any obstructions. One such rig is called the Carolina rig. Worms can be rigged with small corks or floats in front to make them stay on top and pop when retrieved, on a leadhead jig or behind a spinner, spoon, spinnerbait, or even a plug. Today plastic worms are used not only for bass, but also for trout, walleyes, pickerel, steelhead, pike, muskies, salmon, and striped bass.

Plastic Grubs

Grubs are also made from plastic and are similar to plastic worms, but they are usually shorter and have flat or curly tails. Although they can be fished alone, they are usually added to a jig head, spinner, spoon, or spinnerbait. They come in many colors and sizes, with white, yellow, and pink the most popular. When used on a jig, they can be cast and retrieved at various depths. But they are usually allowed to sink and are retrieved by bouncing them along the bottom. Grubs can also be low-

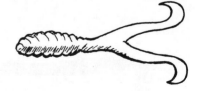

Plastic Grubs

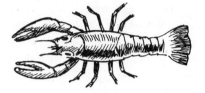

Other Plastic Lures

ered under the boat and jigged up and down vertically. Grubs come in various sizes for taking small and large fish.

Other Plastic Lures

Other plastic lures include the so-called tube lures, which are nothing more than soft, round, hollow plastic tubes with a skirt. They are usually used with jig heads, which are inserted inside, allowing only the eye on the jig to protrude. They come in various colors and sizes, from tiny 1½-inch tubes for panfish up to 5- or 6-inch tubes for larger fish.

Still other plastic lures, often called "naturals" or "lifelike lures," are made to imitate various creatures that fish eat—minnows, frogs, lizards, crayfish, etc.

Flies

Flies were originally created and tied for trout and Atlantic salmon, but today we have many flies that are used for panfish, bass, steelhead, coho and chinook salmon, pike, striped bass, shad, whitefish, and many saltwater fish. There are so many different patterns that it would take several volumes just to list and describe the flies created during the last hundred years.

Flies can be divided into dry flies, wet flies, nymphs, streamers, and bucktails. Flies can also be divided into two other classes: the imitations and the attractors. The imitations represent natural insects or other fish foods as closely as possible in shape, size, and color. The attractor flies are more bulky, often bright colored, and represent no particular creature.

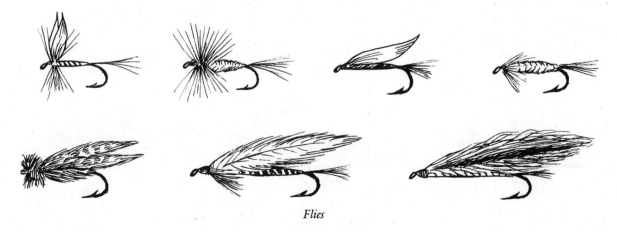

Flies

And although they are called "flies," not all such lures are made to represent insects. Some of them imitate worms, shrimp, tiny crayfish, frogs, eels, leeches, or minnows.

Dry flies are designed to float on top of the water. They are tied to represent various aquatic insects that have just hatched, are laying their eggs, or may have fallen on the water. Dry flies have long, stiff, glossy hackles and tails which support them on the surface of the water. They are tied on light wire hooks and daubed with fly dressing to help them stay afloat.

Wet flies are tied to be fished below the surface at various depths. They represent drowned insects or insects that have submerged to lay eggs. Fish may mistake them for hatching flies rising from the bottom of the stream or other kinds of underwater foods. Wet flies are tied on heavier hooks than dry flies and have soft hackles, which pulse and breathe in the water. They are usually tied sparsely with a minimum of hackle or feathers. The standard wet fly has one or two wings curved low over the body.

Nymphs are tied to represent the larval or pupal stages of aquatic insects that burrow in the mud, hide under stones or in weeds, and rise to the surface to hatch. The majority of nymphs found in streams and lakes are stoneflies, mayflies, dragonflies, and damselflies. The nymphs are generally drab olive-green, brown, gray, or black, with cream or yellowish bellies. Artificial nymphs are made from hair, feathers, fur, wool, yarn, floss, rubber, plastic, wire, and lead in different combinations. The best ones try to imitate a specific nymph, but some are composites which can be mistaken by fish for several kinds of nymphs. Nymphs are often weighted with wire or lead to make them sink faster.

There are also flies tied to represent land insects rather than aquatic, or water, insects. Called terrestrials, they imitate spiders, caterpillars, ants, bees, beetles, cicadas or locusts, grasshoppers, crickets, and other land insects.

Special salmon flies are tied to catch Atlantic salmon. Many standard wet and dry patterns used for trout will also take salmon. And many new patterns of salmon flies have been created in recent years. But the old tried-and-true salmon patterns continue to catch these fish.

Finally, we have the streamers and bucktails, which are called flies, but resemble minnows more than insects, and are used for trout and steelhead. They are usually tied on long-shanked hooks or two hooks in tandem. The name "bucktail" is given to those with wings of hair. The bodies are generally silver or gold, Mylar, or tinsel. The hair is white, yellow, brown, red, green, blue, black, or combinations of these colors. The name "streamer" is used to describe those having long feather wings. The body materials may be hair, silk, wool, chenille, peacock herl, tinsel, or plastic. Although most streamers and bucktails are made to sink, some are tied to float. In recent years, many new designs have appeared, created by innovative fly tiers.

Bass Bugs

Bass bugs are deadly lures for black bass, trout, and panfish. Bass bugs usually have bodies of cork, balsa, foam, plastic, or hair and wings and tails of feather or hair. The smaller panfish

Bass Bugs

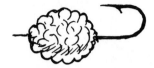  

Salmon Egg Imitations and Ice Fly

bugs often have soft plastic or rubber bodies and flexible rubber legs, and look like spiders. One of the most popular types is the popper, which has an angled or cupped head and a tail of feathers or hair. Another good bass bug is the hair frog. Other bass bugs are tied to resemble a minnow and have a pointed or bullet-shaped head, or are tied to imitate a moth, beetle, locust, or small mouse.

Other Flies and Lures

Finally, we should mention the lures that imitate salmon eggs. They are tied of chenille or other materials to represent a single egg or a cluster of eggs. These are used to catch trout, steelhead, and salmon. Then there are the tiny ice flies with small lead bodies and legs of hair, feathers, rubber, or plastic. These flies are often used with baits to catch panfish through the ice.

In the following chapters, we will recommend flies for specific fish. When it comes to choosing patterns, local preferences and conditions are usually taken into consideration. Any good tackle dealer in the area will tell you which ones produce best in the stream or lake you plan to fish.

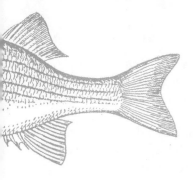

Chapter 3

Natural Baits

From the previous chapter, you might think that most of the fish caught in fresh water are taken on lures. But that is far from true—many fish are caught day in and day out on natural baits. That's because more anglers fishing in fresh water use natural baits than imitations.

There is a common belief among anglers who use artificial lures that fishing with natural baits is too easy and requires little skill or know-how. Actually, fishing natural baits often requires as much skill as fishing with artificial lures.

There is a tendency to get into a rut when using natural baits. Many anglers stick to one or two baits and rarely try other kinds or different ways of using them. But the most successful freshwater anglers know how to use a wide variety of baits, and they experiment with different ways of fishing them. In recent years, new baitfishing techniques have been developed, many of which will be covered in the following chapters on specific fish. In this chapter, we will cover almost all of the natural baits used in fresh water and tell you how to obtain them, how to keep them alive, and how to hook them.

But before you try to fish with bait, check your state and local fishing laws. Many states have laws governing catching or using baits.

Earthworms

Earthworms easily rank number one on the freshwater angler's bait list. For many fish, an earthworm is one of the best baits an angler can use. There are many species of earthworms found in this country, but three are usually used for fishing.

One is the common earthworm, also known as the garden worm, angleworm, garden hackle, or fishworm. It is found in the moist, fertile soil of gardens, fields, and woodlands. These worms can be dug up with a garden fork. Common earthworms average about 3 or 4 inches in length and may reach 5 or 6 inches.

Another worm used for bait is the manure worm, also called the fecal earthworm, stinkworm, or dung worm. This worm is widely distributed but is not now too readily available as it is found mostly in manure, stables, barn-

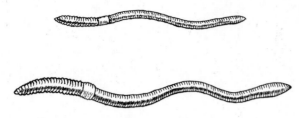

[*top*] *Common Earthworm*   [*bottom*] *Nightcrawler*

yards, and sewage. It has a bad odor and exudes a yellow liquid when handled or cut. But it makes a good bait even though it is only about 4 inches long. It can be dug in the places mentioned above.

The biggest worm used for bait is the nightcrawler, also called nightwalker, rainworm, or dewworm. It is usually found in the soil of gardens, lawns, parks, and golf courses. It averages about 6 inches in length but may reach 10 inches. It comes out at night, especially after a heavy rain, and can be caught by grabbing it near its hole and pulling steadily. But walk softly and do not shine a light directly on these worms, or they will disappear in a hurry.

There are also the commercial, or domesticated, worms which are bred in bins or pits in large numbers and sold to anglers or bait dealers. They are known as redworms, redwigglers, gray nightcrawlers, hybrid nightcrawlers, Canadian nightcrawlers, or African nightcrawlers. You can buy these worms at many tackle stores, from bait dealers, or by mail from worm farms. Look for bait dealers in the classified sections of such magazines as *Outdoor Life*, *Field & Stream*, and *Sports Afield*.

You can raise or keep earthworms in large wooden boxes, metal drums, or plastic containers filled with a bedding of soil, decayed leaves, rotted straw, compost, or manure mixed with soil. The container should be kept outdoors under some kind of cover to prevent rain from entering. Or it can be kept indoors in a cellar, garage, shed, or other cool spot. The worms can be fed cornmeal, chicken mash, bread crumbs, and similar foods; sprinkle these over the surface of the bedding. And

you should keep the soil moist, but don't add too much water, or the worms will drown.

When taking worms on a fishing trip, you can keep them in almost any kind of small container. Many special bait containers are available to hold worms. Be sure to keep your worm container out of the sun as much as possible.

There are many ways to hook worms. For trout and bass, run the hook through the middle of the worm once and let the barb protrude. Or bury the barb inside the worm when fishing around weeds or other obstructions. For panfish, use a small worm and run the point, barb and bend of the hook into the middle of the worm, leaving both ends free to wiggle. Or run the hook through the worm in three or four places along its body. Often two or three small worms can be impaled on one hook. For bullheads and catfish, a gob of several worms on one hook is effective. When drifting, casting, or slow-trolling a big nightcrawler along the bottom for bass or walleyes, just run the hook through the head. There are also tandem rigs on the market for hooking a big worm in two or three places.

Minnows

There are many kinds of minnows in streams and lakes that make great baits for many game fish. Most anglers call any small fish a minnow, but a true minnow belongs to the Family Cyprinidae, which includes the carp and goldfish, and even the squawfish and the white salmon, which may grow to 4 feet and weigh up to 80

Minnow

pounds. But most species of minnows used for bait range from 1 inch up to 10 inches in length. The most popular ones are chubs, shiners, dace, bluntnose and fathead minnows. Minnows are now raised commercially in many areas and can be bought from most tackle stores, bait dealers, or boat stations.

Many anglers prefer to catch their own minnows with a seine. Before using a seine, make sure it is legal. Most states have laws specifying where seining can be done as well as the size of the seine.

Another way to catch minnows is with a drop, or umbrella, net. There are many kinds on the market. The net is lowered into the water where minnows are present and then filled with soaked bread, crumbs, crackers, or oatmeal. When a few minnows swim over the net to feed on this food, it can be lifted quickly to capture them.

Minnows can also be caught in minnow traps. Most are made of wire, glass, or plastic. There are funnel entrances on the ends that allow the minnows to enter but not leave the trap. The traps are baited like drop nets and lowered to the bottom. A trap should be examined every few hours to gather any minnows inside and rebait the trap. If you use more than one trap, you can catch a good supply of minnows in a short time. Here again, it is best to check your state and local laws, which often regulate the size and number of traps and where they can be used.

Some of the larger minnows can be caught on hook and line using No. 16 or 18 hooks baited with bits of worm or a tiny doughball. The doughball bait is made by mixing some flour with water and kneading it into dough. You can also soak some white bread and form tiny doughballs. This is a slow method of obtaining minnows and is usually employed only when extra-large minnows are needed.

Minnows can be kept alive for long periods of time in large tanks or bait cages with running water, or suspended in a stream or lake. For short periods, when taking minnows on a fishing trip, you need a minnow bucket. There are many types of buckets on the market. Some have built-in pumps and aerators for providing oxygen and keeping the water cool. You can also keep minnows alive for relatively short periods of time in a strong plastic bag filled with cool water.

The size of the minnow used depends on the fish being sought. Minnows from 1½ to 2 inches long are good for panfish. For trout, minnows from 2 to 3 inches long are preferred. For bass, walleyes, pickerel, and small catfish, use minnows from 3 to 4 inches long. And for big bass, big walleyes, pike, muskies, lake trout, salmon, and striped bass, use minnows from 4 to 10 inches long.

There are many ways to hook a minnow. For still-fishing, a live minnow is usually hooked through the back, side, belly, or tail. For casting, drifting, or slow-trolling, a live minnow is hooked through both lips. A dead minnow can also be sewn on a hook to make it spin or wobble when retrieved. There are also many types of rigs on the market to hold a minnow in place. Sometimes minnows are used behind a spinner or impaled on the hook of a jig.

Other Baitfish

Other small fish besides minnows can be used for bait.

Different species of suckers occur in many waters. Some can reach up to 2 feet in length, but only the smaller ones—4 to 12 inches— can be fished alive. Larger ones can be cut into strips or chunks. Suckers can be caught in seines or by snagging with treble hooks. Small suckers from 4 to 8 inches can be used for lake trout and pike, bigger ones up to 12 inches for muskies, and small whole suckers or chunks from bigger ones for catfish.

Small bullheads and catfish from 3 to 10 inches in length can also serve for bait. Small catfish are found in creeks and rivers. They can be caught in shallow water by striking the flat stones under which they live with another

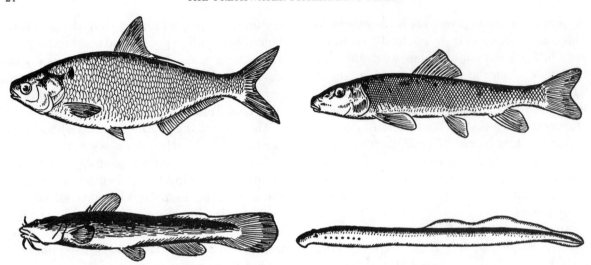

Other Baitfish [clockwise from top right] Sucker   Lamprey Eel   Stone Cat   Gizzard Shad

rock, to stun them, and then, when they are uncovered, scooping them up with a small dip net. Bullheads can be caught on a hook baited with worms or a small piece of fish. Small catfish and bullheads can be used as bait for black bass, especially smallmouths. Large bullheads are effective for pike, muskellunge, and big catfish.

Lampreys, often called lamprey eels, make good bait. They are found buried in the mud bottoms of streams and can be obtained by digging in shallow water and dumping the mud on the shore or in a bucket. They are a tough and slippery bait usually fished for walleyes on a bottom-walking rig or trolled behind a spinner. They are also effective for bass, striped bass, and sturgeon.

Members of the herring family such as the alewife, threadfin shad, gizzard shad, and blueback herring also make good baits. They are found in rivers entering the ocean and are also landlocked in some lakes and reservoirs. They can be caught with seines, cast nets, or on a hook and line with baits or tiny lures. They can be fished alive for bass, striped bass, lake trout, and other big game fish, or cut up and cast to striped bass and catfish.

Anglers also use such small fish as yellow perch, sunfish, and goldfish as bait for bass, walleyes, pike, muskies, and striped bass. But this can be done only in states and waters where it is legal, so check your local and state laws.

Other small baitfish include the common eel, darter, sculpin, smelt, mud minnow, mudsucker, and bowfin. Several kinds of killifishes found in fresh, brackish, and salt water make good baits for pickerel and bass.

Hellgrammites

The hellgrammite is the larval form of the big winged insect known as the dobsonfly and is highly prized as bait, especially for smallmouth bass. It is a long, dark brown or black creature with six legs and many other appendages, and a pair of pincers that can inflict a painful bite. Hellgrammites are found in the fast water of

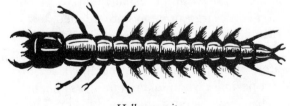

Hellgrammite

streams. They can be caught by turning over rocks upstream of a screen or net and kept alive for long periods in a container or bait box filled with damp, decayed leaves or moss.

The hellgrammite is a tough bait that will stay alive on a hook for a long time. You can often catch several fish on one bait. The best way to hook them is to run the hook under the hard collar just behind the head, or near the end of the tail. Besides smallmouth bass, you can also catch largemouth bass, walleyes, trout, sunfish, yellow perch, and rock bass on hellgrammites.

Other Water Insects

The dragonfly nymph, also called the perch bug or bass bug in various parts of the country, lives in the mud and vegetation on the bottom of ponds, lakes, and in quieter portions of streams and rivers. Nymphs can be obtained with a dip net dragged through the weeds or by digging up the debris on the bottom and can be fished on tiny hooks for trout, bass, yellow perch, bluegills and other panfish.

The mayfly nymph, another good bait, is often called wriggler or seahorse. Several kinds are found in streams and lakes, but only the largest are used for bait. They are obtained by scooping up bottom mud or silt. Mayfly nymphs are also found clinging to stones in riffles or rapids. They are fished on tiny hooks

for trout, bluegills, yellow perch, and crappies.

The stonefly nymph, which somewhat resembles the mayfly nymph, is found in fast-running streams. It clings to the undersides of stones and can be obtained by overturning them. Stonefly nymphs can be fished for trout, whitefish, and panfish.

The larva of the caddis fly, which is called a stickbait, stickworm, caddis worm, or caddis creeper, also makes a good bait. There are many kinds in the streams and lakes of this country. They build a case around themselves from tiny sticks, sand, leaves, and pebbles. They can be found crawling slowly along the bottom and can be picked up easily. To remove the worm, split open the case; then impale the worm on a tiny hook, or use two or three on one hook. They will catch trout, perch, bluegills, and other panfish.

Before you try to take any of the water insects from a stream, check your local and state laws. Some states have laws regulating the taking of water insects from trout streams.

Land Insects

Various kinds of grasshoppers found in gardens and fields can be used for bait. They can be caught by hand or with a small butterfly net. Keep them in a small wooden box with holes or in a can or a special bait container. Grass-

Other Water Insects
[clockwise from top right] Stonefly Mayfly Caddis Larva Dragonfly

Land Insects
[clockwise from top right] Cricket Cicada Caterpillar Grasshopper

hoppers are hooked under the collar or through the body and fished for trout, bass, bluegills and other panfish.

Crickets are also widely used for bait—mainly the large dark-brown field crickets found in grassy fields. They hide under flat stones, or stacks of hay, wheat, rye, or corn and can be caught by hand or with a small net. Crickets can also be raised in large numbers in big boxes or other containers. But most anglers today buy their crickets from commercial bait dealers or tackle stores. Crickets are delicate and soft and should be hooked under the collar with a small, fine-wire hook. Fish them for trout, bass, bluegills, and other panfish.

Caterpillars of various butterflies and moths make good baits. The big catalpa worm, which is the larva of the sphinx or hawk moth, reaches 3 inches and is found in catalpa trees. It can be used whole for bass or cut in half for panfish.

The European corn borer and the corn earworm, which are found in growing corn stalks or in the corn itself, can be used for bait—the large ones for bass or trout, the smaller ones for panfish. Hook them through the head or tie them around a hook with fine thread.

Cicadas, harvest flies, and seventeen-year locusts are sometimes used as bait for big trout, bass, and catfish. There are many species; some appear each year, but others only every so many years. They can be seen flying or landing on trees, fences, or bushes, and make a shrill sound. You can sneak up and grab them quickly.

Other land insects used for bait include mealworms, waxworms, gallworms, grubs, and even maggots and cockroaches. These can be fished for trout, small bass, and most panfish.

Crayfish

This small crustacean, which looks like a miniature lobster, is also called the crawfish, crawdad, craw, and crab. There are many species found in swamps, rivers, and lakes. During the day, they hide in the weeds, under stones, or

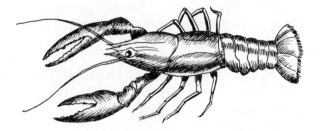

Crayfish

in holes. At night, they come out to feed and can be caught by hand or in small nets. During the daytime, you can turn over stones or drag a net through weeds to catch them. They can also be caught in special traps baited with fish or meat. Crayfish can be kept alive for short periods in a container filled with damp moss.

The best crayfish for bait are the soft-shelled ones that have cast off their hard coverings. But the hard-shelled ones can also be used if you break off the two big claws. A crayfish tail, peeled to expose the meat, also makes a good bait. Hook a hard-shelled crayfish through the tail, running the hook up from the bottom. Or wrap the hook against the body of the crayfish with thread or rubber bands. Crayfish will catch trout, bass, walleyes, and catfish. The meat from the tail section can be used for carp, bullheads, and panfish.

Frogs

There are many kinds of frogs, but the four usually used for bait are the pickerel frog, leopard frog, green frog, and small bullfrog. They can be caught in swamps, streams, lakes, and even in damp fields, by hand or with a net. They are active at night and can be caught by shining a flashlight on them and grabbing or netting them. Keep frogs in wet grass or leaves in a container or bait box. Frogs can be hooked through both lips or in the leg near the crotch. There are also special harnesses on the market to hook and hold them alive. Live frogs make a good bait for bass, pickerel, walleyes, pike, and muskellunge. Dead frogs can also be used for catfish.

Leech

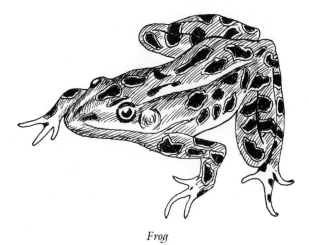

Frog

Salamanders and Newts

Salamanders and newts look like lizards but are amphibians, like frogs. Most are only a few inches long, but the hellbender and mudpuppy reach a foot or more in length. In recent years, the waterdog, which is the larval stage of the tiger salamander, has become a widely used bait. Salamanders and newts are found in springs, streams, and lakes or on land in moist, cool places. During the day, they hide under logs, rocks, or in moss and weeds. At night, they are more active and come out and can be caught by hand or in nets. They are tough baits and can be kept alive in a container lined with damp leaves or moss. Salamanders can be hooked through both jaws for casting, drifting, or trolling. For still-fishing, you can hook them through the base of the tail near the hind legs. You can also fish them on a jig. Salamanders will catch big trout, bass, walleyes, pike, muskies, and catfish.

Salamanders

Leeches

Leeches, also called bloodsuckers, look like worms but have sucking discs on each end of their body. Not all of them suck blood; some of them feed on tiny animals and plants. They can be caught in a trap baited with fresh meat or coagulated blood, or with a net or seine in the shallow water near shore of streams and lakes. If you wade in the water with bare legs and stir up the bottom mud, leeches will often attach themselves to your legs, and you can remove them. Leeches are tough, hardy baits and can be kept alive in almost any container filled with cool water. Leeches make good baits for big panfish, trout, bass, walleyes, and channel catfish. They can be hooked through the head and fished like nightcrawlers or behind a spinner or jig.

Prepared Baits

Salmon eggs are often used as bait for trout, steelhead, and salmon. Large eggs can be fished singly or in pairs, or you can tie a cluster of a dozen or more eggs on a hook with a leader loop or fine thread. Clusters of salmon eggs also are wrapped in maline or other fine netting around a treble hook, the points and barbs allowed to protrude. Salmon eggs can be bought in most tackle stores, packed in jars.

Some anglers use fresh eggs taken from a recently caught female steelhead or salmon. Before you use steelhead or salmon eggs, check your local and state laws. To protect trout and steelhead, some states prohibit the use of salmon eggs statewide or in certain waters.

Prepared baits made into round or pear-shaped "doughballs" are widely used to catch carp, buffalofish, catfish, and panfish. There

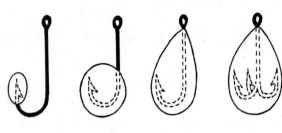

Doughball Baits

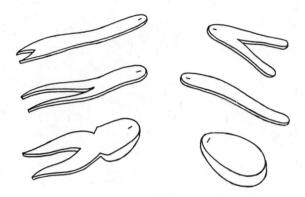

Pork Rind and Pork Chunk

are dozens of recipes, but the basic ingredients are flour, cornmeal, water, and some kind of sweetening or flavoring. You'll find a good recipe for making carp doughballs in Chapter 27. Similar doughball baits are used to catch catfish, but instead of flavoring them with sugar, honey, or gelatin as for carp, they are flavored with strong cheese, oil of anise, rotten eggs, or decayed meat or fish. If you don't want to make your own bait, there are many kinds of prepared baits for carp or catfish available on the market.

Many kinds of meat or congealed blood are also used for catfish. Congealed blood of fowl, cattle, or pigs can be used. Meat or small fish can be kept in a jar and allowed to decompose, or ripen, to make a stinkbait, which attracts catfish. You can buy many kinds of prepared stinkbaits in jars for going after catfish.

Pork Rind and Pork Chunk

Although these pork baits are usually fished like artificial lures or combined with them, they are really a natural bait. Strips of pork rind come in different sizes, dyed in different colors, to affix to most lures. But you can also use them alone, with a bit of weight added,

for pickerel, bass, and panfish. Pork chunks can be used alone or on a spoon with a weedless hook and cast among weeds for pickerel and largemouth bass. Or you can hook a pork chunk or a pork eel on a jig to make a "pig-and-jig" lure for big bass.

Other Baits

Other baits that are popular with anglers include: freshwater clams or mussels for carp, buffalo, catfish, and panfish; snails or slugs for trout, bass, and panfish; freshwater shrimp and small saltwater shrimp for trout, bass, white perch, and catfish; mice and small snakes for big bass; small common eels for black bass and striped bass; larger eels cut into sections for catfish.

Your supermarket carries many products that can be used for bait—for example, marshmallows for trout, carp, and panfish; various berries and fruits for carp and catfish. Most of these baits will be mentioned in the chapters dealing with specific fish.

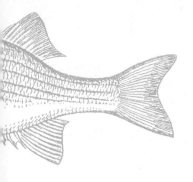

Chapter 4

Largemouth Bass

The largemouth bass is the most widely sought freshwater game fish in the United States. It is especially popular with expert and dedicated anglers who seek a challenging fish that is not too easily fooled.

Fortunately, however, most largemouth bass are also almost always hungry, curious, and pugnacious. If they don't strike a lure or bait because they are hungry, they may strike it because they are curious or angry. Time and again, anglers see bass that seem indifferent to all the lures cast to them. But by continuous casting and reeling past the noses of the fish, they finally succeed in teasing the bass into grabbing the lure. Spawning bass will also guard their homes and nests against all intruders, even if that means chasing and grabbing a bait or lure.

At one time, largemouth bass had a limited range: from southern Canada and Maine, through the Mississippi Valley to northern Mexico, the Gulf States, and Florida, and up

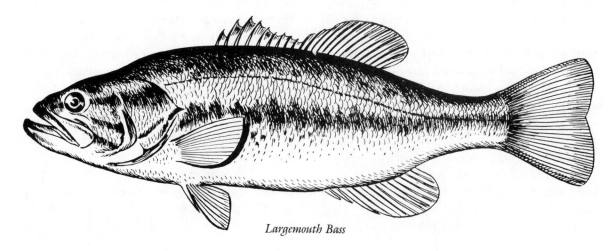

Largemouth Bass

along the East Coast. But extensive introductions have been made through the years, and now you'll find the largemouth bass in almost every state. Together with the bluegill and the catfishes, it has become one of the most commonly stocked fishes in farm ponds and reservoirs. One of the factors in its favor is that the largemouth bass is more adaptable to various waters and water temperatures than the smallmouth bass.

The largemouth bass is also called the bigmouth bass, green bass, green trout, lake bass, mossback, and linesides. Although there are several species of bass recognized by scientists, in this book we'll deal only with largemouth black bass, smallmouth black bass (Chapter 5), white bass (Chapter 21), and striped bass (Chapter 23).

Fishing for largemouth bass has grown tremendously in popularity in recent years. There have been improvements in the design of bass boats and motors, electronic depth finders and fish finders, and tackle. New techniques have been developed, and a great deal more has been learned about the behavior of the largemouth bass. So while the present-day bass angler is better equipped, more knowledgeable, and more highly skilled than his predecessors, he also faces more competition for fewer bass in many heavily fished waters. With more fishing pressure, you have to fish longer and harder to make a decent catch.

You can catch largemouths with a cane or glass pole, spincasting, spinning, baitcasting, or fly tackle, all of which were discussed in Chapter 1. Later in this chapter, we will mention suitable tackle for particular techniques and waters, and for certain lures or baits.

One of the best times to catch bass is in the early spring when the water first starts to warm up and before the fish are ready to spawn. The bass move into spawning areas in shallow water near shore. This usually occurs when the temperature reaches 55 degrees F. or more. They are hungry and will feed and hit lures and take baits.

Bass move on to their spawning beds when the water temperature goes over 60 degrees F. and spawning activity takes place when the temperature reaches around 65 degrees. Largemouth bass spawn as early as January, February, or March in Florida and other southern states and from April to June in more northern climes. If the fishing is open during these months, you can have excellent action on the spawning beds near shore. This is the best time to catch the big female "hawg" bass in the trophy class. Largemouth bass are aggressive at this time and are prone to strike at lures moving near them. But even if fishing is permitted during the spawning season, many anglers prefer to leave the big bass alone, or they keep or mount only one trophy-class fish and release the rest.

As the water warms and water temperature reaches the 70-degree range, bass begin to feed heavily. But as the sun gets bright and strong, they may seek cover or drop back into deeper water. How deep they will go varies according to the type of lake and condition of the water being fished as well as other factors such as preferred water temperature, oxygen content, bottom structure, and presence of food. The bass may return to shallow water at dusk, during the night, and around daybreak. But they may also move into shallow water during daylight hours, especially on overcast, cloudy, rainy days. Small bass are more apt to feed in shallow water than big bass. During the bright daylight hours, deep fishing will be the rule for big bass, especially during the hot summer months. However, night fishing can be very good in shallow water to moderate depths during the summer months, especially in heavily fished or very clear waters.

Then in the fall, as the water and weather cool again, largemouths return to shallow water near shore. September and October can be two delightful and productive fishing months.

In the North, not many anglers fish for largemouth bass during the winter months, but in our southern states, you can still catch bass from December through March, if you fish in deep water where bass are holed up. Of course, in Florida you can catch bass year-round, and winter fishing can be very good.

Locating Bass

The biggest problem confronting the largemouth bass angler is locating the fish. This is especially true if you are fishing a strange lake and are not familiar with the bottom structure, the depths, contours, and hotspots that have produced in the past. The best way to get this information in a hurry and enjoy good fishing is to go out with an angler who knows the waters or hire a fishing guide for a day or two.

If you are on your own, try to find out from the local marina operator, fishing-camp owner, tackle shop, or expert angler which part of the lake is producing. Get a topographic or hydrographic map of the lake you plan to fish, and study the contours and depths, points, coves, and dropoffs shown on it. If possible,

your boat should be equipped with a good electronic depth finder or fish locator to enable you to scan the bottom and know the depth you are fishing, and even pick up schools of baitfish and the bass themselves.

Largemouth bass are easiest to locate when they are in shallow water in the spring and fall, around daybreak, dusk, and during the night. In such shallow water, largemouths like to be under or near some kind of cover. They like shady spots under lily pads, hyacinths, weeds, brush, or overhanging trees, or else they lurk under or near driftwood, rocks, boulders, piers, docks, rafts, and bridges. Any kind of "stick-up," such as saw grass, cattails, reeds, brush, branches, or stumps, also attract them.

Points of land sloping into deeper water, and elevations, ridges, or ledges in shallow water (but close to deep water) are prime fishing spots. If these areas also contain brush, trees, or rocks, so much the better. The mouth of a stream entering a shallow cove is another hotspot. The running water brings food and cool

Standing timber attracts largemouth bass. This is the Toledo Bend Reservoir in western Louisiana.

water into the lake and attracts minnows and small fish, which in turn bring the bass.

Locating largemouth bass in deeper water is more difficult and requires a depth finder to read the bottom and determine the location of schools of fish. Try to pinpoint underwater structure, including channels, old creekbeds, old roads and depressions, elevations, submerged islands, and dropoffs leading to deeper water. Bass often gather along a sharp dropoff or weedbed. Look for rock walls or other deep structure in 15 to 20 feet of water, especially if they are next to a deeper channel. Along channels and riverbeds, the most productive spots are bends, culverts, old foundations, bridge supports, and dropoffs.

Individual bass and small schools of bass may be scattered throughout the lake, at different levels or depths. Bass also move around or migrate to their feeding areas from their resting areas. Most of these movements usually take place in the morning and evening, but at times the bass also move during the middle of the day. However, these movements are limited to a specific range, and bass in most waters move only short distances and for short periods of time. Big bass, especially, spend most of their time in deep water on or near the bottom.

Successful anglers usually don't spend too much time in one spot. They make a few casts and try different lures, but if they get no hits or catch no fish, they move on to the next spot. Expert fishermen, however, do spend many hours on a lake or river and make hundreds of casts during the day.

Bass pros also try to establish a pattern for the day; they try to find out the type of structure or cover the fish prefer, the best depth to fish, the best lure to use, and the action that produces hits or strikes. But they are also alert to conditions that will change the established pattern, such as time of day, moving fronts, wind shifts, waves, temperature changes, fishing activity of other anglers, boat traffic, and other factors that can affect fishing.

In rivers, look for largemouth bass along the edges of fast water where the current is broken and slower—pools, backwaters, coves, eddies, bends, points, bars, rock piles, and especially areas with mud bottoms covered with weeds and logs. Tailraces below dams also attract bass, as well as spillways in canals, especially when water is being released and there is a current. But here again, the bass will not be in the strong current or the main channel. They will seek the quieter water of eddies behind wing dams, boulders, rock piles, points, shoals, bars, and logjams.

In tidal rivers and creeks with brackish water, bass fishing is governed by the rising and falling tides. Bass move up on the flats and close to shorelines when the tide is high, then move back into the deeper pools when the tide falls. Here, too, bass avoid the strong tides and currents and are found behind anything that breaks or slows the current, such as weedbeds, shellfish bars, rock- and sandbars, brush, and logs. Other good spots to fish in tidal rivers and bays are near piers and old pilings.

Whether in shallow or deep water, bass are smart and wary. A sloppy or noisy approach will scare them away or at least alert them. Expert anglers usually cut their motors when nearing a fishing spot and row or drift quietly into the fishing area. Some use a quiet electric motor to reach the area. They try not to get so close that the fish can see them or the boat. Once in a good location, they make long casts from a sitting position, and refrain from banging tackle boxes, oars, or other objects against the boat.

Fishing Techniques

After you have located the bass, your biggest problem will be to discover which lure they want and how it should be presented to bring a strike. In the spring and fall, and at daybreak and toward dusk during the summer months, you can use a surface plug in shallow water—

a popper, chugger, crippled minnow, darter, or gurgler, which creates a commotion on top. Most of these plugs are supposed to imitate a crippled minnow or frog, so an action that duplicates the struggles of such food is best. Good examples of these surface plugs are the Jitterbug, Hula Popper, Devil's Horse, Zara Spook, Crazy Crawler, and Chugger Spook.

For best results, cast a surface plug right next to or into cover. Let it rest for a minute or so, twitch it, let it rest, then jerk and twitch it again. Keep doing this for several feet, then reel in and cast to the same spot or a bit to one side. Some surface plugs such as the Jitterbug can be retrieved slowly and steadily so that they roll, wobble, or crawl along the surface.

Many women like to fish for largemouth bass and become expert in catching big ones and winning bass tournaments. (DuPont Photo)

Other surface plugs such as the stickbaits or the crippled-minnow propeller types can be reeled faster or "walked" on top of the water in a zigzag fashion. They can be fished along shores or cover or out in deeper water when bass are schooled up and chasing shad minnows or other small fish near the surface. Surface plugs are also very good to use at night near shore.

Surface plugs are most effective when the water is warm, clear, and calm, with little or no wind, and on overcast and cloudy days. They work best in shallow water near cover where bass are waiting to ambush their prey.

Shallow-running underwater and minnow-type plugs such as the Rapala, Rebel, and Redfin are designed for shallow water. Some of these plugs run only a few inches to a couple of feet under the surface; others may go down a bit deeper. Slow reeling will keep them close to the surface; faster reeling will make them dive deeper. Most of these plugs have a built-in action—a wiggle, dart, or wobble—but you may also give them some added action by varying the speed of the retrieve at intervals and jerking the rod tip occasionally. Use them throughout the day and also at night. They are often better than surface plugs when the water is choppy or discolored.

Deep-running, diving, and sinking plugs are designed for water from 8 to 25 feet deep. The sinking types go down slowly to even deeper water but must be reeled in slowly to stay there. Some have no built-in action but must be jerked or twitched to provoke strikes. The so-called crankbaits, with big plastic lips that make them dive and wiggle in a lively manner at a certain depth, are effective. They are labeled as shallow runner, medium-shallow runner, medium runner, deep-diving, or extra-deep-diving.

Deep-diving and deep-running underwater plugs are most effective when bass are lying in sunken weedbeds, among logs, over submerged islands, humps, river channels, or rock piles, off rocky points and bars, along dropoffs in holes. Anchor or drift not too far from the chosen spot and cast well beyond it, then reel fairly fast to get your plug down to the structure or cover. The plug can be reeled in steadily if it has a built-in action. But if you are using a floating-type plug, try reeling fairly fast to get it down, then pause and let the plug rise a short distance. Reel fast again, pause, let it rise, and so on during the retrieve. Bass often hit the plug when it stops or as it starts to rise.

The vibrating, or rattle-type, plugs are especially good in roiled or murky water and at night. The sinking types can be allowed to sink to almost any depth before being retrieved. Most bass anglers retrieve them steadily to create a short, snappy wiggle or vibrating action. But they can also be reeled in in a stop-and-go fashion that often brings more strikes than a steady retrieve.

The lure that has really revolutionized largemouth bass fishing is the very popular plastic worm, which usually comes in sizes ranging from 3 inches to the 12-inch-long jumbo "snakes" used for big "hawg" bass. Some anglers in California use plastic worms up to 16 inches long to catch trophy-sized bass. But such big worms are only fished in waters where there *are* giant bass. It must be remembered that in most bass waters, you'll catch more fish

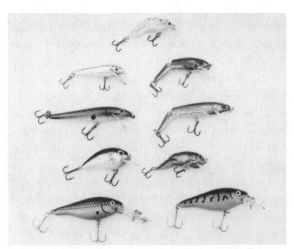

Largemouth bass will hit a wide variety of floating and diving plugs. These are Rebel lures.

of all sizes, including some big ones, on the smaller worms.

As explained in Chapter 2, a plastic worm can be rigged in various ways. For fishing in shallow water, it can be impaled on a single hook, the barb exposed or buried inside the worm. Or the worm can be rigged on a weedless hook. It can be rigged straight or given a curve to make it revolve slowly. Most worms are rigged straight, with the angler imparting action by lifting and lowering the rod. The weedless-type unweighted worm can be cast into heavy weeds or cover; after it sinks a few inches, it is retrieved slowly, or skimmed faster over lily pads or through pockets.

To fish the plastic worm deeper, you can add a clincher or rubber-core sinker a couple of feet above the worm. But the most popular rig for deep fishing is the Texas rig, in which a cone-shaped sinker slides against the worm and rests at its head. The hook is passed through the head of the worm and back into the body so the point and barb are buried inside. When fishing the Texas rig, allow the worm to sink to the bottom, give the rod tip a short jerk, reel in slack line, let the worm settle once more, reel in slack again, let it settle, etc. Try to keep the worm bumping bottom at all times so you will know that you are deep enough. Watch your line where it enters the water to detect a strike. If you get a pickup, lower your rod, reel in slack, and set the hook fast and hard. A stiff rod with a fairly sensitive tip, such as the special "worm" baitcasting rod, is best for deep fishing with plastic worms, but a spinning outfit is adequate.

There are other plastic lures that imitate crayfish, frogs, lizards, snakes, minnows, small fish, or various land and water insects that can be used for bass. Plastic frogs, lizards, and snakes can be retrieved on the surface to imitate the swimming action of these creatures. Plastic crayfish are weighted to get them down deep where they can be retrieved along the bottom. Plastic insects such as grasshoppers, crickets, caterpillars, and bugs can be retrieved on top or underwater.

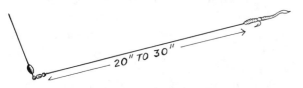

Rig for fishing a floating plastic worm

Another highly effective and versatile lure for largemouth bass is the jig. Formerly used mostly in saltwater angling, the jig has now become a standard lure for bass. The lead head on the jig is dressed with hair or feathers, nylon, rubber, or plastic. The jig heads with short plastic tails are very good. They come in various sizes and colors. The best sizes for bass weigh from 1/8 to 1/2 ounce.

When using jigs, you have to determine the depths you want to fish and the speed of the retrieve. Jigs can be reeled fairly fast, steadily or with short jerks, just below the surface when bass are schooled and chasing shad minnows or other baitfish. When used with a plastic worm or pork chunk and weedless hook, jigs can also be fished in shallow water and reeled fast so they skim on top and through lily pads or other weeds.

But jigs are most effective in deeper water, especially over heavy structure and cover. When fishing over such structure, cast and let the jig sink until it hits bottom, then raise and lower the rod tip. If you're right over the structure you can just lower the jig to the bottom or into the cover and then jig it up and down. Keep a sharp eye on your line; bass usually hit the jig as it is sinking.

Spoons are an old-time largemouth bass lure and are still very effective in many waters and on many occasions. Around lily pads and other weeds, use a silver, gold, copper, black, or purple spoon with a weedless hook and a strip of pork rind, pork chunk, plastic worm, or a rubber skirt on it. Cast right into the vegetation and pull the spoon along on top until it comes to an open pocket of water. Then let it sink a few inches, reel and jerk it until it comes up on the pads again. Be prepared for a jolting strike when the spoon drops off the pad.

You can also cast a plain spoon in shallow water near shore and let it sink, then retrieve it in a darting, stop-and-go fashion with an erratic action of the rod tip. When you see bass schooled up and chasing small fish, you can cast a plain spoon right into them and retrieve it fairly fast just below the surface.

Heavier spoons can be used for vertical jigging in much the same manner as described for jigs. This is especially effective during the hot summer months, when bass are very deep in the daytime, and also during the cold winter months, when they are schooled up in deep water. Some of the spoons used for such vertical jigging include the Hopkins Shorty, Kastmaster, Mann-O-Lure, Slab Spoon, Krocodile, and the heavier Dardevles.

Spinners are also old-time lures that are still effective for bass. In recent years, the weighted spinners with skirts of hair or feathers around a treble hook have become popular. The Mepps is a good example. Most of the time, a bass takes a spinner that is reeled steadily, but at times a stop-and-go action or erratic retrieve with some rod action is better. Spinners are good in murky water because they give off vibrations.

Another type of spinner used for bass is the buzzbait. It is most effective in shallow, calm, or murky water, or at night.

Spinnerbaits are also deadly lures for largemouth bass. When bass are in shallow water, you can fish the spinnerbait near the surface so the blades create a wake. At other times, you can reel the spinnerbait so it travels below the surface. In deep water, you can cast the spinnerbait and simply let it sink, or else you can jig it up and down as it sinks—bass often hit it on the way down. And finally, you can let the spinnerbait sink all the way to the bottom, then raise and lower your rod tip, reeling it in very slowly so the lure bumps the bottom every so often.

Flipping has become a popular and effective way to catch bass when they are in thick cover. For this you use a special, long flipping rod.

Pull some slack line from the reel, leaving about 6 feet hanging from the rod tip. Swing the lure toward you as you lower the rod, then raise the rod and flip the lure toward the target as you release the line and let it run through the guides to gain more distance. After you master the technique you can drop the lure into a small opening quietly and accurately. Plastic worms, jigs, or pig-and-jigs with weedless hooks are usually used for flipping, but you can try other lures and even natural baits.

More and more anglers are discovering the thrills of catching largemouth bass on a fly rod. You'll need a long, heavy fly rod capable of handling a bug-taper line. Bass bugs are great lures to use when the bass are in the shallows near shore. The bug should be worked very, very slowly, with long rests, pauses, short jerks, or twitches to imitate a beetle, moth, dragonfly, other insect, or a small frog struggling in the water. The bullet-shaped, minnow-type bugs (as well as big streamers and bucktails) can be retrieved faster to imitate a frantic minnow trying to escape.

When casting doesn't produce or when you want to locate bass in a strange lake, trolling is often effective. Underwater plugs, spoons, jigs, or plastic lures can be trolled at various depths and speeds until you find the fish. In the morning and evening, troll close to shore and along the edges of lily pads, over weedbeds, around rocky points, and over sandbars or rock bars. During the middle of the day, troll in deeper water over structure with lures that travel near the bottom or even bump it every so often. One of the best lures for this is the Spoonplug, designed by that great bass master Buck Perry. But you can also troll in deep water with crankbaits or other underwater plugs, spoons, or spinners. With light or shallow-running lures, you'll need weights or downriggers to get down to where the bass are lying.

A lot of bass are still caught on natural baits. Worms, either a big single nightcrawler or several smaller earthworms on a hook, make good baits. Frogs in the small or medium sizes are very good baits for big bass. Minnows of various kinds, from 3 to 5 inches for small bass and up to 6 inches for big bass are also effective in most waters. But in Florida and other waters where bass grow huge, anglers use shiners and small fish up to 10 inches. Suckers, small bullheads or catfish, gizzard shad, chubs, yellow perch, and killifish are all effective where legal. Largemouth bass have also been caught on hellgrammites, salamanders, leeches, crayfish, snakes, mice, crickets, grasshoppers, locusts, grubs, and caterpillars.

You can drift or slow-troll a minnow about 60 to 100 feet behind the boat, along lily pads, hyacinths, weedlines, or other cover. In deeper water, you can drift or slow-troll along the bottom with nightcrawlers, leeches, crayfish, or minnows. Anglers often use weighted bottom rigs such as the Lindy rig or the Gapen Bait-Walker rig.

Largemouth bass put up an exciting fight. They should be played carefully until they give up before you attempt to land them. You can lead the bass headfirst into a landing net or grab it by the lower lip. The latter method can be dangerous, however, if you're using a lure with treble hooks.

In most of our northern lakes, largemouth bass run from a pound to 3 or 4 pounds. A 5- or 6-pound bass is a big one in these waters. Farther south, especially in Florida, bass grow much bigger and lunkers are more numerous. In fact, in Florida a largemouth bass isn't con-

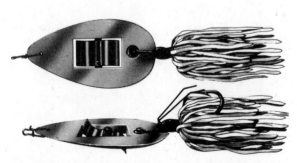

Weedless lures like this Bill Norman Weed Walker II are used to catch bass in heavy cover.

sidered big unless it goes over 10 pounds. Florida-strain bass have also been introduced into the waters of California, Alabama, Louisiana, Mississippi, Tennessee, and Texas. Some big ones close to the world record have already been caught in these waters. The world record on rod and reel is the 22-pound 4-ounce largemouth bass taken by George Perry in Montgomery Lake, Georgia, on June 2, 1932.

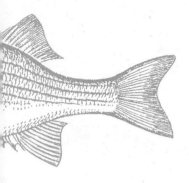

Chapter 5

Smallmouth Bass

Most anglers like to fish for both largemouth and smallmouth bass, but those who have caught both species agree that, when it comes to fighting, the smallmouth has a slight edge. This is especially true when you compare the smallmouth bass of fast, cold rivers to the largemouth bass of warm, muddy lakes. But even when both are found in the same waters, the smallmouth has that extra dash, speed, and stamina that make it the superior battler. And most anglers who have caught both species also agree that the smallmouth bass is harder to fool, more wary, fussy, and temperamental. In other words, these fish offer a real challenge even to the expert angler.

Unfortunately, not every angler gets an opportunity to fish for smallmouth bass, since their distribution is somewhat limited. These fish cannot stand very warm waters, nor do they thrive as well as the largemouth in small, still waters. Smallmouth bass like cool, clean, swift rivers and deep, cool, clear, rocky lakes. Such waters are not as numerous as the warm, muddy, weedy lakes that largemouth prefer. So, while smallmouth bass have been intro-duced into many of our states, there are still many areas in the South and West where they are scarce or nonexistent.

Originally, the smallmouth bass was found from southern Canada south to Alabama, Georgia, northern Mississippi, and Arkansas. But it has been introduced throughout New England, along most of the East Coast, and on the West Coast from California to British Columbia. Smallmouth bass have also been in-troduced into some of the reservoirs in our southern states, and some of the biggest small-mouths are now being caught there.

The smallmouth bass goes by a variety of names, including black perch, brown bass, ti-ger bass, swago bass, gold bass, redeye, bronze bass, and bronzeback. Smallmouths vary in color from a pale yellow to a dark brown, de-pending on where they live. Usually they are dull olive-gold with a bronze luster. The belly varies from creamy white to gray. The sides usually have dark bars, bands, and patches. The eye is bright red. The maxilla, or upper jaw, reaches only to the middle of the eye and not beyond it, as in the largemouth bass.

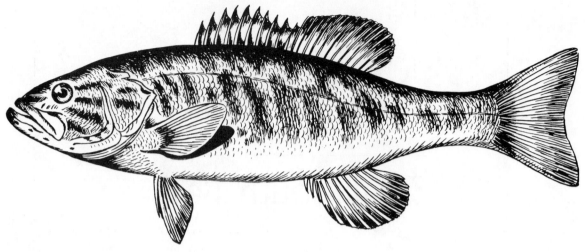

Smallmouth Bass

You can use the same fishing tackle for smallmouth bass as for largemouth bass. However, in most waters you can use somewhat lighter rods and lines to fool the smallmouth in the clear lakes and rivers where it is found.

The same is true of lures. Surface and underwater plugs, spoons, spinners, jigs, plastic worms, plastic grubs, plastic lures, bass bugs, streamers, flies, and pork rind will all catch smallmouth bass, but generally you'll find that the smaller and lighter lures are best.

Smallmouth bass also take many of the natural baits that appeal to largemouth bass. The favorites are worms, minnows, hellgrammites, crayfish, lampreys, salamanders, frogs, crickets, and grasshoppers.

The seasons for catching smallmouth bass are, of course, governed by regional laws. Smallmouths are protected in some states during the spawning season, but where fishing is allowed at this time, it can be out of this world. In southern states, smallmouth bass may be caught during the winter, but fishing usually doesn't begin there until March or April. Farther north, fishing doesn't start until May or June, when the bass in many areas are in shallow water on their spawning beds. June, especially, is considered a top month. Fishing in Canada and in some of our northern states

may be fair to good during July and August. September and October are usually excellent months for smallmouth bass fishing in many areas.

Early in the spring and fall and during the spawning season, smallmouth bass are found in waters ranging from 2 to 15 feet in depth. Even during the hot summer months, they'll often come in close to shore or into shallow water to feed (on minnows, crayfish, frogs, and various bugs and flies) at daybreak, dusk, and during the night. But in the middle of a summer day, smallmouths will be found in waters ranging from 15 to 30 or even 40 feet in depth, usually over structure, along cliffs and sharp dropoffs, over humps, underwater islands, and rock piles, and in the pools and holes in rivers. In Canada and our extreme northern states, smallmouths stay and feed in shallow water more often and for longer periods during the summer, even in the daytime, than in our southern states, where the water is warmer.

In rivers, smallmouth bass are usually found in fairly shallow water. In fact, in many of the smaller streams they haven't much choice because even the pools and eddies are not too deep. Look for river smallmouths in shallow water near shore in the spring and fall and during the spawning seasons. They'll be in

Positions of smallmouth bass around an island

spots flooded by rising water. Fairly deep water with plenty of big rocks and boulders scattered throughout is a good hiding and feeding spot for bass. They'll be found lying behind rocks and under ledges. When actually feeding, smallmouth bass often come into fast rapids, riffles, slicks, and runs, and into the shallow tails and heads of pools. At other times, particularly during the summer months, they lurk in deeper pools, eddies, and runs, or in the shade of a rock, log, ledge, or overhanging tree. Eddies bordering fast water or dropoffs into deeper water from the shallows are good spots. Tailraces below dams or rock jetties jutting into the river are also productive spots to fish. Here smallmouths are found lying close to the main channels and current rather than in the quiet water along the shoreline. And if there are any islands in the middle of the river, look for smallmouths lying along the shoreline. In the bend of a river, they often lie at the deeper side, under overhanging banks.

One of the best ways to fish a big river and locate smallmouth bass is by float fishing from a boat. Here you need two cars, leaving one where you will end the trip. Canoes, johnboats, and even inflatable craft can all be used to float a river. You drift with the current and cast your lure into likely spots. You can beach the boat occasionally and fish from shore or wade.

When a river is low, clear, and warm, wait for a shower or heavy rain to raise the water level, lower the temperature, discolor the water, and wash food into the river. Then bass often go on a feeding spree, and you'll have fast action.

In lakes, smallmouth bass prefer rocky shores, rock, sand, or gravel bottoms, offshore bars and reefs, and underwater islands. Look for shorelines where there are big rocks above or below the surface of the water. Also look for rocky points sloping into the lake. Here the deeper sides and the sharp dropoff on the end of the point are most productive. Sharp ledge rocks formed like steps are also good spots to fish. Smallmouth bass like shady spots, so look for them around brush, sunken tree trunks, bridges, and piers. In some lakes, smallmouths are also found feeding over sunken weedbeds or along weedy shores. Here they often feed on crayfish, minnows, and frogs. Inlets are also hotspots.

When fishing narrow streams, you should approach smallmouths carefully and quietly. These waters are usually shallow, clear, and confined—smallmouths are very spooky here and will take off at the slightest disturbance. So try to avoid wading if possible, keep low or hidden, and make your casts from shore. If you do have to wade, do it slowly without creating too much disturbance and watch where your shadow falls. The same is true when fishing from a boat in shallow water near the shores of big rivers or lakes. Move into a spot quietly and make long casts. When the water is clear and calm, light tackle with light lines and small lures or baits are best.

Because smallmouth bass are so spooky and are often found in clear water, the best fishing is often at daybreak, dusk, or at night. They often move closer to shore at night to feed in shallow water on crayfish or minnows. They are easier to fool at this time; some of the biggest smallies are caught between sunset and sunrise.

Lures and Baits

Plugs aren't used as often for smallmouths as for largemouths, but they can be effective on many occasions. In shallow water, when bass are feeding on minnows or frogs, a small surface plug—a popper or darter—can be deadly. The small, slim plugs with a single or double propeller are among the best. They should be cast near shore or where fish are seen breaking, and twitched in an erratic manner with short jerks and pauses to imitate a crippled minnow. Slim minnow-type plugs such as the Rapala and Rebel can also be fished on top. Do not work a surface plug too fast or too violently. Gentle twitches and jerks are best.

Small underwater plugs are often effective in lakes and rivers. Here the slim minnow-type plugs that float and dive are excellent. In shallow water, they can be worked on top in a snaky, swimming action. Or you can reel them faster so they dive and wiggle below the surface. They have a good built-in action, but sometimes added rod action or a stop-and-go retrieve will bring more strikes.

For deeper waters, deep-diving or sinking plugs are better. Crankbaits in the smaller sizes are often productive, especially the dark-colored ones (black, brown, or dirty green) and others that imitate crayfish. They can be retrieved at various depths in water from 5 to 20 feet deep. Retrieving them close to the bottom is often deadly. In fact, you can even let the plug dig into and stir up the bottom.

Small spoons also account for many smallmouth bass, especially in rivers. Cast upstream and across, let the spoon sink, then reel in fast, stop, lower the rod and let the spoon sink once more, then raise the rod and speed up your retrieve. This gives the spoon a tumbling, sinking-rising action that often brings strikes.

Spinners are old-time favorites for smallmouth bass, and they are still very good, especially the weighted types, such as the Mepps, with hair skirts around the treble hook. These can be fished in rivers and lakes at various depths. Retrieve them straight or give them action with the rod tip so they rise and fall in an enticing manner.

You can also use spinnerbaits. During the daytime and when fishing for smaller bass, use small spinnerbaits of ¼ or ⅜ ounce. When fishing for big smallmouth bass or at night, use larger spinnerbaits. Because they give off vibrations, they make especially good lures not only at night but also in roiled or murky water. Spinnerbaits can be fished in shallow water as well, worked near or even through cover. They should be fished just under the surface by holding the rod tip high and reeling fast to make the blades bulge the surface. Spinnerbaits can also be fished at various depths through schooled or suspended smallies or retrieved along the bottom, raising and lowering the rod at regular intervals.

The small tail-spinner lures such as Little George are highly effective when smallmouth bass are deep. Keep a tight line while the lure is sinking so you can set the hook if a fish hits it. If you get no hits on the way down, let it sink to the bottom and then retrieve it along the bottom with an up-and-down action of the rod tip.

Jigs are one of the prime smallmouth lures. They should be small and fairly short, with the feathers or hair not much longer than 3 inches, and should weigh from ⅛ to ⅜ ounce. The best jigs are those with black, brown, or gray bucktail hair or marabou feathers. Add a short strip of pork rind, a pork eel, or a piece of plastic worm on the hook to make the jig even more effective. You can also fish jigs with plastic grubs or curlytails on them.

Cast the jig upstream and across, and let the current swing it around and down deep where the bass are lying. Then retrieve it with short, gentle twitches of the rod tip. In quiet pools or in lakes, let the jig sink to the bottom, then reel it in steadily so that it crawls along the bottom like a crayfish. If a steady retrieve doesn't produce, let the jig hit the bottom, slowly move the rod up and to the side, then let it settle back to the bottom. You can also try shaking the rod as you lift the jig so that it quivers and pulsates and looks alive.

For big smallmouth bass, especially in southern reservoirs, fish larger, more heavily dressed jigs and add a pork eel, pork frog, or pork chunk on the hook. This jig-and-pig

Imitation crayfish lures, fished on a jig, are effective on summer nights. This is a Strike King Babe-E-Craw.

combo appeals to trophy smallies, which frequent the deep waters of the impoundments. A variation of this lure is to add a plastic lizard or plastic crayfish imitation on the hook. Such lures are especially effective when fished during the summer months at night. The best way is to swim them just off the bottom or bouncing bottom at regular intervals.

Smallmouth bass in deep water can also be caught by vertical jigging. Such lures as Little George and the Hopkins, Sonar, Kastmaster, Krocodile, and other heavy spoons—and even jigs—are productive. You have to try different techniques to get strikes. Some days, depending on their mood, the fish want the lure barely moved up and down. Other days, a vigorous upward sweep of the rod and quick drop are required.

Plastic worms catch smallmouth bass, but not as often as they do largemouths. They are usually more effective impaled on jigs or other lures than fished alone. Worms should be short—no longer than 6 inches. In fact, short plastic grubs and curlytail lures are usually better than longer plastic worms. If you do use long plastic worms, try rigging them on a tandem rig with one hook near the head and the other one near the tail. If you rig the worm with a hump or curve, it will have more action. Cast the worm into pockets, below rapids or riffles, or behind rocks and be prepared to set the hook quickly.

Flyrodders find that bass bugs, popping bugs, streamers, bucktails, wet flies, big nymphs, and, at times, dry flies are very effective for smallmouths. These usually work best in the early morning and in the evening when flies are hatching and bugs are flying. But bass bugs that imitate baitfish, or streamers and bucktails, are also good when smallies are feeding on minnows in the shallows or tails of pools. These should be cast and retrieved by stripping in line in short spurts in an erratic manner to simulate a frightened baitfish. When you see smallmouths rising for insects and making rings on the surface, cast to the disturbance with your bug or dry fly. Then twitch it several times so that it acts like a bug or fly on top of the water. When smallmouths are deep, you can still catch them on streamers, bucktails, wet flies, and big nymphs on a fast-sinking fly line. Buoyant flies are best because, while the line touches bottom, the fly will float higher and is less likely to foul on rocks, weeds, or logs.

Trolling is often very effective when smallmouth bass are in water from 6 to 20 feet deep. Fly rods should be equipped with sinking or lead-core lines. Streamers such as the Muddler, Gray Ghost, Black Ghost, Blacknose Dace, Mickey Finn, Nine-Three, or one of the marabous are effective. In rivers, you can troll very slowly against the current. In lakes, you can troll not too far from shore over structure. If you prefer spinning or baitcasting tackle, you can troll with underwater plugs, spinners, spoons, and jigs with the lines anywhere from 30 to 150 feet out behind the boat. For best results, the lures should travel close to the bottom. It requires some experimentation to find out which lures are best, the right speed to troll, and how much line to let out. In

Plastic worm rigged with two hooks

deeper water, you may also have to add a trolling weight about 3 or 4 feet in front of the lure to get it down near the bottom. And, of course, when trolling deep lakes, you can use outriggers to hold the lures at the depths at which smallmouths are lying.

Smallmouth bass are not always easy to catch with artificial lures, and there are times when natural baits are more effective. Nightcrawlers or garden worms are productive. Worms can be fished on a free line, under a float, or on the bottom.

Hellgrammites are a deadly bait for smallmouth bass, especially in streams and rivers where they are naturally found. Hook the hellgrammite under the collar and cast across and upstream, letting it drift freely through good holding water. Most of the time, you can fish without a sinker, but there are places (particularly fast currents) when you may have to add some split shot or a clincher sinker above the hook. Or you can fish in the deeper pools with a bottom rig and sinker and let the hellgrammite lie on the bottom.

In lakes and in the quiet pools of big rivers, you can also cast worms from a boat into shallow water near shore. Shady spots and cover such as rocks, logs, and overhanging branches are especially productive. Let the bail of your spinning reel remain open so the bait sinks naturally with plenty of slack line.

When smallmouth bass are deep in a lake you can drift or slow troll a single nightcrawler on a Lindy or other slip-sinker rig. Or you can use the Gapen Bait-Walker rig, which is less likely to snag. You should feel the sinker hit bottom and slide along it. Keep the bail on your spinning reel open (or on free spool with a baitcasting reel) and keep the line from running out with your finger. But when a bass picks up the worm, let out line and give the bass a chance to swallow the bait. Then set the hook. A live minnow or leech can be fished the same way.

While many smallmouth bass are caught from shore or by wading, you can cover more territory in a boat. (Arkansas Dept. of Parks Photo)

In the tailwaters of rivers in Alabama and Tennessee, big smallmouths are taken on minnows. Anglers anchor above a good spot, impale a shad minnow through both lips on a No. 1 or 2 hook, and let it out in the fast current. If the current is too fast, they add a couple of split-shot sinkers about 18 inches above the hook. Here again, the reel should be on free spool or with the bail open to allow the bass to take line when it picks up the minnow.

In lakes and deep pools, a similar minnow rig with a couple of split-shot sinkers or a clincher sinker can be cast, allowed to sink to the bottom, and retrieved slowly along the bottom. When you feel a pickup, give the bass some slack line so that it can swallow the minnow before you set the hook.

One of the best baits for smallmouth bass is a live crayfish. The soft-shelled variety is preferred, but it is hard to keep on a hook. You have to attach it to the hook with thread, rubberbands, or plastic tie. A hard-shelled crayfish can be used, but the two big claws must be removed. You then simply hook the crayfish through the tail.

In a lake or deep pool, one of the best ways to fish a crayfish is to add a split-shot sinker or two a couple of feet above the hook, then let the bait out from a drifting boat so it moves slowly and bumps bottom. Or you can cast the crayfish and let it sink deep, then retrieve it slowly with occasional twitches. During the summer months, use the crayfish in water from 10 to 30 feet deep along underwater points, reefs, bars, ledges, and submerged islands.

In streams and rivers cast your crayfish across and upstream and let it drift into good holding water. Here you usually don't need a sinker; if you cast well upstream of your target, the crayfish is heavy enough to sink, even in a current.

Small frogs also make good bait for smallmouth bass. Hook the frog through both lips with a No. 1/0 or 2/0 hook and cast it near shore around logs, weeds, rocks, and under overhanging bushes and trees. Let it swim around until a bass grabs it. In deeper water in lakes, or in deep pools in rivers, you can add some split shot or a clincher sinker on the line about 3 feet above the hook to take the frog into the depths. Here again, best results are obtained when fishing over structure. Salamanders, small lizards, or newts are also good bait and are fished in the same way.

Other effective smallmouth baits at times are live grasshoppers, crickets, and locusts. They can be hooked lightly with a small, fine-wire hook through the neck or body and cast on top of the water where they can kick around. If that fails, add a split shot or two on the line and let the bait sink slowly to various depths, even to the bottom.

A smallmouth on the end of a line in a fast river puts up a fight that will remind you of a big trout. It often makes a long, fast run or leaps out of the water, or bores down toward

Although not big, smallmouth bass this size put up a great fight on light tackle and make good eating afterward. (Mercury Marine Photo)

rocks or snags. In the deeper water of quiet pools or lakes, it may do most of its fighting below the surface, but even here it shows more speed, flash, and endurance than the largemouth bass.

Most smallmouths in rivers run from about ½ pound to 3 pounds in weight. They may average somewhat larger in lakes, but any fish going 4 or 5 pounds is a big one in northern waters. In southern waters, they may attain larger size because of the longer feeding and growing season and the abundance of shad minnows. The rod-and-reel record smallmouth bass, 11 pounds 15 ounces, was taken in Dale Hollow Lake on the Tennessee-Kentucky border by David L. Hayes in 1955.

Where to Go

Most southern lakes and reservoirs are usually better habitat for largemouths than for smallmouths. If you want good smallmouth fishing, you're better off in our northern states and Canada. Michigan has excellent smallmouth fishing in Lake Michigan and off the Les Cheneaux Islands in Lake Huron as well as in many other lakes and rivers. In Minnesota, Lac La Croix, the Mississippi River, and the Quetico-Superior wilderness (to name only a few of the state's bass waters) are noted for smallmouth bass. In Missouri, the Ozark region has many streams and impounded waters for fishing. In Ohio, the Maumee River and central Ohio streams such as the Big and Little Darby, Big Walnut, and Whetstone are good. Pennsylvania has Lake Erie, Allegheny Reservoir, Kinzau Bay, the Susquehanna River, and the Delaware River. New York has the St. Lawrence, Niagara, and Delaware rivers, Finger

Lakes, and many lakes and reservoirs in the Catskill Mountain region that contain smallmouth bass. In New England, the state of Maine ranks high for smallmouth bass, with such noted waters as Third Machias Lake, Big Lake, Scraggly Lake, Great Lakes Flowage, Spednic Lake, Pocomoonshine Lake, Crawford Lake, Meddybemps Lake, and the St. Croix River. The upper reaches of the Penobscot and Kennebec rivers are also good. New Hampshire has many lakes and rivers that contain smallmouth bass; among the best are Lake Winnipesaukee, Lake Wentworth, the Connecticut River, Lake Winnisquam, and Sunapee Lake. Vermont has the Connecticut, White, West, Williams, Black, Missisquoi, Lamoille, and Winooski rivers. Lake Champlain also contains smallmouth bass. Maryland has several reservoirs in addition to the popular Potomac River. In West Virginia, the Summerville Reservoir and such streams and rivers as the Greenbrier and New rivers, south branch of the Potomac, Shenandoah, Little Kanawha, Cacapon, and Ohio all contain smallmouth bass. Arkansas has the Buffalo and Beaver rivers. Kentucky has the Dale Hollow Reservoir, and Tennessee has Center Hill Reservoir, Woods Reservoir, and Norris Lake. Smallmouth bass in Alabama are concentrated in Pickwick Lake, Wilson Lake and Dam, Wheeler Lake, and the Tennessee River. There are also some smallmouth waters in California, Oregon, and Washington. And, finally, Canada offers some great smallmouth fishing, especially in Ontario, Quebec, and New Brunswick.

Of course, there are many more smallmouth rivers, lakes, and reservoirs in the states mentioned above. Write to the state tourist bureau or conservation department to find out which waters contain smallmouths.

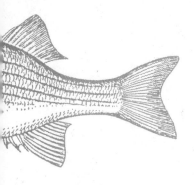

Chapter 6

Atlantic Salmon

Ask any expert freshwater angler which fish he considers the greatest game fish and chances are he'll say the Atlantic salmon. This big fish is esteemed by anglers not only in America but also in Europe and other parts of the world where it is found.

Through the centuries, the Atlantic salmon has been highly prized both for sport and food. In England, Scotland, and in this country, Atlantic salmon were once so plentiful that they were served to servants and workers nearly every week. Some complained if they had to eat salmon more than twice a week.

That, of course, was in the good old days when Atlantic salmon swarmed up coastal rivers as far south as the Connecticut River. But during the past century, Atlantic salmon have been depleted by commercial and sport fishing, pollution, dams, lumbering, and other conditions affecting our coastal rivers.

Today Atlantic salmon are found in the United States, Canada, the British Isles, Norway, Sweden, Finland, Iceland, France, and Spain. Salmon fishing can be expensive on most European rivers and on some rivers in Canada. You can pay up to several thousand dollars a week to fish a certain stretch of river,

not including the cost of a guide. After you add air fare or other transportation and lodging, it becomes obvious that this is not a poor man's sport. But in recent years more sections of salmon rivers in Canada have been acquired by the provinces and have been opened to public fishing. This brings the cost down quite a bit, and the average angler can usually afford a few days of fishing on a public salmon river. But such sections of a river are often crowded, and you may have to wait your turn to fish a productive stretch.

Because Atlantic salmon are so highly prized for food, they are caught commercially in many rivers throughout the world and on the high seas off Greenland. Even though they are protected in most of the rivers where they are found, poaching is still a problem, and many salmon are taken illegally. But in recent years, fish farms in Sweden, Norway, Scotland, and Canada have started raising Atlantic salmon for food. It is hoped that this will result in less pressure on the rivers where the wild salmon are found.

As almost everyone knows, Atlantic salmon ascend freshwater rivers to spawn after spending from one to six years in the ocean. Those

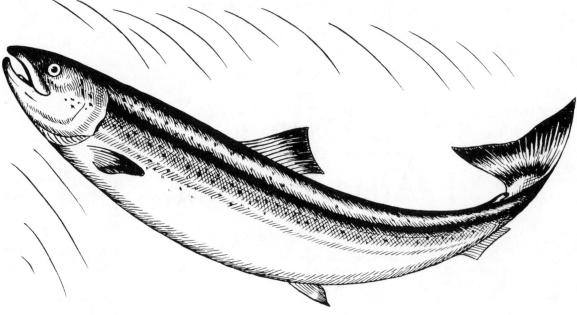

Atlantic Salmon

that return to the stream after one year in salt water are called grilse and range from 3 to 6 pounds in weight. The fish that spend two or three years in the sea are much larger when they return to spawn, sometimes reaching 30 pounds or more. The longer a salmon lives and feeds in the ocean, the heavier it will be. Atlantic salmon do not die after spawning as the Pacific salmon do, but may return to spawn again.

An Atlantic salmon just entering the fresh waters of a river is a handsome fish. It has a dark steel-blue back, silvery sides, and white belly. Small black spots may cover the back and sides. After spending some time in fresh water, the salmon loses its silvery hue, turning dull and reddish or gray. The spots grow larger toward spawning time. After spawning, the fish become even drabber and tend to lose weight. At this stage, they are called black salmon, or kelts. These spent fish are often caught in the spring on their way back to the ocean. But most expert anglers consider them inferior in fighting ability and endurance to the "bright" salmon fresh-run from the sea.

Tackle

Atlantic salmon are caught in this country and Canada mostly on fly tackle and can be taken only on fly rods in the United States. At one time, rods from 12 to 16 feet long and weighing up to 26 ounces were used. A few such rods are still being used in Europe, especially Norway, for big fish in fast, heavy waters. But now long fly rods can be made of graphite that are powerful and lighter than rods of bamboo or glass; and the trend in recent years has been toward shorter (8 to 10 feet) and lighter fly rods. Longer, heavier, more powerful rods are best for making long casts on big waters for big fish or for casting into strong winds. For dry-fly fishing on smaller rivers, shorter, lighter fly rods are adequate.

The single-action fly reel for salmon fishing should be bigger than most trout reels. There are now many fine fly reels made especially for salmon or saltwater fishing. The reel should hold your fly line with at least 150 to 200 yards of Dacron backing line testing around 20 pounds.

Atlantic salmon are found in broad, scenic rivers. These anglers are casting flies on a classic salmon stream in New Brunswick. (New Brunswick Dept. of Tourism)

Lines for salmon fishing are usually No. 8, 9, or 10 weight. A floating, weight-forward fly line is good for all-round salmon fishing and allows you to make long casts. For dry-fly fishing, some anglers prefer double-tapered lines. Still others like sinktip or sinking fly lines for wet flies. In rivers with strong, fast currents or deep pools, where salmon are lying deep, the sinking fly lines will get the fly down to where the fish can see it. These lines are also effective when the water is cold and salmon are sluggish and not inclined to rise or move far for a fly.

The traditional Atlantic salmon flies originated in England many years ago. They are heavily dressed wet flies made of many materials, often gaudy in color, difficult to tie and expensive to buy. They include such classics as the Jock Scott, Black Dose, Durham Ranger, Thunder and Lightning, Green Highlander, Silver Doctor, Blue Charm, Silver Wilkinson, Lady Amherst, Mar Lodge, and Dusty Miller. They are still used a lot in Europe, but in this country and Canada they have been largely replaced by the simpler, more subdued hairwing flies. Some of these patterns imitate the older classic flies, but many are new creations. They include such flies as the Black Bear Red Butt, Black Bear Green Butt, Green Groundhog, Cosseboom, Butterfly, Colburn Special, Rusty Rat, Silver Rat, Blue Rat, and the popular Muddler.

Wet-fly patterns in the larger sizes, from No. 3/0 down to No. 2, are used in the spring when the water is fast, high, and roily. Later on, Nos. 4, 6, and 8 can be used, the smallest being especially effective when the river is low and clear. Even trout flies in sizes 10, 12, and 14 have been used in low water during the hot summer months.

There are also times on certain rivers and under certain conditions when Atlantic salmon take streamers and bucktails. Such patterns as the Governor Aiken, Mickey Finn, Tri-Color, Thunder Creek, Gray Ghost, and Warden's Worry have all been successful.

You can also try nymphs when salmon are present in a river during low-water conditions. Favorite patterns include the Black Nymph, Brown Nymph, Gold Nymph, Leadwing Coachman Nymph, March Brown Nymph, and Olive Nymph.

There are also the so-called tube flies, which consist of a long, slim, hollow tube made of plastic or light metal and dressed with long strands of bucktail or polar bear hair with a treble hook at the tail end. They are popular in Europe, where fishing with treble hooks is allowed on many waters. Use of such hooks is not permitted when fishing for salmon in this country and on most Canadian rivers.

Tactics

The key to success in Atlantic salmon fishing is to time your fishing trip to coincide with the upstream runs of the fish. The exact day when this occurs varies from river to river and from year to year. It depends on many factors, such as the weather, water temperature, water level and flow, and time of year. Salmon like to move into rivers when they are high and the current is strong from recent rains. Then they move upstream fast, from pool to pool, often covering many miles in a short time. When the river is low, the salmon may not enter at all, but rather wait in the estuaries. Or they may move up to a deep pool or hole and wait there for the river to rise.

Good salmon fishing can be had as early as May on some rivers and as late as October on others. The spring run is usually the best, with May and June being two good months on many salmon rivers. During July and August, the fishing may be fair to good if the river isn't too low. September may be a good month on many rivers, especially when the fall rains raise the level of the water.

Once you are on a salmon river and have established that the fish are present, you still have to locate the spots where salmon are lying. Casting blindly, as is often done when fishing for trout, rarely pays off in salmon fishing. Expert anglers like to locate a fish first and actually see it or at least have an indication of its presence before they start casting.

Naturally, the natives of the area or anglers who have fished a certain river for many years have a big advantage. They have seen many fish or have caught them in certain spots and know where to look for them. That is why an angler fishing a certain river for the first time will get much quicker results if he hires a guide. Guides are familiar with the river, know the habits of the salmon, and know where they are lying under various water conditions. On certain rivers in Canada, you *must* hire a guide, especially if you fish from a boat. But even when fishing from shore, a guide can be a big help.

If you are on your own, you can try to locate a fish in shallow water ranging from 3 to 8 feet. It is usually best to concentrate on the pools, especially the swift, shallow pools rather than the deep, quiet ones. Look for rocks or boulders around which the current flows. The eddies behind or below such rocks will often hold salmon. Or they may be lying alongside a rock or boulder that splits the fast current. The areas around gravel bars, the tails of pools, and along the deep-cut banks and ledges are also productive spots. If a river forms a lake, look for salmon at the inlets and outlets. When the water is very high or very low, salmon will usually change their positions and hold in different spots than when the river is normal.

At times you can see salmon leaping or rolling on the surface. A high-leaping salmon is less likely to take your fly than one that barely shows its back or fins above the water. But whether salmon show at all, at least you know they are present, which means you won't waste time casting over empty water.

The basic method of presenting a wet fly to salmon is to cast across and downstream, al-

Classic Salmon Fly
Hairwing Salmon Fly

lowing the fly to swing in an arc. If you see the salmon or know which way it is facing, try to present the fly broadside. At the end of the drift, the fly is retrieved in short pulls against the current.

When fishing a long pool where the exact position of the fish is uncertain or where several fish may be lying scattered in different spots, start with short casts and then lengthen them to cover all the water. Then move to a new position 2 or 3 feet downstream and repeat the casts in a series of arcs to cover all the water.

As a general rule it is best for the wet fly to travel just below the surface. However, there are times in deeper pools or runs when it pays to let the fly sink and drift close to the bottom. This is especially true when the water is cold and big fish, which are more apt to take a fly that travels slow and deep, are present. Most of the time, let the fly drift naturally with little or no drag. You may have to raise or lower your rod tip to control the line. Or you may have to mend your line by rolling it upstream so that it makes a curve on the upstream side to enable the fly to drift without drag or an unnaturally fast swing.

The speed at which a fly travels is very important in salmon fishing. It has to be moved just right for a particular salmon to take it. Too slow or too fast and it doesn't interest the fish. And this correct speed can vary from day to day. Salmon usually do not move too far for a fly, and are more likely to take a fly that is only 2 or 3 feet in front of them. And they are more apt to take a fly the first time they see it. Sometimes, though, a salmon will follow a

fly and take it later during the swing or when it reaches the end of the drift. The smaller salmon or grilse will take a faster-moving fly than the slower-moving bigger salmon. If you can see the salmon, cast your fly and watch the fish's reactions. If it shows interest, keep casting.

Salmon often strike a fly that is retrieved rapidly just below the surface or is skated or skittered on top to create a small V-shaped wake. To do this, tie two half hitches behind the head of the fly and tighten so the fly is almost at a right angle to the leader. Then cast across and downstream and skate the fly on the surface just fast enough to leave a slight wake. Make short casts and hold the rod high so that most of the fly line is off the water.

During the summer months when the water is low, clear, and warm, salmon will often rise to a dry fly more readily than a wet one. Such patterns as the Ratfaced McDougall, McIntosh, Irresistible, Whiskers, Bomber, Curt Hill's Haystack, Elk-Hair Caddis, White Wulff, Gray Wulff, Royal Wulff, and the various skaters, bivisibles, and spiders. Many of the other standard trout flies can also be used. And in recent years, flies tied to imitate terrestrials—ants, bees, dragonflies, grasshoppers, and other bugs—have been used. The hooks used for dry flies should generally be small and light—Nos. 6, 8, and 10.

When fishing a dry fly, you can cast across and slightly upstream, well above the fish so that the fly drifts over it. Salmon aren't as frightened as trout at seeing an angler nearby. So you don't have to sneak up on them or use too long a line. However, it is wise not to get *too* close, or make unnecessary movements or create vibrations. Also, when entering a pool, make sure there are no salmon lying close to shore that will be frightened by your approach.

The dry fly should be fished without drag most of the time. But here again, there are times when you can deliberately skate a fly with a short twitch or pull to try to induce a strike. Salmon often rise and play with a dry fly. Some simply approach it, while others move it out of the water with their head. When this happens, keep casting and changing fly patterns, because your chances of hooking the fish at this time are excellent.

The thing to remember is that Atlantic salmon feed little if at all in fresh water, so they aren't too interested in your offering. With luck, you may get a strike early, after just a few casts—or you may have to make a hundred casts before a fish suddenly decides to take your fly. Of course, in rivers where salmon are fairly plentiful and you have many spots to fish, you don't have to make too many casts over the same fish. You can make, say, a couple of dozen casts with different flies and then move on. But in rivers where fish or productive fishing spots are scarce, you may have to spend a lot of time casting to one or two fish.

To increase your chances of catching salmon, it's a good idea to spend at least a week or more fishing a river. For a shorter trip, a guide or a knowledgeable local angler familiar with the river can lessen the odds. But since weather and water conditions play a big part, together with the number of salmon entering the river or holding in the pools, the timing of your trip is very important. Avoid the low-water summer months if possible, and plan your trip for the spring or fall.

Salmon are slower and more deliberate than trout about taking a fly. So don't react too fast when you see the fish rise or flash. Wait a second or two, until you feel the pressure of the fish, before you set the hook.

Once hooked, a salmon may make a long, fast run, leap high out of the water, or walk on its tail. Fight a salmon directly from the reel instead of holding the line as you would do when fighting a small trout. And keep a light drag on the reel in the beginning, to permit the fish to take line freely during its runs. Try to stay abreast of or below the fish at all times. If the fish takes off downstream, you will have to follow it until you come abreast of it again. Many big fish are lost in fast, shallow rapids when they tear off downstream and

Roger D'Errico, a fishing guide in Maine, is holding an Atlantic salmon he caught in the famous Bangor Salmon Pool on the Penobscot River. (Roger D'Errico Photo)

take all the line or break off altogether.

If there's a sandbar nearby, you can often beach the fish in shallow water and then pick it up under the gills. Landing nets are used by many guides, whether fishing from a boat or shore. A tailer that snares the fish around the tail by means of a wire noose is preferred by many salmon anglers. Gaffs are also used, but they may injure a fish that later escapes. And, of course, gaffs are not used if the salmon will be released. Some expert anglers and guides simply grab a salmon around the narrow part of the tail.

Most of the salmon you catch will range in weight from 3 to 20 pounds. Big salmon from 20 to 50 pounds are not too plentiful in most rivers these days. The largest ones are usually caught in Europe, especially in Norway. The rod-and-reel record is a 79-pound 2-ounce salmon caught in 1928 by Henrik Henriksen in the Tana River in Norway. One of the largest ever recorded weighed 103 pounds and was killed by Scottish poachers at the mouth of the Devon River in 1902.

Atlantic salmon make fine eating, but most anglers don't fish for them for their food value. Salmon are sought after because most freshwater anglers find them unpredictable and difficult to hook and land. They offer a challenge not provided by other freshwater fish.

Where to Go

In the United States, Atlantic salmon are found primarily in the state of Maine, in the Penobscot, Machias, Dennys, Narraguagus, Pleasant, Sheepscot, and Union rivers. The total catch of salmon in all the Maine rivers is improving but is not too high—less than one thousand fish are caught during the season. Since there are not too many spots to fish on each river, things can get crowded. Most of the salmon are caught by local anglers who spend a lot of time fishing.

Restoration projects of the Atlantic salmon are being made in other New England rivers, such as the Connecticut, Merrimack, Pemigewasset, and Westfield rivers. So far, the most successful of these has been the Connecticut River, where more and more salmon have been returning each year.

Atlantic salmon have also been stocked in rivers entering the Great Lakes, and fishing for them may develop in these waters in the future. They have also been stocked in some lakes in Oregon, such as Mud Lake and Hosmer Lake, where they have been caught in the past from boats.

In Canada, New Brunswick offers some of the best salmon fishing in North America.

There the famed Miramichi River system is the most productive. Other salmon rivers include the Cains, Dungarvon, Renous, Tobique, Upsalquitch, Tabusintac, Restigouche, Sevogle, Bartholomew, Hammond, Alma, Black, Jacquet, Bartibog, Big Tracadie, and St. John. In New Brunswick, most of the salmon waters are private or leased, but more and more stretches on certain rivers have been opened to the public in recent years. Nonresident anglers are required to hire a licensed guide to fish for salmon in New Brunswick.

Nova Scotia has over forty salmon rivers, all of them open to the public for the price of a fishing license. Such rivers as the Medway, Tangier, Gold, Margaree, Tusket, Moser, Wallace, Philip, French, Waugh, Stewiacke, Grand, and St. Mary's are best known.

In Quebec, not too long ago, all salmon waters were private or leased, but now there are more public waters. Atlantic salmon are found in such rivers as the Matane, Port-Daniel, Petite Cascapédia, Petit-Saguenay, Laval, Moisie, St.-Jean, Cap-Chat, Dartmouth, York, George, and Whale rivers.

In Newfoundland, most of the rivers are open to the public, and the best ones are the Humber, Grand Codroy, Little Codroy, Serpentine, Portland Creek, Placentia, Trepassey, Castors, Torrent, Highland, Exploits, and Gander. Most of the salmon caught in these rivers are the smaller grilse, which average about 5 pounds.

In Labrador, all the rivers are also open to the public, and the top waters are Sand Hill Creek, the Forteau, Pinware, Eagle, Hunt, and Adlatok rivers.

Elsewhere, Iceland has about sixty salmon rivers. Salmon do not run too big here but are plentiful in the Grimsa, Langa, Laxamyri, Hofsa, and Nordura rivers. There is also Atlantic salmon fishing in the British Isles, France, Spain, Norway, Finland, and Sweden.

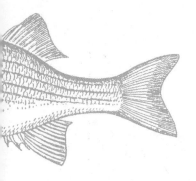

Chapter 7

Landlocked Salmon

Every spring, thousands of anglers in our New England states and in Canada eagerly await the cry "the ice is out." Then, regardless of the weather, which can be raw and cold in April, they converge on their favorite landlocked salmon lake and spend hours trolling or casting from small boats for one of their favorite fish.

The fish they are seeking—the landlocked salmon—is almost identical to the great Atlantic salmon, which runs up rivers from the sea to spawn. The main difference is that the landlocked salmon, as its name implies, is trapped in fresh water and doesn't migrate to the sea. Landlocked salmon are also smaller than the Atlantic salmon and never reach the weights of their seagoing relatives.

The landlocked salmon looks a lot like the Atlantic salmon except that it has larger eyes, longer fins, and double-X black spots on its back. Its back is blue-green, and there is a reddish tint over its silvery sides.

Landlocked salmon are also called Sebago salmon, Sebago trout, Schoodic salmon, lake salmon, and *ouananiche*. The last name comes from the parts of Canada where this salmon is found.

Landlocked salmon are most common in Maine, New Hampshire, Vermont, New York, and Canada. Originally they were found in only a few Maine lakes and rivers and in Lake Ontario, Lake Champlain, and in Canada. Then during the 1800s they were stocked in other Maine lakes and rivers and also in many of our states as far west as California and south to South Carolina. But these transplants were most successful in Maine, New Hampshire, Vermont, and New York. Landlocked salmon thrive best in cold, northern lakes that are fairly large, deep, and have tributary streams for spawning. And they should contain smelt or other forage fish on which landlocks feed. Landlocked salmon have also been introduced into some foreign countries, but with little success except in Argentina.

But no matter where you find them, landlocked salmon rate among the top freshwater game fish. They are fast, tough, spectacular fighters guaranteed to provide plenty of thrills. The landlocked salmon is also one of the largest

Landlocked Salmon

game fish taken in many waters, and it makes fine eating.

Tackle

Many anglers choose a fly rod for landlocked salmon fishing, usually a light- or medium-weight rod from 8 to 9 feet in length. It should be matched with a fairly large fly reel with a good drag and a capacity to hold 100 to 150 yards of backing line. Such a rod can be used for casting or trolling. For casting streamer flies, a weight-forward sinktip or sinking fly line is recommended. For fishing dry flies, of course, a double-tapered fly line is best. For trolling, a sinking fly line is good, but some anglers prefer a reel filled with 10- to 15-pound-test monofilament.

More and more landlocked salmon anglers are using spinning tackle for trolling and casting lures. A medium-weight freshwater spinning rod and a spinning reel filled with 8- or 10-pound-test line can be used for trolling or casting. A few anglers prefer baitcasting rods and reels for trolling or casting. For deep trolling with weights, somewhat heavier freshwater or light saltwater rods and reels are needed.

Streamers and bucktails, wet flies, nymphs, and dry flies are all effective for landlocks.

Streamers and bucktails for trolling are large (Nos. 4, 6, and 8) and are often tied on tandem hooks. The most popular and effective streamers and bucktails include the Black Ghost, Gray Ghost, Supervisor, Mickey Finn, Nine-Three, Silver Doctor, Highlander, Barnes Special, Brook Trout, Blacknosed Dace, Red-and-White Bucktail, Edson Light and Dark Tiger, Green Queen, Green King, Ballou Special, Joe's Smelt, and Warden's Worry. Marabou streamers with silver bodies or Mylar strips or tubing with white or yellow feathers can also be deadly.

Dry flies are called for when landlocks are feeding on top. The Gray Wulff, White Wulff, Green Drake, Black Gnat, Adams, Red Fox, Light Cahill, Quill Gordon, March Brown, as well as spiders and bivisibles, in sizes from 8 to 14, should be carried for this fishing.

When casting or trolling with spinning or baitcasting rods, you can use spoons such as the Little Cleo, Krocodile, Kastmaster Sidewinder, Dardevle, and Mooselook Wobbler. Weighted spinners are also good. In recent years, the slim, minnow-type plugs such as the Rapala and Rebel have proven very effective when trolled shallow or deep. The Flatfish is an old favorite for trolling.

Landlocked salmon are also caught on smelt, alewives, or minnows sewn on a single- or double-hook rig. The smelt is bent slightly so that it wobbles and flashes when trolled anywhere from 50 to 80 feet behind the boat. A light keel sinker is added a couple of feet ahead of the smelt to keep the line from twisting. You can also drift or slow-troll with a live smelt, alewife, or minnow by hooking it through the lips and then letting it out with a couple of split-shot sinkers or a small clincher or rubber-core sinker on the leader. Keep the reel in free spool or with the bail off so that when a landlock grabs the bait you can let some line flow off for a few seconds before setting the hook.

Seasonal Tactics

The best time of the year to catch landlocked salmon is, as stated earlier, just when the ice breaks up on a lake and for about two to six weeks after that. When the water temperature on the surface hovers between 45 and 55 degrees F. during the day, landlocks often go on a feeding spree. This may occur as early as April in New York and the southern part of Maine. But in the northern part of Maine and in most of Canada, you usually have to wait until May.

When smelt are moving into streams to spawn, landlocks congregate to feed on them at inlets, outlets, the mouths of feeder streams, and in the shallow water along shore. Later on, in late June, July, and August when the water warms, landlocks go into deeper water and are harder to locate and catch. In early fall, landlocks move into rivers to spawn, and good fishing can be had at times in shallow water at the mouths of the streams and in the rivers themselves if the season is still open at that time. In the extreme northern waters of Quebec, Labrador, and Newfoundland, landlocks often feed on top and in shallow water, even in the summer. And in southern Canada and in Maine, you can often have good fishing on top and in shallow water if you fish around daybreak and dusk.

When the season first opens and the ice breaks up on the lake, the weather is often raw and cold, and the water, rough. But good landlocked salmon fishing can be had on such wet, cold, windy days. In fact, most landlocked salmon anglers agree that rough water provides better fishing than calm water, since landlocks come to the surface when the water is rough and go down when the water is calm. You can also have better luck on calm days if you fish early in the morning and toward dusk. If the water is choppy or rough, you can often take salmon during the middle of the day. A dark, overcast day is usually better than a bright, sunny one.

As we have seen, landlocked salmon often congregate around the mouths of streams entering a lake. Troll for them there or along rocky shorelines, ledges, and sharp dropoffs. Rocky points, bars, and shoals extending well out into the lake and then dropping off into deeper water are also good spots. Landlocks tend to gather and feed on the side where the waves pile up. At other times, they may be scattered all over the lake and are even caught in the middle. Sometimes they can be seen chasing smelt or other small fish to the surface.

The most popular and effective method of catching landlocks is to troll streamer flies, spoons, spinners, or plugs. Usually two or three anglers share a boat. Two fly rods are placed in rod holders at each corner of the stern and a spinning or baitcasting rod in the middle. The streamers are trailed from 40 to 100 feet behind the boat, the lure about 20 to 30 feet. Landlocks are not boat-shy but rather seem to be attracted by the wake of a moving boat.

Tandem-hook streamer fly for trolling for landlocks.

In trolling, you will, of course, cover the hotspots where landlocks are believed to be present. Or you can follow the contour of the lake near shore. One man often casts toward shore from the moving boat. A landlocked salmon may follow his lure toward the boat, then see one of the lures on the other rods and grab it.

When the water is choppy, no rod action is necessary to obtain strikes. But when the water is calm or when the fish refuse to take a straight-trolled lure, you can impart some rod action to tease the fish into striking. Raising and lowering the rod tip is one way to do this. Another is to pull back and forth on the line to make the lure dart forward, then drop back. Usually a fast trolling speed of 4 to 5 miles per hour is best. But you can also vary the speed of the boat or even zigzag at an angle to see which maneuver brings the most strikes. Another trick is to troll two or three flies on the same line to see which one the landlocks hit.

Many expert anglers prefer to cast rather than troll in the early spring when the salmon are on top. They work the mouths of streams and the shorelines, casting streamers with a fly rod. Anglers with spinning or baitcasting tackle cast spoons, spinners, or underwater plugs. Your chances are increased if you can find landlocked salmon feeding on smelt and chasing them to the surface. Work your lure at different depths and try different retrieves. Later on, during the summer and early fall, dry flies, wet flies, and nymphs are productive. The best times to fish dry flies are early morning or evening when salmon are feeding on hatching insects. You can see rings on the surface as the fish rise to feed. At such times, cast your dry fly toward the rings and let it lie motionless for a second or two. Then give the fly some movement by skating it across the surface in short twitches or even short hops.

Some of the best fly fishing occurs when landlocked salmon enter rivers. Landlocks enter cool, well-aerated rivers even during the summer months. But the best fishing usually is in September, when they enter the rivers to spawn. Then a rising river fed by recent rains will bring them in, and good fishing can be had below falls, rapids, and dams. You can work flies in much the same manner as for trout, allowing them to drift through pools, pockets, and runs.

During the hot summer months, landlocked salmon go down deep and are caught mostly on live bait, either cast or trolled. For trolling you need lead-core or wire lines on fairly heavy tackle with a series of spinners, and baits such as smelt, minnows, or worms. Instead of bait, you can troll a small underwater plug or a spoon. Monel lines testing about 20 pounds are often let out anywhere from 60 to 200 feet to reach the ledges and spring holes preferred by the smelt and salmon. This means that the lure or bait has to reach anywhere from 30 to 150 feet down. Experiment with different trolling speeds, depths, and line lengths until you get a strike. Of course, if your boat is equipped with a depth finder or a fish finder, you can locate the bottom structure and even the baitfish and fish themselves. If your boat has downriggers, you can troll deep and still fish with light tackle to get the most sport with landlocks.

When hooked on top or near the surface, a landlocked salmon is a fast, flashy scrapper that hits a lure hard, runs, leaps, twists, circles, and dives all around the boat. Many fish are lost during the fight, or right at the boat itself. A big, wide-mouthed net is needed when boating a salmon, and even then, great care must be taken. The safest procedure is to fight the fish as long as possible, until it turns over on its side—then net it *head* first.

Landlocked salmon in most waters don't grow as big as Atlantic salmon. Usually they range from about 2 to 6 pounds. A 10- or 12-pound landlock is a big fish. The rod-and-reel record is a 22½-pound fish caught in Sebago Lake, Maine, on August 1, 1907, by Edward Blakely. There are records of big landlocked salmon, weighing up to 36 pounds, caught in weirs or nets. But such big fish are extremely

Al Raychard holds a beauty of a landlocked salmon taken by trolling along the edge of the ice in Lake Winnipesaukee, New Hampshire. (Bob Harris Photo)

rare in this country and even in Canada. The biggest landlocked salmon caught nowadays are found in Argentina, where fish over 15 pounds are fairly common, and a few going over 20 pounds have been caught on rod and reel.

Where to Go

In Maine, there are over two hundred lakes and rivers containing landlocked salmon. Some of the best waters include Sebago Lake, Moosehead Lake, Mooselookmeguntic Lake, Grand Lake, Big Lake, Pococumas Lake, Pleasant Lake, Dobsis Lake, Spednic Lake, Schoodic Lake, West Grand Lake, Green Lake, Eagle Lake, Square Lake, Lake Chesuncook, Rangeley Lakes, and Fish River chain of lakes, Moose River, Kennebec River, Union River, and the branches of the Penobscot River.

New Hampshire has landlocks in Lake Winnipesaukee, Sunapee Lake, Merrymeeting Lake, Big Dan Hole Pond, Big Squam Lake, Bow Lake, Newfound Lake, Ossipee Lake, Pleasant Lake, Silver Lake, the Connecticut chain of lakes, and some of the rivers entering these lakes.

Lakes in Vermont with landlocks are the Caspian, Willoughby, Big and Little Averill, Seymour, Memphremagog, Champlain, Dunmore, Crystal, Echo, Maidstone, East Long Pond, and Harveys.

Farther south, landlocked salmon have been stocked in the Quabbin Reservoir in Massachusetts. In New York State, they are found in Schroon Lake, Lake George, Lake Champlain, and the Bouquet, Saranac, and Oswego rivers. In Pennsylvania, landlocks have been stocked in Raystown Lake. They have also been stocked in Hosmer Lake in Oregon.

Landlocked salmon are found in Canada in New Brunswick, Ontario, Quebec, Labrador, and Newfoundland. Here the more remote northern areas provide the best fishing both in lakes and rivers, even during the summer months.

The landlocks stocked in Argentina have done very well in such rivers as the Traful. They have also been stocked in New Zealand, and there are various strains of landlocked salmon found in Norway, Sweden, Finland, and Russia. These grow bigger than our landlocks, reportedly up to 50 or even 60 pounds! Some salmon from Sweden were stocked in Lake Michigan in 1975 and a few have been caught weighing over 30 pounds. But in the following years, they died out and are rarely caught now.

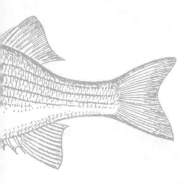

Chapter 8

Coho and Chinook Salmon

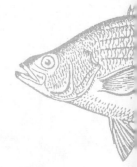

The introduction of the coho and chinook salmon into Lake Michigan and other waters is a success story in modern fish culture. An entirely new sport fishery has been created in the Great Lakes area and other waters. Today, vast armies of sport fishermen descend on these waters with one purpose in mind: to hook a big, wild, silvery coho or chinook salmon.

The amazing part of the whole story is that this fishery developed in only a few years— the first coho salmon were planted in 1966 in creeks and rivers entering Lake Michigan. The first chinook salmon were stocked in the same lake a year later. The results were almost immediate and quite surprising: Only ninety days after stocking, a 5-inch coho salmon had grown to 15 inches and weighed 1¼ pounds. In eighteen months, some of the salmon grew to 15 pounds!

Evidently both the coho and chinook found the deep, cold waters of Lake Michigan to their liking, and the abundance of alewives and smelt in the lake provided plenty of food for the new arrivals. Since then, coho and chinook

salmon have been stocked successfully in most of the other Great Lakes and in many other lakes, reservoirs, and impoundments in various parts of the country.

Neither the coho nor the chinook salmon are new fish; both have always been present in Pacific salt waters and are very popular game fish all along the West Coast of the United States and Canada. Actually, there are five species of Pacific salmon that ascend the rivers of the coastal states to spawn. With the exception of some fish caught in rivers during their spawning runs, until recently, most of these salmon were caught in salt water. But now, thanks to human intervention, coho and chinook salmon provide good fishing (until they die after spawning) in fresh waters throughout the country.

In recent years, salmon fishing in Lake Michigan has declined somewhat, and fewer and smaller fish are being caught. This has been blamed on the stocking of other species, which also feed on alewives and other baitfish, leaving less forage for the salmon. Disease, pollution, commercial fishing for other species

Coho Salmon   Chinook Salmon

and an increase in lampreys have also been blamed for the decline in salmon catches. Whatever the reason, steps are being taken by fishery biologists to improve the salmon fishing. There is still good fishing for coho and chinook salmon in the Great Lakes if you know when, where, and how to fish for them.

The coho salmon, also known as the silver salmon because of its predominantly silvery color, has black spots on its back and upper part of its tail. The interior of its mouth is usually gray or black, with whitish gums. The body of the coho is usually smaller and more slender than that of the chinook salmon, and the coho doesn't grow as big.

The chinook is also called the king, spring, and tyee salmon. It too has black spots on its back and on the top half of its tail, but the spots may also appear on the lower half of the tail and on the fins. The interior of its mouth is gray or black, with black gums. The body of the chinook is usually deeper than that of the coho salmon, and the chinook grows much bigger in size.

Coho and chinook salmon fishing varies with the seasons and with the water temperatures of a lake. In the southern part of Lake Michigan, off the shores of Illinois and Indiana, especially near Michigan City, the season starts in April as the water begins to warm up. This early fishing is usually close to shore and near river mouths. By May, the salmon start moving north along both shores of Lake Michigan, and a bit farther offshore into deeper water. During June and July, they move still farther out in the lake to colder and deeper

waters. By August and September, the salmon
are in the central part of Lake Michigan. Then
by October and November they reach the
northern part of the lake and start entering the
streams and rivers for spawning.

The key to locating salmon is water temperature. Their movements from shore and
from the surface to deep water will depend on
the thermocline—that is, the layer of water
whose temperature is most suited for the fish.
This layer will rise and drop depending on the
season, the weather, the wind, currents, and
the time of day. Both the coho and chinook
feed most actively when the water temperature is from 45 to 55 degrees F. An electronic thermometer is a big help in finding the
layer where the salmon are feeding. A depth
sounder or graph recorder also aids in locating
salmon, baitfish, and structure in the deep
waters of the lake.

Find the baitfish and you'll find the fish—
in this case coho and chinook salmon. And the
baitfish could be smelt, alewives, ciscoes, or
chubs. In recent years, salmon in Lake Michigan have been feeding more and more on
chubs rather than on the alewives, which are
not as plentiful as in former years. So the

salmon will follow the schools of baitfish wher-
ever they go. Since the baitfish are found in
different areas and depths throughout the season, you have to do a lot of searching to locate
them and the salmon following them.

Tackle and Tactics

In the spring of the year, when the salmon are
smaller and can be caught closer to shore and
near the surface, you can use light tackle. A
trolling or spinning rod from 7 to 9 feet long
is best. It should have a fairly limber tip; the
reel should be filled with 8- to-20-pound-test
line. The lighter lines can be used with spinning rods and reels, the heavier lines, with
baitcasting or light saltwater revolving-spool
reels. The most popular reel is a revolving-
spool, level-wind reel holding at least 200
yards of line. Most anglers trolling with downriggers use lines testing from 12 to 20 pounds.
Of course, lighter lines can be used for casting.
Most of the tackle designed for muskies, lake
trout, and striped bass can also be used for
salmon. Today many fishing tackle companies
make special trolling rods and reels for salmon
fishing.

Since in the early spring salmon are in shallow water, and in the upper levels in 30 or 40
feet of water, you can troll with little or no
weight on the line but can control the depth
by letting out line or using lures that run deep.
Occasionally you may have to add a light trolling weight or sinker to get down deeper. You
can let out anywhere from 50 to 250 feet of
line, depending on the lure used, the location
of the fish, boat speed, and water conditions.
As a general rule, you'll find the cohos feeding
closer to the surface and less boat-shy than the
chinooks. In fact, cohos will often rise to the
surface to feed on alewives or smelt. Chinooks
will stay deeper and farther away; they hit best
early in the morning and in the evening.

The lures used in spring for salmon tend to
be somewhat smaller than those used in summer and fall. Spoons, both freshwater and salt-

*Chinook salmon put up a good fight, especially on a light,
limber rod.* (Michigan Travel Commission Photo)

water types from 3 to 5 inches long, are productive in silver, gold, brass, and copper finishes. Fluorescent yellow, orange, pink, red, and light-green spoons are also effective. Popular spoons include the Andy Reeker, Alpena Diamond, Williams Wobbler, Westport Wobbler, Loco, Miller, Northern King, Dardevle, and Flutterspoon. Use the lighter, thinner spoons for trolling and the heavier ones for casting. Spoons must be trolled at the correct speed to bring out the right action.

Salmon also hit single-blade or tandem spinners. Plugs such as the Flatfish, Tadpolly, J-Plug, Rapala, Rebel, Redfin, Pikie Minnow, Dandy Glo, Lucky Louie, Hot Shot, and the various crankbaits are highly effective lures. Streamers and bucktails or coho flies with Mylar strips can also be fished. Some lures can be tied behind a series of spinners or other metal attractors called cowbells, dodgers, or flashers. You can also troll a sewn alewife, smelt, or minnow behind these rigs.

In recent years, a lure called the squid has become very popular and is deadly for catching salmon. This is a long plastic skirt with a pointed head rigged with a single or treble hook that is trolled behind a flasher or dodger.

During the summer months, when both coho and chinook salmon are down deep, trolling in depths from 50 to 150 feet may be required to reach the fish. First you have to locate the area in which the fish are present and then troll at the correct depth. With so many boats fishing for salmon these days, you can easily locate the fleet and join them. When going it alone, it can be difficult to locate salmon since they are often scattered in deep water, often 10 to 15 miles from shore. And they move around a lot, often averaging several miles a day and swimming as far as 20 miles on some days. So a good sonar unit is a must for deep-water salmon fishing.

Some anglers use various types of metal or plastic diving planers. When trolled, these dive and pull the lure down. When a fish is hooked, the planer releases the line, allowing the angler to fight the fish. There are also side

Multiple-spinner rigs are trolled in front of a lure or bait.

planers, which are attached ahead of the lure and angle the line and lure away from the boat 80 feet or more, enabling an angler to cover a lot of water. A line with planer and lure is less apt to frighten salmon than a boat moving over them, especially when they are in fairly shallow water or feeding near the surface.

All serious salmon anglers, fishing guides, and charter-boat captains today depend on downriggers on their boats to reach the depths where salmon swim and feed. Downriggers are superior to other methods because you can locate and control the depth at which the lure or bait travels. The fishing line can be let out to troll a lure or bait anywhere from a few feet to 200 feet or more behind the boat at any depth you want. The line is released from a heavy weight when a fish takes the lure. Lighter tackle can be used when fishing with downriggers than with the other methods requiring weights for deep-water trolling.

There are many different kinds of downriggers on the market. Most smaller boats can accommodate two downriggers; bigger boats, four—two with short arms and two with longer arms to spread the lines. In addition to downriggers, you can use side planers, outriggers, and even flat lines. Extra lines can be run out from the side planers or stacked one above the other on the downriggers. The combinations and number of lines are endless and are up to an angler's ingenuity and skill.

When salmon are deep, you can also try drifting in a boat and jigging vertically at the depth where fish are located or believed to be feeding. The lure is worked up and down and allowed to flutter in an erratic manner. Such lures as the Hopkins, Krocodile, Kastmaster, Mr. Champ, Slab Spoon, and the thicker Dardevles can be used for jigging.

When the salmon are in shallow water near shore in the early spring and again in the fall, they can often be caught from shore, from breakwaters, jetties, or piers. A long, light, saltwater surf rod can be used to cast heavy spoons, spinners, and plugs.

When Great Lakes coho and chinook salmon start moving in the fall, into shallow water near shore at the mouths of streams and rivers prior to entering them for spawning, they can be caught by shallow-water trolling or by casting from boats and shore. You'll often see the fish concentrated around the stream outlets and "porpoising," or showing on the surface.

Once the coho and chinook enter a stream or river for spawning, they stop feeding but will still hit a lure or take a bait. These are big, mature fish that can be caught during October and November in the upper reaches of streams and rivers in very shallow water. Look for individual fish lying in the water or on the spawning beds and wade quietly below the fish until you are within casting distance. It is also possible to approach a fish from upstream until you can reach it with a cast.

Most anglers use spinning or baitcasting tackle for cohos or chinooks in rivers. They'll take spinners, spoons, plugs, or jigs; also salmon or steelhead eggs, and worms. Other anglers use a fairly heavy fly rod, 8 to 10 feet long, with a No. 9 or 10 fly line, and an 8- or 10-pound-test tippet on their leader. They cast gaudy steelhead flies, streamers, bucktails, or specially tied salmon flies on Nos. 4 to 3/0 hooks.

Chinook can also be caught by trolling alewives, smelt, and other small fish impaled on a two-hook rig to give them a bend so they wobble. A gob of nightcrawlers or fresh salmon eggs on a weighted bottom rig also produces, especially near shore around river mouths and coves where the salmon gather before entering streams to spawn. Best times to fish are evening and night.

Big chinook can also be caught in freshwater streams and rivers along the coasts of California, Oregon, Washington, British Columbia,

Chinook salmon run big even in fresh water. This hefty fish puts up a hard fight and will make a stunning trophy. (Michigan Dept. of Natural Resources Photo)

and Alaska. They hit spinners, spoons, cherry bobbers, plugs, and jigs. But here, too, some anglers like to go after chinook with fly rods. Big chinook up to 50 pounds or more will hit special Pacific salmon fly patterns tied on No. 8 or 10 hooks. These usually have long tails and no wings and chenille or tinsel bodies. One of the most effective flies for chinook is the Teeny Nymph. But they also take many steelhead or trout flies. For most of this fishing, shooting-head sinking fly lines are needed to get down to the deep water in fast currents where the big salmon are lying.

Most of the big chinook salmon in these Pacific Coast rivers are found in the deeper pools; when the water is low and clear, often you can see them. When rain discolors the water, the salmon hit more readily. The best fishing is usually early in the morning or in the evening. The best approach here is to get above the spot where the salmon are lying or showing, cast across and slightly downstream, and let the current take the lure down to the level of the fish. When it does reach the fish, start retrieving in short, quick jerks.

Both coho and chinook salmon enter Pacific coastal streams from June to November, depending on weather and water conditions. Usually the best fishing is in August, September, and October. During dry spells, the salmon are often held up at the river's mouth, in salt water, and cannot enter the river itself until heavy rains raise the water level. Once in the river, the salmon become wary, moody, and unpredictable fish—difficult and challenging to catch.

No matter where you catch them in fresh water—in a river or a lake—coho and chinook are big, powerful fish that make long runs, bore down, and do not give up quickly. They make good eating if caught in a lake or soon after entering the mouth of a river. Later on, when they reach their spawning beds, their flesh turns soft and dark and they aren't very good for the table.

Most of the coho you will catch will range from about 2 to 20 pounds. Smaller fish caught in the Great Lakes in spring will run from about 2 to 6 pounds; in fall, they will range from 4 to 12 pounds. Several coho salmon over 30 pounds have been caught in weirs in rivers during their spawning runs. The biggest reported was a 39-pound 2-ounce fish caught in the Manistee River in Michigan.

Chinook range from 15 to 40 pounds in weight. Fish from 50 to 70 pounds have been caught in rivers entering the ocean along the Pacific Coast. Some of the biggest ones, up to 90 pounds, have been caught in British Columbia and Alaska. Chinook can reach over 100 pounds in weight. The present rod-and-reel world record is the 97-pound 4-ounce lunker caught in Alaska's Kenai River in 1985.

Many of the streams and rivers entering the Great Lakes are now stocked with coho and chinook salmon. Fishing is good along the lake shores of Michigan, Wisconsin, Illinois, Indiana, Ohio, Pennsylvania, and New York as well as in many rivers and streams in these states. You can find many lake ports where you can charter or rent a boat for this type of fishing. Or you can launch your own boat from many ramps along the shores of the Great Lakes.

There is also some coho salmon fishing in New Hampshire along its ocean coast and in the Lamprey and Exeter rivers. Massachusetts, Rhode Island, South Dakota, and several other states have been introducing coho and chinook salmon into some of their lakes and rivers.

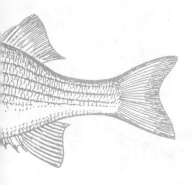

Chapter 9

Brown Trout

The brown trout is a relative newcomer to the American continent compared to the native brook trout and rainbow trout, which were on the scene long before the white man or, for that matter, the Indians appeared. The first brown trout were sent to this country from Germany in 1883 by Herr F. Von Behr. At that time, 80,000 brown trout eggs were sent to Fred Mather at New York's Cold Spring Harbor Hatchery on Long Island. Some of the brown trout eggs were forwarded to the Caledonia hatchery in New York State. The rest were sent to the United States Fish Commission's hatchery at Northville, Michigan. During the following years, additional shipments of eggs of a different variety of brown trout called the Loch Leven arrived from Scotland and England.

From the year 1886 the distribution of young brown trout expanded rapidly to various New York State waters. Later, other shipments of brown trout were sent to other states and Canada. By 1900, brown trout had been introduced into the waters of thirty-eight states. Nowadays the brown trout is found na-tionwide except in some deep southern states where it is rare or absent. Actually, the brown trout is an international fish, found in most of Europe, parts of the Middle East, North and South Africa, North and South America, Asia, Australia, and New Zealand.

When brown trout first appeared in numbers in American waters, they weren't welcomed with open arms by most trout fishermen. In fact, many protested loudly that the brown trout was ugly, not good to eat, and not much of a fighter on the end of a line. They also said that the brown trout was a cannibal that ate other trout and was responsible for the disappearance of the brook trout in eastern streams.

But as the years went by, the genuine qualities of the brown trout revealed themselves, and today this immigrant is revered by countless serious fly fishermen. It's still not too popular with the casual angler or the clumsy, unskilled novice. They'd rather fish for the rainbow trout or brook trout, which are easier to catch. The brown trout is wary and soon learns to survive in hard-fished, civilized

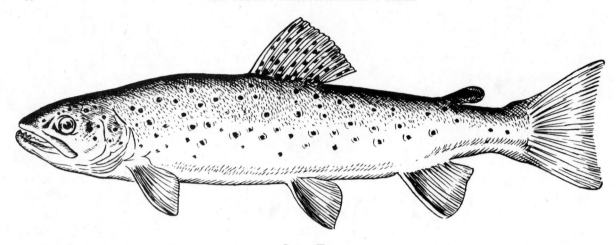

Brown Trout

streams and lakes. As streams become warmer, more polluted, and more heavily fished, brook trout and even rainbow trout tend to decline or even disappear. But brown trout manage to survive and even thrive in many such waters. Brown trout are also more aggressive than the native trout and take over in most waters. The result is that more and more streams end up containing mostly brown trout.

This situation is welcomed by serious trout anglers. To them, the brown trout presents a challenge unmatched by other trout. It rises more readily to the dry fly than either the rainbow trout or the brook trout. It is also more selective in its feeding and thus harder to fool with ordinary flies, lures, or baits. Brown trout are now found in many waters near big cities and towns where other trout are scarce or absent. Catching a brook, rainbow, or any other trout is considered fun and sport, but catching a good-sized brown trout on a fly is considered an achievement.

At one time, scientists used to differentiate among European brown trout, German brown trout, Lock Levens and others, but today they are all lumped under the name of *Salmo trutta*. Most anglers call it the brown trout or brownie.

The name indicates the general color of the fish. This may range from a pale dirty yellow to olive brown or greenish brown. These colors become lighter toward the belly, which is creamy white or yellowish. There are dark spots on the head, dorsal fin, and the back above the lateral line. Orange or reddish spots are often found along the sides. Brown trout that run to the sea or live in lakes usually are bright silver. Large, old brown trout develop big heads and a hooked, undershot lower jaw.

Tackle

Fly rods from short, light 7-footers to long, heavy 10-footers are used for brown trout, depending on the waters being fished and the flies or lures used. Brown trout are also caught on spinning, spincasting, and baitcasting tackle, even with cane or glass poles. For trolling deep in lakes, heavier rods and reels are often used with weights, lead-core lines or wire lines, and diving planes. Outriggers are also used for deep trolling in big lakes, and with these you can use lighter tackle.

The angler who seeks brown trout with a fly rod has to carry a wider selection of fly patterns and sizes than he usually needs for other trout. A wise old brownie that has been approached on many occasions or has even been hooked and gotten away becomes "educated"—highly suspicious and selective. Even smaller brown trout will often demand a fly that matches closely in size, color, and shape the naturals they are feeding on at the time.

Some of the more popular and tested dry flies that can be used for brown trout include the Adams, Light Cahill, Quill Gordon, Blue Dun, Olive Dun, March Brown, Black Gnat, Hendrickson, Light Blue Quill, White Miller, Ginger Variant, Ginger Quill, Pale Evening Dun, Goofus Bug, Irresistible, Royal Wulff (and others in the Wulff series), and the various bivisibles, spiders, and skaters, in sizes 8 to 18.

During the summer and early fall, when brown trout are feeding on terrestrials (land insects) such as ants, beetles, crickets, grasshoppers, or caterpillars, your flies should imitate these creatures. Some of the best patterns are the Letort Hopper, Michigan Hopper, Deer Hopper, Joe's Hopper, Letort Cricket,

Most brown trout are caught on flies in good-sized streams. This angler is wading the famed Battenkill River in Vermont. (Vermont Travel Division Photo)

Muddler, Black Ant, Black Beetle, Crowe Beetle, Inchworm, and the Jassids. These are usually tied in sizes 4 to 22.

There are also times when brown trout feed on tiny midges, which, again, should be imitated by your flies. The most popular and effective are the Black Midge, Brown Midge, Olive Midge, and Blue Dun Midge, tied in sizes 20 to 28.

An assortment of wet flies such as the March Brown, Gray Miller, Cahills, Leadwing Coachman, Black Gnat, Ginger Quill, Woolly Worm, Quill Gordon, and Hendrickson should also be carried in sizes 6 to 14.

Nymphs also take many brown trout early in the spring and throughout the year. There are many patterns available such as the Brown Stonefly, Ted's Stonefly, Brown Bomber, March Brown, Hare's Ear, Gray Nymph, Breadcrust, Dragon, and Caddis Larva, usually tied on Nos. 8 to 14 hooks. Some of these nymphs should be weighted.

A good assortment of streamers and bucktails should also be carried when you fish for big brown trout, since they often feed on minnows or other small fish. In this instance, it's a good idea to use streamers that imitate the minnows or small fish found in the stream being fished. Some of the proven streamers and bucktails are the Mickey Finn, Blacknose Dace, Brown-and-White, Black-and-White, Black Ghost, Gray Ghost, Golden Darter, Grizzly King, Muddler Minnow, and the marabous in different colors. These can be tied on hook sizes 2 to 10.

The flies mentioned above are tried-and-true patterns that have withstood the test of time. But in recent years, many innovative fly tiers have come out with new patterns that are as good or better than the older flies. So it's a good idea to buy flies that are recommended by anglers and tackle dealers in the locality you plan to fish. Rather than carry hundreds of different flies, it's far better to select a few patterns that have produced on a certain stream or lake and make sure you have two or three sizes of each pattern.

When you use spinning, spincasting, or bait-casting tackle, various kinds of small lures such as spinners, spoons, underwater plugs, and plastic lures will take brown trout. These lures are especially effective for big fish in larger rivers and lakes.

Many anglers fishing for brown trout have found that jigs can also be very effective for these fish when cast with a spinning or spin-casting outfit. The lighter jigs weighing ¼64, ⅓32, and ⅟16 ounce are best for streams. Larger jigs can be used for big brownies in rivers and lakes. Such colors as white, yellow, char-treuse, brown, black, and various combinations are productive. Fish the smaller, darker-colored jigs during the middle of the day and the larger, lighter-colored ones toward dusk and at night.

You can also use wet flies, nymphs, and streamers with a light spinning outfit by adding a couple of split-shot sinkers or a small rubber-core or clincher sinker on the line about a foot or two in front of the fly. Dry flies can also be cast with a plastic bubble float.

Bait for brown trout includes nightcrawlers, earthworms, minnows, crayfish, frogs, and various land and water insects.

Seasonal Tactics

Brown trout can be caught during most of the trout-fishing season, but certain times are better than others. The bait fisherman and spinning angler usually do best early in the year, during April and early May. This is also a good time for fishing with streamers and bucktails as well as wet flies and nymphs. And with a spinning outfit, you can use spinners, spoons, plugs, or jigs in the early spring.

Later on, from about the middle of May through early July, the dry-fly fisherman usually does best. But the farther north you go and the higher the altitude, the better the fishing during the summer months. Many lakes and streams in our northernmost states and in Canada provide good brown trout fishing in July and August.

Some big brown trout are also caught during the fall months when they move up streams to spawn. If the trout season is still open at this time, you can have some great fishing in pools below dams, logjams, and waterfalls. Brown trout will often gather in certain pools a month or two before spawning.

Early in the spring when the water is still cold, your best fishing will be during the middle of the day. This is also true in the late fall, when the water turns colder. Then as the water warms in the spring and insects begin to hatch toward evening, your best fishing will be during the late afternoon and toward dusk. During the hot summer months, early morning, dusk, and night provide the best fishing. In fact, big brown trout are noted for their night feeding habits during the summer months.

Reading the Water

The best way to locate brown trout—or any trout, for that matter—is to live by the stream or visit it often, and spend many hours observing the fish and their favorite hiding, holding, and feeding spots. Brown trout, especially, are known for choosing a good spot and staying there. Recent studies and observations have shown that brown trout choose a certain, specific spot in a stream and stay there all or most of the time. These "feeding" locations depend on the flow of the current bringing food, and the obstructions and bottom formations that enable trout to lie and wait for food being swept by without having to fight the strong current. They do not move too far from such spots to take any food floating on top or underwater. Several trout may occupy the same pool or run in different feeding stations. Brown trout may leave their favored locations because of very low or very high water or when frightened by a predator or an angler, until the danger is past. And, of course, they also leave them when moving upstream in the fall to spawn.

Brown trout hide in and even feed from spots that provide cover, safety, and security—under rocks, ledges, logs, undercut banks, in roots of trees, under bridges, and in submerged weeds. This is especially true of the larger brown trout, which often lie hidden during the day and then emerge toward dusk and at night to feed in the bigger pools and runs. They will cruise around seeking food or lie at the heads and tails of pools. Many anglers like to fish for these big trout at night during the hot summer months. Or they wait until rain causes the stream to rise and discolor. Then big trout often go on a feeding spree and are easier to catch.

Of course, the obvious, easy way to locate brown trout is to actually see them lying in the water on the bottom or rising to feed on hatching flies or on insects falling into the water. You'll often see only dimples or wakes made by the feeding fish.

Once a fish is located or a specific spot is suspected of harboring a trout, caution must be observed in approaching the fish. In shallow, clear water and in small streams, especially, you must keep out of sight, avoid casting a shadow, and move as slowly and quietly as possible. Try to avoid wading, and fish from shore, if possible, when working a narrow stream. If you do wade, move very slowly and carefully and stand still for long periods of time so that you don't create waves or vibrations. Stocked or hatchery trout are less wary of human beings than wild trout, and you can often approach them and catch them even if they see you or are aware of your presence. But wild trout with their keen eyesight and senses that pick up vibrations are difficult to approach and are usually aware of an angler's presence.

Dry-Fly Fishing

Dry-fly fishing is most effective when flies are hatching and brown trout are feeding on them.

Or when trout are in a feeding location and are waiting to see what the current brings their way. During a hatch it is important to match the size, color, and general shape of the natural insects the fish are feeding on. As a general rule the larger flies are better early in the year and the smaller ones later on, when the water is low and clear. And long leaders, up to 12 feet, with fine tippets may be needed to fool the fish and make the fly drift naturally.

Proper presentation of the dry fly is important; it should be dropped lightly and accurately a few feet in front of the trout so that it drifts naturally with the current. The line should float and the leader should sink. The slack line should be gathered with your hand but not so fast as to cause the line to pull on the fly. This would create a drag and should be avoided because it gives the fly an unnatural movement and speed. In most dry-fly fishing, you cast upstream and across. But if you see a fish or a rise or can pinpoint the location of a brownie, you can cast a few feet above it so that the dry fly drifts toward it. You can also cast downstream if you are standing directly above the fish's position. But here plenty of slack is needed to allow the fly to drift down naturally.

However, there are times when brown trout will take a dry fly that is deliberately pulled or skated across the top of the water. Spider and skater flies are best for this. Cast them like any dry fly and let them drift naturally until they are downstream. Then retrieve them by holding the rod high so the fly skims on top of the water or even hops occasionally. On big pools or quiet stretches, cast across stream and immediately begin a smooth, even retrieve, causing the fly to skim or skitter on the surface.

Fishing Wet Flies and Nymphs

Brown trout, especially the big ones, feed more underwater than on the surface, so day in and day out, wet flies or nymphs are usually more effective than dry flies. Both wet flies and nymphs can be fished by casting across and slightly upstream and then letting them drift naturally without pull or drag during most of the drift. When the fly reaches the end of the drift or swing, let it pause and rise, then retrieve it in short pulls or jerks. Often two wet flies or a combination of a wet fly and a nymph on the end of the leader will be more effective than just one. Some anglers also attach a dry fly above a wet fly or nymph and watch the dry fly to detect a strike. But most anglers fish just the wet fly or nymph and develop a sort of sixth sense to detect a strike and to set the hook at the right moment. You can also watch the floating fly line if you are fishing wet flies or nymphs not too deep. Or you can look for the flash of a fish underwater and then set the hook. But wet flies and nymphs usually produce best when fished deep with sinking fly lines, in which case it is very difficult to detect a strike.

Streamers and bucktails are often deadly for brown trout and are usually best early in the spring or in the fall. In summer, streamers produce well right after a heavy rain or shower that raises a stream and discolors the water a bit. But they can also be used early in the morning, in the evening, or at night when brownies are chasing minnows in the shallows or tails of pools. At other times, you can fish the deeper pools, holes, deep pockets, and runs. A streamer or bucktail can be cast quartering upstream and allowed to drift down with the current on a fairly slack line. When it reaches the end of the drift, let it pause and flutter a few seconds, then bring it back in spurts or short darts. You can also cast downstream and hold the streamer in the current in a good spot and work it back and forth. Or you can retrieve it on top of the water fast to make it look like a frantic minnow. At other times, in deep pools and in lakes, you can let the streamer or bucktail sink to the bottom and then retrieve it in slow, short spurts. Weighted streamers and sinking fly lines are most effective for reaching the depths fast and holding the fly there.

In the late summer and early fall, terrestrial flies often attract big brown trout. At this time, especially along meadow streams on windy days, trout often lie close to the banks waiting for land insects to be blown into the water. If you see fish rising, cast to them. At other times, you can float the fly along the banks, under overhanging tree branches and bushes, and through rapids, riffles, runs, glides, and pockets.

Lures and Baits

The spinning or spincasting rod is a highly effective weapon for big brown trout, particularly on the larger streams and lakes. With such a rod you can reach broad runs, pools, pockets, overhanging banks, deep-cut banks, and other spots where brown trout may be lying or feeding. Spinners, spoons, jigs, small plugs, and even weighted streamers can be cast at almost any angle and worked at varying speeds and depths. Sinking lures can be retrieved fast near the surface or allowed to sink toward the bottom and retrieved slowly, in an erratic manner.

More brown trout have probably been caught on an earthworm or nightcrawler than on any other natural bait. This is especially true during the spring of the year, but a skillful angler can take big brown trout throughout the year on worms. You can fish the worm with a fly rod or a long, light spinning rod, but whichever tackle you use, try to drift the worm deep and as naturally as possible under stumps, tree roots, fallen trees, and undercut banks; around boulders, rocks, and ledges. The best procedure is to cast the worm well upstream of the spot to be fished and let it drift down with the current. In slow- or medium-flowing water, you usually don't need a sinker or weight. But in faster, deeper water you may have to add

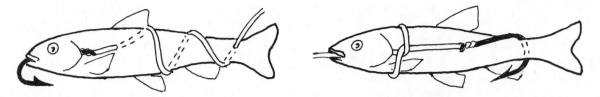

Two ways to sew a minnow on the hook

a split-shot sinker or two on the leader to get the bait down.

A minnow sewn on a single or double hook is often deadly for big brown trout. The minnow is rigged so that it has a slight curve or bend and is cast across stream and allowed to drift and sink toward the bottom, then it is retrieved slowly with short jerks to make it dart, wobble, and flash. Split-shot or light clincher sinkers are often added to the leader about 18 or 20 inches ahead of the minnow to provide more weight for casting and to allow the bait to sink in the deeper pools and fast runs. The weight also makes the minnow rise when pulled, and allows it to sink down when you stop the retrieve. The result is an effective crippled-minnow action.

Some of the biggest brown trout are now caught in large rivers, lakes, reservoirs, and impoundments. On our larger trout-inhabited rivers in Montana and other Western states, float trips are popular to reach spots that are rarely or never fished by shore anglers. Here you can fish from the boat itself with fly tackle or spinning gear, or you can beach the boat and fish from shore and from islands and bars. The tailwaters below dams often contain big brown trout that can be caught on flies, spoons, spinners, small plugs, and natural baits. This fishing is often good even during the summer months because of the cool water being released.

Brown trout can be caught in many lakes and reservoirs in the early spring, when they will often be seen feeding on alewives, smelt, or minnows close to the surface in shallow water near shore. Fishing can be especially good soon after ice-out and for a few weeks thereafter as the baitfish gather near the mouths of tributary streams. Anglers casting from shore use weighted spinners, small spoons, and small plugs to catch brown trout. From a boat, you can fish with a live alewife or minnow and cast it toward feeding fish or near the shore. Later on, when the water and weather warm up, you can fish live baitfish in deeper waters from 15 to 35 feet. In this case, you may need a weight or sinker to take your baitfish down and hold it at those depths.

In the Great Lakes and other big lakes, trolling is a very effective method for taking big brown trout. Here you can use spinners, spoons, or plugs such as the Flatfish, Rapala, and Rebel and troll these on long lines (up to 300 feet) in shallow water near shore. Or you can use a side planer, which angles the line and lure away from the side of the boat. This way, your lure can be traveling in shallow water near shore, but your boat will stay farther out in deeper water where it will not frighten the trout. You can troll at the mouths of streams, over rocky shoals, sandbars, along dropoffs, off points, and over submerged trees, rocks, and weedbeds. Shallow-water trolling is best in the spring, early summer, and fall.

During the summer months, as we have seen, brown trout go deep, in water from 20 to 50 feet, depending on the thermocline and presence of baitfish where the water temperature ranges between 55 and 60 degrees F. This means using lead-core or wire lines, or diving planers or downriggers, to get the lures or baits down to where the fish are. Lures are

Bob Harris, outdoor writer, holds a 13-pound brown trout he caught in Lake Ontario, New York. (Bob Harris Photo)

trolled slowly most of the time, but, since big brown trout will often follow a lure and make passes at it, you can try speeding up the boat for a few feet every so often to provoke a strike. Or you can try to give the lure extra action with up-and-down sweeps of the rod. A zigzag pattern is often better than steering a straight course.

Brown trout aren't spectacular fighters, although they'll occasionally leap out of the water. Usually they prefer to slug it out below the surface and try to snag your leader or line around a rock, log, or tree root. Big brownies have the weight to give you plenty of trouble, but after the first run or two, they can usually be handled easily.

In the smaller streams, brown trout will run

from about half a pound up to several pounds in weight. In the larger rivers, they'll often reach 10 to 20 pounds. But the biggest ones are caught in our larger lakes and reservoirs. A 31-pound 8-ounce brown trout was caught in Lake Michigan by John Duffy on July 3, 1976. A 33-pound 10-ounce brown trout was caught in Utah's Flaming Gorge Reservoir by Bob Bringhurst on March 4, 1977. Robert Henderson caught a 34-pound 6-ounce brown trout on May 14, 1984, in Arcadia Lake, which is connected to Lake Michigan. One of the biggest brown trout caught on rod and reel in this country is the 39-pound 9-ounce fish taken by Mike Manley from the North Fork River in Arkansas on August 6, 1988. But it was not recognized as a world record because it was caught on a treble hook instead of a single hook. The official rod-and-reel record is a 35-pound 15-ounce brown trout caught by Eugenio Cavaglia in Nahuel Huapi Lake in Argentina, on December 16, 1952. The Utah Division of Wildlife once gill-netted a 44-pound brown trout in the Flaming Gorge Reservoir. There have been reports of brown trout weighing over 50 pounds taken commercially in nets, or on lines in European waters.

Brown trout are now present in so many waters in most of our states that there is no space to list even a fraction of them in this book. Your best bet is to check with local tackle shops or write the state fish and game department and obtain a list of the best brown trout waters in the area you plan to fish.

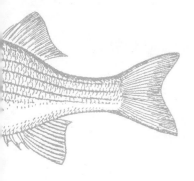

Chapter 10

Brook Trout

When the first white people settled in North America, the only trout they found in the East was the brook trout. This colorful trout was the true native trout and the only one known to these early settlers. Until the rainbow and brown trouts were introduced into eastern waters, the angler who went trout fishing caught only brook trout.

The brook trout was a great favorite of those early fishermen. Abundant in almost every stream and in many lakes, it provided both sport and food. Early accounts tell of the wonderful brook trout fishing in many areas in New England, New York, and other eastern states. The brook trout ranged in those days from Labrador west to Saskatchewan in Canada, and south through the Alleghenies to northern Georgia. Then it was introduced in the West from California to Alaska and later in the Rocky Mountain states.

Today the brook trout is still a popular fish in those areas where it is fairly plentiful. It is the most cooperative of the trouts, feeding on a wide variety of foods and almost always willing to take a properly presented fly, lure, or bait. The brook trout is usually caught in scenic, wild, cool, clear streams or in cold northern lakes, especially in the mountains.

Unfortunately, brook trout waters are becoming scarce, and those that remain are often in remote wilderness areas, difficult to reach. With the advance of civilization, and the attendant pollution and siltation, the brook trout is becoming increasingly scarce. In addition, water temperatures in most streams have become too warm for brook trout. Of course, fish hatcheries keep producing millions of brook trout for the put-and-take fishing practiced in many states, but most serious anglers want to catch wild brook trout.

Brook trout have been called eastern brook trout, speckled trout, native trout, mountain trout, red trout, squaretails, and brookies. The brook trout actually isn't a true trout, but belongs to the char family, which also includes the lake trout and the Dolly Varden trout.

Anyone who has seen the brook trout in its fall spawning colors will admit that it is one of the prettiest of trouts. The back is usually blue-green or bronze-green with wormlike mark-

Brook Trout

ings on the back and sides to the lateral line, and red dots outlined in blue on the sides. The fins have dark bands and are edged with pink blending into white. In small brooks, deep forests, and some big, deep Canadian rivers and lakes, the brook trout is very dark all over. Those that run to sea turn silvery, but soon revert to their original colors when they return to fresh water.

Tackle

Brook trout can be caught on the same tackle used for brown trout. Fly rods are used for fishing flies or bait. For fishing the smaller streams where small brook trout predominate, you can use a light, short fly rod, 6 to 7½ feet, with No. 3, 4 or 5 weight fly line. Short rods are easier to carry in woods or heavy brush. Some anglers prefer longer fly rods even in such spots. They find that longer rods (from 8 to 9 feet) allow them to flip a fly or bait from a safe distance without casting and scaring the fish. Long fly rods are also better for trolling or for fishing for big brook trout in Canada.

For fishing lures and baits in small streams, an ultralight spinning rod with a small reel filled with 2- to 4-pound-test-line is ideal. Spincasting and baitcasting outfits can be used on larger streams for big brook trout.

Brook trout, especially in wilderness waters, often go for more colorful, gaudier wet-fly patterns—for example, the Silver Doctor, Parmachene Belle, Red Ibis, Royal Coachman, Montreal, Grizzly King, Professor, Black Gnat, Gray Hackle, and McGinty in sizes 6 to 14.

Of the dry flies, the Black Gnat, Royal Coachman, Light Cahill, Dark Cahill, Quill Gordon, Hendrickson, Adams, Gray Hackle, Brown Hackle, Irresistible, Blue Dun, and Woolly Worm are good. You can also try the Wulff flies, spiders, bivisibles, and a few terrestrials. Dry flies in sizes 8 to 18 are usually used.

Various nymph patterns such as the Tellico, March Brown, Gold-Ribbed Hare's Ear, Stonefly, Caddis, and Zug Bug, sizes 4 to 16, also take brook trout.

Streamers and bucktails for brook trout include the Red-and-White, Mickey Finn,

Blacknose Dace, Dark Edson Tiger, Light Edson Tiger, Green Ghost, Black Ghost, Supervisor, Nine-Three, White Marabou, Yellow Marabou, Warden's Worry, Matukas, and Muddler Minnow. These can be carried in sizes 2 to 10, the larger ones for big brookies in wilderness rivers and lakes, the smaller flies for small brook trout in small, heavily fished streams.

With spinning, spincasting, or baitcasting tackle, you can use spinners, spoons, jigs, small plugs, and plastic lures. Brook trout are also among the easiest trout to catch on natural baits such as worms, minnows, grasshoppers, crickets, grubs, and nymphs.

Seasonal Tactics

Brook trout start feeding early in the spring, soon after the ice is out. April, May, and June are usually good months. In colder northern lakes and in mountain lakes and streams in Maine, Canada, and our western states, you can often have good fishing in July and August. In more southern waters, however, the summer months are not too good.

Brook trout prefer cool, clean, turbulent waters. In small streams, look for them beneath undercut banks or overhanging trees, around brush, logs, tree roots, logjams, rocks, and under ledges, and in the deeper holes and pools. They usually like to lie behind a rock, log, or other obstruction. During the warmer months, they may lie in the deepest pools in streams and rivers and around spring holes or the mouths of cool brooks. Many brook trout at this time will also move up into the cooler brooks and tributaries.

In lakes, big brook trout are often found close to shore in the early spring, soon after ice-out, or around the mouths of streams entering a lake. They feed on smelt, minnows, and other small baitfish that congregate there.

Today, the best brook trout fishing is found in cold, northern wilderness lakes and streams. (Travel Manitoba Photo)

Later on, as the water warms up, they often move into cooler streams and into the running water connecting lakes.

During the summer months in large, deep, clear lakes, brook trout are often at depths ranging from 20 to 50 feet. They prefer a temperature range from 50 to 60 degrees. Here they usually hang out over structure such as underwater plateaus or islands, points sloping into deeper water, and along dropoffs and ledges. Cool underground springs entering a lake also attract them during the hot-weather months.

Beaver ponds, especially those in the more remote forests, often contain brook trout. You can locate beaver ponds by studying topographic maps or by following streams through the woods. Since most beaver ponds are on the small side and usually calm and clear, brook trout are very wary and easily spooked in these waters, so they have to be approached carefully and quietly. The best fishing in beaver ponds is usually in the spring, but if the water in the pond stays cool, brookies can also be caught during the summer. Most of the action occurs around daybreak and a bit later, and then again toward evening and dusk. Rainy, overcast days are usually better than bright, sunny ones. Heavy showers often trigger good fishing in beaver ponds.

Brook trout from certain Atlantic coastal streams and rivers migrate to the sea, live there in salt water for a few years, and then return to the same river or stream to spawn. The Canadian Maritime Provinces often offer good fishing for these sea-run brookies for a short period in June when they begin their run up the rivers. These fish often move in schools, and you have to find a spot where they stop for a day or two. Usually early morning and evening fishing are best for these sea-run brook trout.

In late August and September, big brook trout leave the lakes and enter the tributary streams to spawn. You can often see them moving upstream, leaping over small falls and lying at the heads of rapids in pockets. If fish-ing is permitted in the stream during these spawning runs, it can be very good.

Although brook trout will often hit flies or lures or take baits with abandon, they can also be difficult to catch in our hard-fished waters, and must be approached with care and caution. Try to sneak up to each spot quietly and avoid wading in the water. Instead, fish from the bank and hide behind a treetrunk or bush, or crouch low.

The brook trout is mostly an underwater feeder and can be caught on wet flies fished below the surface. Cast the wet fly across and slightly upstream and, while keeping the slack line under control, let it drift naturally in the current. At the end of the drift, lift the fly out of the water for a new cast, or retrieve it upstream in short spurts. You can even try skittering it on top of the water. If a shallow-working fly doesn't produce, let it sink to the

The brook trout can be caught on a wide variety of flies. As it generally feeds underwater, it takes wet flies and nymphs readily. (Bob Harris Photo)

bottom and keep it moving deep. You may have to cast farther upstream to get it to sink deep enough. In fast water, you should add a split-shot sinker or two on the leader to get the fly down near the bottom, or you can use a sinking fly line in fast, deep waters. Nymphs also take brook trout and can be worked in basically the same way as wet flies.

At times, brook trout will take a dry fly, especially when they are feeding on surface insects. The fly is drifted naturally with the current over rising fish. Since most brook trout streams are narrow, with trees and overhanging limbs on their banks, long casts or false casting should be avoided. You have to flip out the leader and a short length of fly line or even just dap the fly on the water a short distance from the tip of the rod. The fly should be a good floater and be dressed with a floatant.

Streamers and bucktails are often effective for large brook trout, especially on big rivers and lakes. The trout here often feed on smelt, minnows, or other baitfish running up a stream to spawn, and any streamers or bucktails resembling these baitfish will work. Give them an erratic, hesitant retrieve in 2- or 3-foot spurts and try them at different depths, from surface to bottom.

Some big brook trout are also taken at times on small spoons, weighted spinners, jigs, and underwater plugs. Here too, lures that resemble the small fish prevalent in the waters being fished are best. When fishing a spoon, cast it out and let it sink a few feet; then start reeling, stop and let it flutter down again, and repeat. Big brook trout often follow a spoon and hit it as it flutters and sinks.

Retrieve a spoon in stop-and-go fashion so it flutters up and down in the water.

Brook trout can also be taken by trolling on the larger rivers and lakes. Trolling with fly rods and streamers or bucktails, in the same way as for landlocked salmon, described earlier in this book, is often effective in the spring near shore and near the mouths of streams. In fact, while trolling for landlocked salmon, anglers often hook brook trout. You can also troll spoons, spinners, and small plugs near shore in the spring and fall. Later on, during the summer months, these lures should be trolled deep with weights on lead-core or wire lines.

When brook trout are deep in lakes, you can also try jigging up and down close to the bottom. Such lures as the Swedish Pimple, the Ugly Bug, and other small jigs in ¼- to ½-ounce sizes are good for such jigging. You can add a worm, a minnow, or a small plastic worm to the jig to make it even more effective.

Anglers find the ordinary garden worm a fine bait for brook trout, especially in the spring. At this time when the trout are hugging bottom, the worm should be drifted in the current along the edges of fast water, under overhanging banks, around sunken trees and logs, and in pockets and deep holes. Follow the drift of the worm with your rod and allow plenty of slack line for a natural drift. When you feel a bite or pickup, wait a few seconds, then set the hook. Grasshoppers and crickets can also be fished for brook trout and are especially effective on small meadow brooks. You can also use worms, minnows, crayfish, and small frogs for big brook trout in lakes.

A good-sized wild brook trout in fast water puts up a strong, stubborn battle. It rarely leaps out of the water like the rainbow trout or even the brown trout. And brook trout are not noted for making long runs. But they usually bore deep, twist, roll, and try to foul your line.

Unfortunately, most of the brook trout caught these days in small streams rarely go more than 12 inches. In some tiny brooks and mountain streams, they are fully grown at 8 inches. However, in large rivers and lakes of remote wilderness areas, trout weighing up to

Good-sized brook trout can still be caught in some waters.
This one was hooked in the Lamoille River in Vermont.
(Vermont Travel Division Photo)

8 pounds are still caught. Though most of these waters are in the northern sections of Canada, some of the biggest brook trout are now caught in Argentina and Chile, where they were introduced. The world record on rod and reel is the 14½-pound brook trout taken by Dr. W. J. Cook on the Nipigon River, Ontario, Canada, in July 1916.

Wild, fresh-caught brook trout make delicious eating. The flavor and texture of their flesh cannot be matched by the other trouts.

The best brook trout waters in the United States are found in Maine, New Hampshire, Vermont, and other northern states. The mountain states, along the Appalachians and the Rockies, are noted for their brook trout streams. Some of the best fishing is found in the streams and ponds of the national parks in higher altitudes. Canada still has good brook trout fishing, especially for big fish, in many waters in the provinces of Quebec, Ontario, Manitoba, New Brunswick, Nova Scotia, and Newfoundland (especially in Labrador).

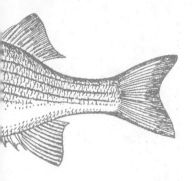

Chapter 11

Rainbow Trout

The spectacular rainbow trout is one of the world's most popular game fish. It is found from Alaska to California, throughout our northern and western states, in most of our eastern states, and in Canada, Europe, Asia, Africa, New Zealand, and South America.

Rainbow trout are also known as California trout, Pacific trout, salmon trout, western rainbow, and steelhead. The last name is applied to a rainbow trout that goes to sea or into large lakes and then returns to the rivers to spawn. (See the next chapter for information on these migrating rainbow trout.)

A rainbow trout is a colorful and beautiful fish when first removed from the water. The back is usually greenish or bluish, shading into silvery green on the sides. The whole upper surface of the body is covered with small, dark spots. A wide band of crimson or pink runs along the lateral line from head to tail. This stripe is most evident in large mature fish and in males at breeding time. The female rainbow may lack this pink stripe and appear silvery all over. The rainbows that live in lakes or in large, deep bodies of water often turn dark steel blue on the back and silvery on the sides.

Tackle

To catch rainbow trout, you can use the same tackle that was discussed in detail in the chapter on brown trout. However, on large rivers and lakes that hold big rainbows, heavier tackle is required.

Although rainbow trout do not rise to a dry fly as readily or as often as brown trout, they can be taken on many of the same dry-fly patterns. Of the dry flies, the Grizzly Sedge, Ginger Quill, Green Sedge, Quill Gordon, Light Cahill, Adams, Hairwing Royal Coachman, Hendrickson, Black Gnat, Elk-Hair Caddis, and the various Wulff patterns are effective. On western waters when the salmon flies hatch, you can fish the Bailey Salmonfly, Kolzer Orange, and Sofa Pillow. Bivisibles, spiders, and variants are also good at times. Dry flies in sizes from 10 to 18 are best suited to rainbow trout.

In wet flies, stock such patterns as the Brown Sedge, Green Sedge, Coachman, Royal Coachman, Alexandria, Skykomish Sunrise, Parmachene Belle, McGinty, Gray Hackle Yellow, Black Gnat, Mosquito, and Woolly

Rainbow Trout

Worm. Yarn flies in white, yellow, orange, pink, red, and green fluorescent colors, or combinations of these colors, are highly effective in discolored or murky waters and for rainbows that run up rivers to spawn. Wet flies in sizes 8 to 16 are most productive.

Nymphs are very good in low, clear rivers and in many lakes. The different patterns used for other trout often work for rainbows too. Some of the popular nymph patterns are the Montana Nymph, Troth's Black Stonefly, Bird's Brown Stonefly, Box Canyon, Olive Dragonfly, Black Dragonfly, Hare's Ear, and Girdlebug. Some of these are gaudy and, therefore, are good in murky water, but in clear water, drab or dark-colored nymphs are better. In mountain lakes, nymphs with fur-dubbing bodies are effective. Weighted nymphs that go down deep, or sinking fly lines are often needed when fishing the fast, big rivers where rainbows are found. Sizes 4 to 14 are the most popular and effective.

Streamers and bucktails such as the Mickey Finn, Red-and-White, Brown Bucktail, Black-nose Dace, Gray Ghost, Black Ghost, Warden's Worry, the marabous, and the Muddler Minnow will also take rainbow trout. In waters where sculpin are present and form an im-portant part of a rainbow trout's diet, patterns tied to imitate this bottom-dwelling fish are highly effective. Most of the streamers and bucktails used are tied on hooks from No. 6 to No. 3/0, depending on the pattern and the size of the baitfish being imitated.

And various grasshopper, cricket, beetle, and ant imitations can be carried for late-summer and early-fall fishing, when land insects are falling on the water. (See the chapter on brown trout for terrestrials that can also be used for rainbow trout.)

With spinning, spincasting, or baitcasting tackle, spinners, spoons, jigs, small plugs, plastic worms, and other plastic lures will take rainbows. They are especially effective on the larger rivers and lakes for big rainbows early in the season when the water is cold. Lures are deadly for spawning rainbows that enter streams from large lakes.

Rainbow trout are also caught on salmon eggs, worms, crayfish, hellgrammites, grubs, and minnows. Where salmon eggs are illegal, anglers often use substitutes such as pink or red yarn on a hook; cooked tapioca dyed red; tiny balls shaped from cheese, marshmallow, or dough; and rubber or plastic imitations of fish eggs.

Seasonal Tactics

Fishing is usually best early in the spring right after ice-out. Late March, April, and May are good months in most areas, when the big rainbows head upriver to spawn. Another good period is September through November, when big rainbows return to the rivers from the larger lakes. But smaller rainbow trout can be caught during the summer months in many waters that remain cool. There is often excellent fishing in our extreme northern states, including Alaska, and Canada during the hot summer months. Rainbow trout are most active in water temperatures above 50 degrees F. and up to about 65 degrees F. They may move into warmer water to feed for brief periods, but soon return to cooler water to hide or rest.

This angler is holding a good-sized rainbow trout. In large rivers and lakes, these fish can reach 20 pounds. (Bob Harris Photo)

The time of day when fishing is best for rainbow trout will depend on the season, water conditions, and water temperatures. Early in the spring and fall, the fishing is often good during the middle of the day. In colder climates and in high-altitude mountain lakes, the middle of the day is a productive time through most of the fishing season. In warmer climates and during the summer months in our more southerly states, early morning and evening hours are usually better.

Rainbow trout like the faster portions of rivers and streams. Thus you'll find them in the rapids, riffles, fast glides, runs, and pockets. The white water at the heads or tails of pools and under waterfalls will also attract them. But even in this fast water, they like to lie along the edges of strong currents and around obstructions: in front, behind, or alongside a rock, boulder, stump, log, or treetrunk. Fast water running along undercut riverbanks or shorelines will also hold them. Big rainbows can often be seen on their spawning beds in the shallow water, especially early in the morning and evening. During the day, they often hide in deeper water and pools. And, of course, you can also look for rainbow trout rising and feeding on hatching insects.

In lakes, early in the spring, rainbows cruise the shallows near shore and gather at the mouths of streams and rivers prior to entering them. During the warmer months, they hang out in deeper water along dropoffs and rocky points sloping into the lake. They are also found around spring holes bubbling up from the bottom of the lake. They feed on smelt, alewives, ciscoes, threadfin shad, and minnows.

Rainbow trout are mostly underwater feeders but will rise to a dry fly when insects are hatching on a lake or stream. For lake-dwelling rainbows, fish weighted wet flies and nymphs deep on a sinking line and retrieve them in short pulls. Most of the time, you have to cast blind, trying different depths until you start getting hits. In clear, calm mountain lakes, where you often see rainbows cruising near

Rainbow trout like to lie in front of or behind a rock, where the current is weak.

shore, cast a wet fly or nymph from 10 to 15 feet ahead of the fish, let it sink slowly until the trout gets close enough to see it, then start retrieving it in short jerks.

When fishing with streamers or bucktails, you can try stripping in the fly on top across the stream so that it leaves a tiny wake on the surface. But most of the time, you have to get down deep to interest rainbow trout.

When using a spinning outfit, make up a rig with a tiny three-way swivel: tie a 2-foot leader and the fly to one eye of the swivel; tie the fishing line to the second eye; and tie a 6-inch dropper with two or three split-shot sinkers to the third eye. Cast the rig and allow it to sink to the bottom where it can move or drift along the rocks. The lead weights will keep the fly just off the bottom.

You can also fish deep with lures, especially for big rainbows that run up rivers from lakes in the spring and fall. Use a spinning or bait-casting outfit with spinners, spoons, cherry bobbers or drifters, small plugs, jigs, or plastic lures. Cast across and well upstream and allow the lure to sink and tumble and drift in the current. It should travel as close to the bottom as possible without fouling. When the lure reaches the end of its drift, retrieve it slowly and erratically against the current. Lures can also be fished in lakes for rainbows. Cast from shore or a boat and retrieve the lure at various depths until you locate feeding fish.

You can also float down a big river in a boat and catch big rainbows in spots that can't be reached from shore. In the past, anglers usually floated our big western rivers, but in re-cent years float fishing has become popular and highly effective on rivers in Arkansas, Alabama, North Carolina, South Carolina, and Tennessee. The best fishing is just below dams in the tailwaters and up to 30 miles downstream. The water released below the dam is cool throughout the year and attracts big rainbows and other trout. The best fishing is when the water is high and moving. Then look for obstructions or bottom formations that slow the current and enable the rainbows to lie there without fighting the strong flow—eddies, shore points, rocks, or holes.

Baitfishing is often deadly for rainbow trout in many streams. Anywhere from one to five salmon eggs or a cluster or spawn sac are used for bait. Nightcrawlers and earthworms are also good, especially in the spring. These baits should be cast upstream and across and allowed to drift along the bottom with the current. You can fish these baits with a fly rod without any weight. But usually you need a sinking fly line or two or three split-shot sinkers on the leader to get the bait down deep enough in a strong current.

The most effective rig for big rainbows when you are baitfishing or even using lures consists of a 2-foot leader tied to a small three-way swivel, with a small sinker on a short dropper tied to another eye of the swivel. Slim, pencil-type sinkers are also used because they hang up less often than other styles. This rig is bounced along the bottom with the baited hook on a tight line so you can feel a bite or a change in movement and set the hook accordingly. See the chapter on steelhead for

These anglers are float-fishing a large river in Montana that is too deep and swift in parts to wade.

more details on how to fish baits and lures near the bottom.

Trolling is a good way to take rainbow trout on larger rivers and in most lakes. You can use wet flies, streamers, and nymphs on a sinking or lead-core fly line and troll them at slow or moderate speeds, giving the flies action. In the spring and fall, troll in shallow water close to shore and around the mouths of streams entering a lake. Later on, as the water warms, use spinning, baitcasting tackle, or trolling outfits. One of the most effective lures is a series of spinners in front of a worm, minnow, or lure. You can also troll weighted spinners, spoons, and underwater plugs. When rainbow trout are deep, you may have to troll with weighted lines, lead-core lines, wire lines, diving planers, or downriggers to reach the depths where they are lying.

In smaller streams and lakes, rainbows average from 1 to 5 pounds, but in larger rivers and lakes they often reach much heavier weights. The rainbows that have access to a big body of water containing abundant baitfish often grow to 20 pounds or more. The Kamloops rainbows found mostly in Idaho and British Columbia, reach a giant size. One of the largest taken on rod and reel went 37 pounds and was caught in Lake Pend Oreille, Idaho, on November 25, 1947. Many other fish in the 30-pound class have been taken from these and other waters. Even bigger Kamloops rainbows have been reported from British Columbia, where fish going over 40 pounds have been trapped by the game commission for eggs. Two huge rainbows weighing 48 and 52½ pounds were reportedly taken from Jewel Lake, British Columbia, back in 1931 and 1933.

Rainbow trout caught from wilderness streams and lakes make excellent eating. Hatchery trout are not as good, but after they live in a lake or stream for a few months, they improve. Many rainbow trout are raised for the market and are served in restaurants or sold to the public.

Rainbow trout are found in so many waters in this country and in Canada that it is impossible to list even a fraction of the best waters. The best fishing is in Washington, Oregon, northern California, Utah, Montana, Michigan, Wisconsin, Minnesota, and New York. There is excellent rainbow trout fishing in the Great Lakes region and in the many streams entering the lakes. Many rivers and lakes in Canada offer fine rainbow trout fishing, with British Columbia tops for big fish. Rainbow trout fishing in Alaska is fabulous. Argentina, Chile, and Peru have some huge rainbow trout in mountain lakes and rivers. They are also present in some of the rivers in New Zealand.

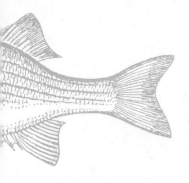

Chapter 12

Steelhead

The steelhead is a rainbow trout that migrates down a coastal river to the sea, spends a few years there, and then returns up the river to spawn. Anglers along the Pacific Coast from California to Alaska have no Atlantic salmon in their rivers but are perfectly content with the steelhead as a good substitute. In fact, since both fish are very similar in appearance, habits, and fighting ability, it is difficult to determine which is superior. Steelhead from the Pacific have been introduced into the Great Lakes and other waters. One strain of steelhead called the Skamania provides good fishing in many lakes and streams where it has been introduced.

Most steelhead rivers are open to the public, and the fishing seasons are long. (You can catch steelhead most of the year.) In addition, you are not restricted to the kind of tackle you can use, as is true with Atlantic salmon, which can only be taken on fly rods in this country.

All this makes the steelhead highly popular with Pacific Coast anglers, who seek this fish in rain, snow, sleet, and freezing weather dur-ing the winter months. But while steelhead are much more numerous than Atlantic salmon, they are not always easy to catch, and they offer a challenge to most anglers, whether novice or expert. It takes skill to locate steelhead, to cast and present the bait or lure, and to hook and fight them successfully. In the rushing rivers where they are found, they are real tackle-busters. And to complicate things even more, steelhead reach a good size. So you can consider yourself lucky if you land a large majority of the steelhead you hook.

A steelhead looks like a rainbow trout, which, of course, it is, except that a steelhead may be bigger, longer, more streamlined, and different in color when it first comes in from the sea. Fresh from the ocean, a steelhead, as its name implies, has a steel-blue or greenish back, silvery sides, and some dark spots on the back and tail. After it has been in fresh water for a while, it reverts to the original rainbow trout colors. (Many steelhead, however, are now being caught in inland waters and spend all their lives without touching the sea.)

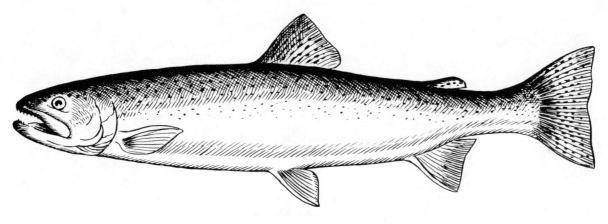

Steelhead

Tackle

Steelhead are caught on a variety of fishing outfits, from light fly rods up to heavy surf-fishing rods. Years ago, the most popular outfit was a two-handed baitcasting rod and baitcasting reel. Such outfits are still used, but most anglers now prefer spinning rods ranging from 7 to 10 feet in length. These rods have limber and sensitive tips for casting the lighter lures and baits and for feeling pickups or strikes. Spinning reels are usually filled with lines testing from 8 to 15 pounds. Heavier spinning rods with 15- to 20-pound-test lines are preferred for casting from the shore, piers, or jetties in streams and lakes. They are also used for "plunking" bait and sinkers on the bottom. Other outfits favored for trolling on the larger lakes are similar to the trolling rods and revolving-spool reels used for chinook and coho salmon.

For fly fishing, you need a heavy salmon rod 8 to 10 feet long that can handle a No. 7, 8, or 9 weight fly line. Weight-forward floating fly lines are best for dry-fly fishing, even for wet-fly fishing in low water during the summer. But when fishing fast, deep, cold rivers in the early spring, late fall, or winter you need a shooting-head sinking fly line. Many expert steelhead anglers carry at least three extra reel spools, each filled with a different sinking fly line to match specific fishing conditions. A

single-action fly reel to match the rod should have a good drag and hold at least 100 to 150 yards of 20-pound-test backing line.

The angler who prefers to use artificial lures for steelhead should carry spoons in various sizes, colors, and weights. Silver, gold, and brass spoons, as well as those painted in bright fluorescent yellow, pink, orange, or red are all good. Lighter spoons such as the Dardevle, Pet Spoon, Evil Eye, and flutterspoons are used for trolling and river casting. For casting from shore, heavier spoons such as the Kastmaster, Mr. Champ, Krocodile, Little Cleo, Hopkins, and Rok't-Devlet are better. Some of these heavier spoons in the smaller sizes can also be fished on large rivers when the water is high and fast, and you have to get down deep.

Weighted spinners are also good for casting and probing the bottom where steelhead lie. The Cherry Bobber spinner, which has a balsa body to keep it high in the water, can be fished with a sinker rig, often to deadly effect. Equally good are various other lures with imitation egg clusters, such as the Oakie Drifter and the Spin and Glo. Jigs are also effective for deep fishing. Underwater plugs such as the Tadpolly, Flatfish, Rapala, Rebel, and similar minnow-type plugs in the smaller sizes are also productive. Other plugs such as the J-Plug, Hot Shot, and various small crankbaits can be fished with side planers, either from shore or from a boat when trolling.

Many steelhead are now being caught in inland rivers and lakes and spend all their lives in fresh water. (Minnesota Dept. of Natural Resources Photo)

For the flyrodder, there are numerous productive wet flies and streamers; some are standard trout patterns, others are tied especially for steelhead. Flies for steelhead include the Royal Coachman, Silver Doctor, Gray Hackle, Queen Bess, Van Luven, Skykomish Sunrise, Polar Shrimp, Umpqua, Silver Ant, Orange Optic, Thor, Silver and Golden Demons, Harger's Orange, Comets, Governor, Burlap, Babine Special, Skunk, Fire Fly, and Kalama Special. Atlantic salmon flies also take steelhead, and there are special steelhead patterns tied for fishing the streams entering the Great Lakes.

Another variety of steelhead fly is made from yarn tied around the hook. These flies are often bright fluorescent yellow, orange, pink, or red. Some are wrapped in the shape of a small ball to look like a big salmon egg or a small cluster of several eggs. Called Glow Bugs, they are highly effective, especially in cold and murky waters. Wet flies tied on Nos. 8 to 1/0 hooks are usually the most effective. Nymphs such as the Hare's Ear, Stonefly, Dragonfly, Teeny, and caddis-larva imitations in sizes 2 to 10 can be used for steelhead.

When steelhead take dry flies, you should have on hand the Gray Wulff, Black Wulff, March Brown, Adams, Royal Coachman, Light Cahill, Pink Lady, Irresistible, Steelhead Bee, and the caddis patterns, in sizes 4 to 12.

Steelhead are also caught on salmon eggs. The eggs from a fresh-caught chinook salmon are especially good; they are smaller, firmer, and stay on a hook longer than those of other species. Fresh eggs taken from a female steelhead are also very good. These eggs are encased in a tiny bag of thin maline. Place the eggs in the center of a 3-inch square of the netting, gather the corners together, and tie them with thread to form a small bag.

Steelhead also take crayfish tails or nightcrawlers drifted along the bottom or allowed to lie still in a quiet pool. Other effective baits include grasshoppers, crickets, caterpillars, grubs, hellgrammites, nymphs, and small shrimp and prawns.

Tactics

The key to success in steelhead fishing is to time your fishing trip to coincide with the run of fish up the river. Since this may vary from river to river and from year to year, it requires constant checking to see if there are steelhead in the section you plan to fish. Some rivers have only one main run of fish, such as the summer run, which may start in April in some rivers or as late as August or September in others. Other rivers may have a summer run and a winter run, which may begin in October or later and last until February or March. On

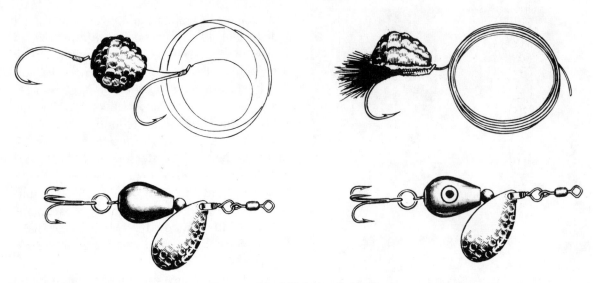

Lures used in drift-fishing for steelhead

still other rivers there are continuous runs from early spring to winter as fish keep entering at various times. Before planning a trip it's a good idea to get in touch with someone who lives near the river and can tell you if the steelhead are running.

On short rivers, the runs may last only a few weeks, the fish moving upstream rapidly without pause. On longer rivers, the runs spread out over a longer period of time, with different sections of the river producing fast fishing as the steelhead move upstream. Here you have to follow the fish or intercept them if you want to catch them. Large stretches of the river may be barren of fish or contain only a few strays, while others provide hot fishing.

Even when the steelhead are moving in the river there is no guarantee of good fishing. A sudden storm, prolonged rain, or drop in water temperature may put a stop to the fishing. It has been found that when the water temperature is below 39 degrees F., steelhead are inactive and feed little. Also, a rapidly rising river that becomes discolored is usually unproductive. But after the river starts to clear and the water becomes a milky green or blue, the fishing picks up again.

After a heavy rain, the upper portions of a river clear first, then the lower portions. In some rivers, it may take two, three, or more days for the fishing to return to normal; in others, several days to a week or more before it pays to go fishing. At such times, try some of the smaller tributaries entering the main river, which usually clear faster.

During the summer, the best time to fish for steelhead is on overcast, cloudy days. If it is sunny, bright, and hot, your chances are better early in the morning and again in the evening. During the winter months, if the weather and water are cold, fish in the middle of the day and into the afternoon when the water may have warmed up a bit.

Even after you arrive on a river and are assured that steelhead are present, there is another important hurdle to overcome. You have to locate the fish. If you have fished the river before and know the locations and spots where steelhead like to lie, this is not a big problem. But if you are fishing a strange river, then you have your work cut out for you.

The main point to keep in mind is that steelhead are usually found in holding, or resting, spots where they are protected from the main force of the current. So in a riffle or rapid, they will be found along the edges of the fast water at the head or tail of the run. If there are rocks, look for the fish in front, behind, or along the sides. Along the banks of a river, they may lie behind rock outcroppings, rock ledges, beneath undercut banks, or behind logs. In pools, look for them at the tails or heads rather than in the deeper, quieter middle portions. Fish pools from the shallow side, casting toward the deeper side.

Steelhead anglers also look for holes where up to a dozen or more fish gather and rest before moving upstream to the next favorable spots. During the summer months, when the water is low, the fish tend to concentrate in these holes, in water from 4 to 8 feet deep. They also seek shade from overhanging trees, undercut banks, brush, and bridges. Bottoms lined with big rocks and boulders that slow the force of the current are favorite spots for steelhead to lie. Another good summer spot is at the head of a pool where white-water rapids enter.

Most expert steelhead anglers study their favorite river during low-water periods. They memorize the location of every boulder, rock, log, hole, depression, and obstruction that may harbor a steelhead later on when the river rises. Then they can cast their lure or bait to these spots even though they cannot see the structure below the surface. Once they take some fish from these spots they know they can return and catch some more as new fish replace those that have been caught or have moved upstream.

The favorite method of fishing for steelhead is to drift a bait or lure close to the bottom. One of the best rigs for this is made by tying a three-way swivel on the end of your line; then tie a 20-inch leader to another eye, and the hook or lure to the end of this leader. Attach a short length of surgical tubing to the remaining eye, and insert about a 3-inch length of lead-pencil sinker into the surgical tubing. The beauty of this rig is that if the lead gets caught, you can free it with a hard yank. However, since you probably will still lose some rigs, it pays to make up a couple of dozen in advance and take them with you.

This rig is often baited with egg clusters.

The proven technique is to cast across and somewhat upstream and let the bait drift downstream on a tight line so the sinker bounces bottom at all times. That's the main secret—keep the sinker sliding or bouncing along the bottom so the bait passes through the resting or holding spots where steelhead are lying. Keep taking up slack line, raise and lower the rod tip, feed line as the situation demands, and always be on the alert for the slightest pause or nibble. Then raise the rod tip smartly to set the hook. It may only be fouled on the bottom, but you still have to set the hook at every indication of a bite in order not to miss a genuine bite.

Carry plenty of lead wire or sinkers and keep changing lengths and weights to match the current and depth you are fishing. Either trim the lead or add a longer length until your bait or lure moves a little slower than the current and keeps hugging the bottom.

Although salmon eggs and worms are popular, spinners, spoons, jigs, imitation eggs, plastic lures, and plugs are also used for drift fishing. Natural baits are usually best when the water is high and somewhat roily or discolored. Lures work better when the water is clear and low. Heavy spoons and jigs are often fished in many spots along the bottom without the help of a sinker. But lighter lures are fished with the same rig and lead-pencil sinker used with natural baits.

Fish a lure by casting upstream and across and letting the current take it down along the bottom. Steelhead often hit the lure as it is swinging in the current if it has some action or flash. At other times, you can reel the lure slowly and even give it additional jerks with the rod tip. If you can wade out above a good holding spot, let your lure go down with the current, and hold it there while working it back and forth in a small area.

In recent years, anglers have started using bobbers on their line above a bait or lure. Small jigs especially designed for steelhead, such as Leo's Jig, Big Jig, and Jig-A-Lou, are especially good for this fishing. Small panfish

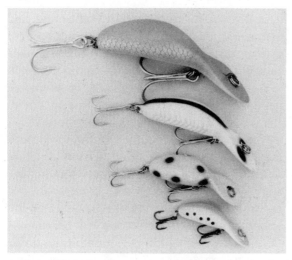

The Heddon Tadpolly plug comes in different sizes and is popular with steelhead anglers for casting and trolling.

On big rivers, the best steelhead spots are reached by boat. The lure is let out downstream while the boat moves slowly. You may need a sinker or trolling weight in front of the bait or lure to get it down close to the bottom. Or use a crankbait or other deep-diving lure that digs deep into the current and runs near the bottom.

Some sections of steelhead rivers, especially the lower portions, are wide, slow-moving, and have deep pools. Or they may be muddy from recent rains. Here still-fishing or "plunking" is the most effective method. A plunker chooses a spot on the bank and stays there most of the time. From there, he casts his bait on a bottom rig with a sinker and lets it rest on or near the bottom. Then he puts his rod in a holder or forked stick on the bank and sits down to wait for a bite. A fairly long, heavy baitcasting or spinning rod with lines testing 15 to 20 pounds is suitable for this type of fishing.

Anglers fishing for steelhead in large lakes use the same tackle and techniques. But they do a lot more trolling during spring, summer, or fall when steelhead move closer to shore to feed or to enter tributary streams to spawn. The same tackle and techniques used for coho

jigs are also good, but make sure the hooks are strong. The bobber is attached to the line just high enough so the bait or lure travels a few inches above the bottom. For fishing deep water or pools, rig a sliding bobber to get the bait or lure close to the bottom.

Still other anglers use a Hot Shot side planer, which is fastened on the line above a plug and let out in the current to carry the lure toward the middle of the river.

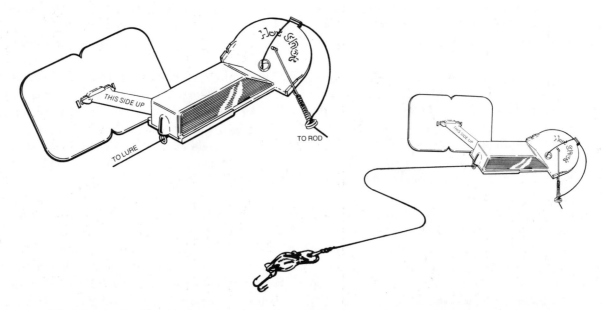

A Luhr-Jensen Hot Shot side planer is used to work a lure into the current and carry it across and downstream.

or chinook salmon also take steelhead. Trolling is done with flat lines, weighted lines, planers, or downriggers. Trolling near tributary streams, river mouths, along dropoffs, and over any fish located by sonar is most productive. In recent years, anglers fishing Lake Michigan have discovered that steelhead can be caught during the summer months in deep water 20 or more miles from shore. The fish feed on insects blown or carried by currents to the middle of the lake. Many steelhead are caught there by trolling flies, spoons, or plugs.

Anglers fish for landlocked steelhead in big rivers from an anchored boat by letting out plugs about 50 to 100 feet to reach spots where fish are present. Other anglers in the Great Lakes cast heavy lines from shore, piers, and breakwaters. Many anglers also fish midwestern rivers that steelhead enter to spawn.

For real sport, nothing beats hooking and fighting a big steelhead on a fly rod. Unfortunately, fly fishing is often limited to certain rivers and certain seasons. It is most effective during the summer and early fall when the water is low and clear. However, with sinking lines it is now possible to catch steelhead on flies even during the cold winter months when stream conditions are favorable.

Wet flies and streamers are fished in much the same manner as for other trout. Cast across and upstream and allow the fly to sink close to the bottom as you take up slack line. If you see a steelhead or know where one is lying, keep casting so the fly drifts and swings in front of its nose. Steelhead often ignore the fly or even move out of the way, but suddenly may decide to take it after several casts. Usually the fly is taken at the end of the swing. While steelhead will hit a fly drifting naturally, you'll get more strikes if you give it some action with short pulls or twitches to make it pulsate and quiver.

To cover the most water with a fly rod, start fishing upstream with short casts and gradually progress to longer casts until you have covered most of the holding spots. Then move downstream a short distance and repeat this procedure. It is important that the fly moves as close to the bottom as possible during the drift. This may mean changing lines often to match the speed of the current and the depth of the water. Weighted fly lines in various sinking speeds can be carried on extra spools.

You can catch steelhead on dry flies on the surface at times when the water is low and clear in summer or early fall. Late afternoon and evening are usually the best times. The dry fly is allowed to drift naturally in the current, but steelhead also take a fly that is skated or skittered along the surface. In fact, many anglers often deliberately skate the fly on the surface to create a wake. Steelhead may make several passes at a skated fly.

Once you hook a steelhead on any kind of tackle you can look forward to a fast, spectacular fight. Smaller fish leap out of the water again and again. Steelies of all sizes make long, fast, powerful runs, often forcing you to follow them downstream in a strong current. The safest way to land a steelhead is to fight it until it gives up and then beach it on a rock or shore. When you are fishing from a boat, or from shore with deep water at your feet, use a wide-mouthed net or a gaff.

Steelhead caught during the summer range from 2 to 8 pounds. Winter fish are much larger, often going up to 15 or 20 pounds. Steelhead up to 30 pounds have been caught in many rivers. The rod-and-reel record is a 42-pound 2-ounce steelhead caught in Alaska at Bell Island on June 22, 1970, by David White. The largest steelhead caught was a 47½-pound fish netted in Alaska.

Where to Go

In California, steelhead are found in the Klamath, Trinity, Mad, Eel, Sacramento, Russian, American, Yuba, Feather, Smith, Mattole, and Navarro rivers. Oregon has many steelhead rivers, among which are the Rogue, Umpqua, Destuches, Coquille, Siletz, Siuslaw, Sandy, Alsea, Wilson, Big Nestucca, and

This angler proudly displays two trophy steelhead from the Sheena River in British Columbia. (Gov't. of B.C. Photo)

Columbia. The last named also flows through the state of Washington, whose other steelhead rivers include the Duckabush, Kalama, Stillaguamish, Snoqualmie, Washougal, Wind, Quinault, Dosewallips, Green, Lewis, Puyallup, Skagit, Skykomish, Nisqually, Chehalis, Cowlitz, Wenatchee, Rogue, Queets, Naselle, Willapa, Nooksack, Bogachiel, and Toutle. Idaho's steelhead rivers include the Snake, Salmon, Boise, and Clearwater. Alaska also has many rivers in its southeastern section that can be fished for steelhead. In British Columbia, the Fraser, Kispiox, Cowichan, Skeena, Cooper, Sustut, Babine, Dean, Thompson, Vedder, and Bella Coola rivers offer great steelhead fishing, as does the famed Campbell River on Vancouver Island.

Steelhead have also been stocked in most of the Great Lakes, and there is good fishing not only in the lakes themselves but also in many tributaries entering them. So there is steelhead fishing in many of these streams in Michigan, Wisconsin, Minnesota, Ohio, New York, Pennsylvania, Indiana, and Ontario, Canada. Steelhead have also been stocked in some of the larger reservoirs and lakes in other states.

For the latest information on river conditions, it's a good idea to contact local fishermen, tackle stores, the outdoor writers of local newspapers, or your state fish and game department. It also pays to visit the river yourself to see firsthand if water conditions are right and to find out if fish are being caught.

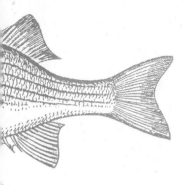

Chapter 13

Lake Trout

Lake trout are unfamiliar to many anglers and not too popular as game fish, mostly because their range is limited and fishing for them is usually best during inclement weather. Also, the best lake trout fishing is found in remote, northern, wilderness areas accessible only by float planes. And even here, the fishing season may only last about two months. Thus, only a small percentage of freshwater anglers have had firsthand experience with this fish.

The lake trout is a char like the Dolly Varden trout and brook trout. It is also called the Mackinaw, togue, Great Lakes trout, forktail trout, gray trout, salmon trout, namaycush, or just plain laker.

The lake trout varies from gray to light green, brown, or almost black, with a cream-colored or white belly. The whole body is covered with lighter, irregular spots. The laker has a large head, a large mouth with strong teeth, and a forked tail.

Originally the lake trout was found from Labrador to Alaska, throughout the Great Lakes, and in northern New England. But it has been introduced into waters in many other states as far west as California and Utah and as far south as Tennessee. It has also been stocked in several foreign countries. Lake trout thrive best in large, clear, cold and deep northern lakes, where good fishing is often found from spring to fall.

Tackle

Spinning, spincasting, baitcasting, and even fly tackle are all used for lake trout. Formerly, most trolling was done with fairly heavy tackle, lead-core or wire lines, and weights to get down deep where lake trout are usually found. But today downriggers with lighter tackle have become popular for deep trolling. With this method, you get more fight from the fish because the weight is released when a laker is hooked. In general, tackle and techniques for lakers are similar to those for coho and chinook salmon.

Lures for lake trout include spoons up to 6 inches long, spinners of various types, and long, light plugs such as the Rapala and Rebel,

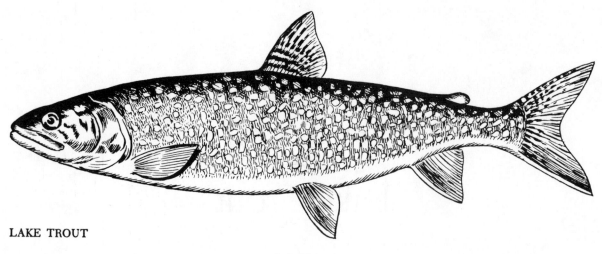

LAKE TROUT

Lake Trout

as well as jigs, big streamers, and bucktails.

Lake trout feed on smelt, ciscoes, tullibees, whitefish, yellow perch, sculpin, suckers, darters, alewives, chubs, shiners, and other small fish and minnows. These can all serve for bait. You can also use strips cut from fish or even worms behind spinners or on jigs.

Seasonal Tactics

Lake trout fishing is best early in the spring, soon after the ice is out, and then again in the fall when the fish return to the shallows to spawn. During these times, the trout are in shallow water and close to the surface. In the summer months, when lake trout are deep, the fishing is slow, except farther north in Canadian and Alaskan waters, where the ice may not break up until June or even July, and good fishing is often had during July, August, and early September. Lake trout are also caught through the ice during the winter months, but more on this later.

Lake trout can be caught on almost any day, but many anglers prefer windy, rainy, cloudy days for the fastest fishing. This is especially true when the lake trout are in shallow water. When they are down deep, you can often catch them during the middle of the day.

Finding lake trout in the spring is easy because they are usually feeding near shore at the mouths of inlets and along reefs and points. They prefer reefs with deep water nearby and a rocky bottom. The smaller fish venture into the shallows, but the larger ones usually prefer somewhat deeper water. At this time, the waters are cold inshore and at the surface throughout the lake. Lake trout usually follow regular predictable routes when they move about a lake. These routes can provide fast fishing if you are there when the lakers are moving through.

During the summer months, locating lake trout presents more of a problem since they are in very deep water. You may find them in some lakes only 50 feet down, while in others they may be down 100, 150, and even 200 feet deep. They like a water temperature ranging from 42 to 55 degrees F., so a thermometer is a big help in finding them. The layer with the preferred temperature and sufficient oxygen will vary in depth from lake to lake and according to the season, but if it lies over a reef, shoal, rocks, or a depression, you have a prime spot for lakers. That is why a depth finder is needed for locating such bottoms and even finding baitfish or the lake trout themselves.

In the extreme northern lakes of Canada and

The biggest lake trout are caught in Canada. This one was taken in Great Slave Lake in the Northwest Territories.

Alaska, you can often find lake trout in shallow water near shore and in the upper layers even during the summer months. At this time, they also may be caught in some rivers that feed these lakes. Here you'll usually find the best fishing below rapids and at the mouths of streams entering the lake.

When lake trout are in fairly shallow water near shore, you can catch them by casting from shore or from a boat. A boat is best because you can move around, trying different spots and covering deeper water. Spoons and underwater plugs and spinners should be retrieved at a slow or medium speed with plenty of rod action to make them rise and sink and flutter. Try a few casts with the lure traveling just below the surface. If you get no strikes, let it sink a bit deeper, reel it in, and work it at that level. On the next cast, let it sink still deeper and retrieve it at this deeper level. Keep doing this until you get a strike. Move the boat around and cast over a reef from different angles.

When lake trout are in shallow water or near the surface, or when, at times, you see baitfish being chased by lake trout or see terns or gulls diving over feeding fish, casting jigs, spoons, or plugs with a light spinning rod provides top sport. Or you can use a fly rod and cast big silver-bodied streamers or bucktails on a weight-forward sinking fly line. Many flies tied for saltwater fishing are excellent. Instead of casting, try trolling streamers or bucktails.

Spoons, spinners, and plugs can be trolled at different depths and different speeds until you find the right combination. You can also troll a smelt, alewife, or minnow sewn on the hook so that there's a curve in its body. If your boat isn't equipped with downriggers, troll with a lead-core or wire line. Let it out until you feel the lure or bait hit bottom, then reel in a couple of feet and troll at that depth. Once you locate the depth where the fish are, you can mark your line with plastic tape so that you can let out the same length every time. Even when using lead-core or wire line, you usually need weight a few feet in front of the lure or bait to get down deep enough.

The best trolling speed for lake trout is very slow and against or across any current. You'll get more strikes and hook more fish if you raise the rod in a quick, short sweep and then lower it at regular intervals. This causes the lure or bait to rise and dart forward and then settle back toward the bottom, giving it a crippled-fish action. Long, thin flutterspoons are especially good for such trolling. And by raising and lowering your rod and bumping bottom with the weight every so often, you will know that you are deep enough.

Although plain lures or baits will catch lake trout, they often become more effective if trolled behind a series of spinners, called "cowbells," or behind a metal dodger or flasher. These act as attractors, giving off vibrations, flashing, and imparting an extra action to the lure or bait. They work especially well with a sewn baitfish behind them; also in front of spoons, flash flies, plugs, and the Michigan squid.

In recent years, the older methods of deep trolling for lake trout have been replaced by the use of downriggers. With one to four mounted on a boat, you can troll a lure or bait at exactly the depth you want. When you get a strike, the line is released and you can fight the fish without any weight, allowing you to use lighter tackle and have more fun and sport.

Many anglers also jig for lake trout. For this you need fairly light spinning or baitcasting tackle. Almost any heavy, quick-sinking lure is effective—big white or yellow leadhead jigs to 3 ounces or heavy spoons such as the Hopkins, Kastmaster, or Krocodile. A strip of fish added to a jig is an extra attraction. Jigging can be done from a boat drifting over the rocks, shoals, or reefs where lake trout like to lie or feed. Send the lure down to the bottom, and when it hits, reel in a couple of turns, then start working it up and down. Or after it hits bottom, jig for a while near the bottom, then start reeling it toward the surface as you work the rod tip up and down to make the lure flutter and flash.

Lake trout can be caught in the winter through the ice. Here, too, jigging is the best method. Tackle consists of a short baitcasting rod, a reel with about 20-pound-test mono line, and a silver or gold spoon, plain or dressed, with a dead minnow or a strip of fish on the hook. Some anglers also use a combination rig with two spoons. You have to develop the right jigging speed to get strikes. The spoon should rise and then flutter down in an enticing manner.

Lake trout can also be caught throughout

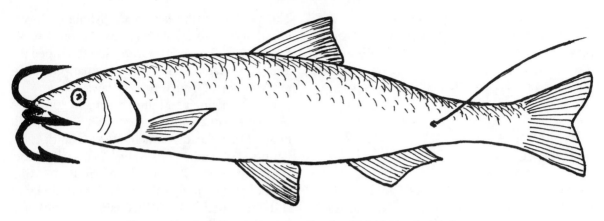

How to rig a dead big minnow or small sucker for ice fishing for lake trout.

the season by fishing live minnows or other small fish on the bottom. A live smelt or alewife, small sucker, or chub from 4 to 6 inches long is hooked through the back. You need a bottom rig with a sinker just heavy enough to reach the bottom. Let the baitfish swim around until a lake trout comes along and swallows it.

A lake trout hooked on light tackle will put up a good fight, especially in shallow water. (Quebec Tourist Branch Photo)

Lake trout hooked on or near the surface on light tackle provide an exciting battle. They run fast and occasionally kick up a fuss. But a laker hooked on wire line or rigs with heavy sinkers at great depths is another thing. A disappointing fight usually ensues, with the fish giving up long before it reaches the surface. Then you just have a dead weight to raise to the top, which, of course, is why most anglers use downriggers and light tackle nowadays.

If you catch really big lake trout in the Far North you'll get a long, stubborn fight even on fairly heavy tackle. But big lakers are rare in most waters in the United States, where most of the fish taken run from 5 to 15 pounds. However, in parts of Alaska and in Canada, lake trout up to 30 pounds are fairly common. The rod-and-reel record is a 65-pound lake trout caught by Larry Daunis in Great Bear Lake in the Northwest Territories in Canada. A few others in the 60-pound class have also been caught by sport fishermen. But lake trout grow much larger, and there have been reports of fish up to 104 pounds caught on handlines or in nets.

The lake trout has a fine-flavored flesh that can be fried, baked, broiled, or smoked. Eskimos in Alaska prefer the taste of lake trout over rainbow trout, and in Canada, lakers have appeared on restaurant menus. However, lake trout grow very slowly; in northern lakes it may take fifty years for a lake trout to reach 50 or 60 pounds. So more and more anglers are releasing big fish and keeping only one as a trophy or a couple of small ones to eat.

Where to Go

As stated earlier, lake trout are found in many lakes and rivers in Alaska. In Canada, Saskatchewan is noted for its lake trout fishing. Some of the best lakes are Waterbury, Kingsmere, La Ronge, Black, Little Bear, Cree, Reindeer, and Athabasca. In Manitoba, Gods, Nueltin, Reed, Clearwater, and Athapapuskow are productive but have to be reached by plane. In the Northwest Territories, Great Bear and Great Slave lakes are noted for their big lake trout. In Alberta, you can fish Cold, Gris, Wentzel, Peerless, and Swan lakes. In Quebec, St. John, Wakonichi, Mistassini, and Chibougamau lakes can be fished, as well as most of the extreme northern part of the province bordering Hudson Bay and Ungava Bay.

There is also some lake trout fishing in Newfoundland, Labrador, Nova Scotia, and New Brunswick. For information about a specific area in Canada, write the Canadian Government Office of Tourism in Ottawa.

In this country, Maine has many productive lake trout waters, including Beech Hill Pond, Moosehead, Branch, West Grand, East Grand, Schoodic, and Sebec lakes. In New Hampshire you'll find lake trout in Big Greenbough Pond, Silver, Tarleton, Squam, and Newfound lakes. Wisconsin's Green Lake is well known for its lake trout fishing. In Michigan, you can try Torch, Elk, Crystal, and Higgins lakes. And as mentioned earlier, lake trout have made a comeback in most of the Great Lakes. In Idaho, lake trout are found in Priest Lake. Utah has Fish and Bear lakes and the Flaming Gorge Reservoir. In New York, lakers can be caught in Lake George and in Seneca, Raquette, Cayuga, Keuka, and Canandaigua lakes. In Massachusetts, Quabbin Reservoir contains lake trout. They have also been stocked in Tennessee in Dale Hollow Lake. And lake trout are also found in Lake Tahoe on the California-Nevada border.

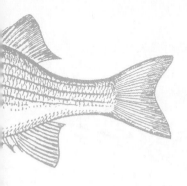

Chapter 14

Muskellunge

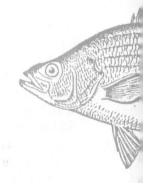

Most freshwater anglers would like to catch a muskellunge because it is big and makes an impressive trophy. It also puts up a tough fight that strains the tackle and provides plenty of thrills. But not many anglers are willing to pay the price of catching a muskellunge. The musky is a moody, temperamental, unpredictable, tricky fish that is rarely easy to catch. It takes a lot of patience, persistence, and know-how to hook one, and plenty of skill and a bit of luck to land one. Many big muskies manage to break the line or straighten the hook and are therefore lost to the angler. You may also have to fish for days or even weeks before you get so much as one solid strike from a musky. Even expert musky anglers and guides claim that it usually takes a week of hard fishing to catch one or two fish. Many anglers have pursued muskellunge for years and have yet to catch their first fish.

There are some anglers and fishing guides who have acquired reputations for their musky catches. These men and a few women catch dozens of big muskies each season, often winning contests with the bigger fish. Some of these anglers have even caught two or three fish in one day or several in one week. These skilled anglers are usually the musky "specialists" who fish only for these big fish and waste little time on other species. Most of them live close to the waters they fish and concentrate on the lakes or rivers they know best and which contain plenty of big muskellunge.

The average freshwater angler usually has to confine his fishing to a weekend or a brief vacation period, often during the poorest time of the year for musky fishing. This may be sufficient to catch trout, bass, or panfish, but to catch a musky you have to allow plenty of time and make repeated trips to your fishing site throughout the season (from spring or early summer to late fall). To be frank, if you can't spend the time or don't have the patience and persistence to seek out muskellunge you'd better confine your fishing to easier-to-catch species.

Let's take a close look at the muskellunge, which, as most anglers know, is a member of the pike family, related to both the northern

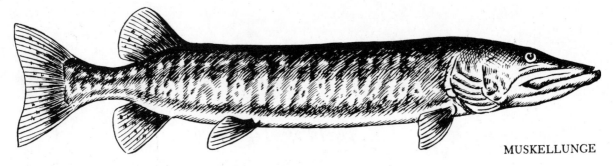

MUSKELLUNGE

Muskellunge

pike and the pickerel. It has the same big al-ligatorlike jaws, sharp teeth, and long, slim body. The back is green or olive fading into gray, and the belly is white. There may be darker spots or stripes on the sides and tail, but these are often indistinct in the larger fish.

The muskellunge is known by many differ-ent names, which are usually spelling varia-tions of the more popular one. They are called maskinonge, masquenonge, masquealonge, muskalonge, muskallonge, moskallonge, etc. They are also called the great pike, lunge, and musky. Most anglers like to use the last name.

Muskellunge are found in the Great Lakes region north to Canada. They are also found in the St. Lawrence River system (including parts of western New York) and in the Ohio and Tennessee river systems. Many waters in Wisconsin, Minnesota, Michigan, and Penn-sylvania also have them. Although they have been stocked as far south as Virginia, North Carolina, Kentucky, Tennessee, and Alabama, muskies prefer the cold northern lakes and rivers.

Tackle

Many muskies are hooked each season on light tackle by bass fishermen, but only a small per-centage of these are landed; the majority are lost. Yet too many anglers insist on using light bass tackle for this king of freshwater game fish with a reputation as a tackle-buster.

If you are really interested in catching some big muskies, you should get special tackle for them. Special baitcasting rods are labeled "musky" rods. These are stiffer and heavier and often longer than baitcasting rods used for most bass fishing. If you plan to cast very heavy lures or baits, a rod from 6 to 8 feet long with about a 20-inch handle is best since it can be cast with two hands. Similar rods, for trolling, can accommodate either heavy-duty baitcast-ing reels or light saltwater revolving-spool reels. Lines for trolling test from 18 to 30 pounds.

You can also use a stiff, heavy spinning rod from 6 to 8 feet in length for muskies. Such a rod calls for a good-sized spinning reel with lines testing from 12 to 20 pounds. Many of the spinning rods and reels designed for coho and chinook salmon and striped bass serve equally well for muskies.

Muskies have also been caught on fly rods from 8 to 9½ feet long capable of handling No. 8, 9, or 10 weight-forward fast-sinking fly line. But you have to know how to handle such an outfit. Fishing for muskies often requires long casts and a fast retrieve. And although big flies and bugs can be cast with a fly rod, muskies, especially the large ones, prefer even bigger lures. So for most anglers and those who fish only occasionally, a baitcasting or spinning out-fit is more practical.

Rods for muskellunge are on the stiff and heavy side for a number of practical reasons. First, muskies have a tough mouth, and a stiff rod and strong line are needed to set a big

This musky was hooked on a spoon, an old favorite for this species. They also hit plugs, spinners, jigs, and spinnerbaits. (Ontario Ministry of Industry & Tourism Photo)

of big muskellunge. Old-time topwater favorites such as the Lucky 13, Crazy Crawler, Muskie Jitterbug, and Flaptail are still good. Newer plugs such as the Hawg-Wobbler, Creeper, Woodchopper, and Mouldy's Topper are popular. Floating minnow-type plugs such as the Rapala, Rebel, and Redfin can also be used on top or underwater. Other underwater plugs include the larger Creek-Chub Pikie Minnow, Cisco Kid, Bomber Long-A, Bagley's Bang-O-Lure, Storm Big Mac, Uncle Josh Burmek B-1, and Jointed Believer. Plugs up to 10 inches or longer have been used to catch big muskies. Flyrodders use big streamers or bucktails tied on Nos. 1/0 to 4/0 hooks. Two good patterns are the Larry Dahlberg diving jerkbait fly and the Muddler Minnow tied extra large. You can also try big saltwater flies and bugs.

Many of the larger crankbaits designed for bass often work well on muskies. So do jerk baits such as the Suick, Teddie Bait, and Bobby Bait, which are especially made for musky fishing. In recent years, anglers have had luck with large jigs, big plastic worms, curlytails, and grubs.

Whichever lure or bait you select, it's a good idea to tie it on a wire or heavy monofilament leader. Muskies have strong jaws and big teeth and often break regular monofilament. For casting, short 6- to 8-inch wire or nylon-covered braided wire leaders are recommended. For trolling, leaders of wire or 30-pound-test mono up to 3 feet long are better.

When artificial lures fail to produce a strike, try natural baits such as big minnows, suckers, carp, yellow perch, small walleyes, or other fish that are legal. The big salamanders called waterdogs also make good musky baits. But the favorite natural bait is a live or dead sucker from 8 to 12 inches long.

Seasonal Tactics

You may be able to catch muskies as early as March or April along their southern range if

hook. Lures and baits for muskies are usually big and heavy and require a sturdy rod to cast. And finally, you need a strong rod to turn or at least slow down a big musky heading for cover.

Lures for muskies include the old-time fluted spoon with feathers, and spinner and big bucktail combinations, especially those with black hair. The Mepps Musky Killer is a good spinner-bucktail lure that has accounted for many muskies. In recent years, anglers have been achieving excellent results with large spinnerbaits. Spoons up to 8 inches long are also old-time favorites that still catch muskies.

Various types of surface plugs such as poppers, swimmers, gurglers, crawlers, and crippled minnows with propellers will raise a lot the legal season has started at that time. But farther north, fishing doesn't usually begin until May or early June. June is a good month in most areas to start fishing for muskies. July and August have traditionally been the top months, probably because that is when most anglers take their vacations and can spend the most time on the water. But some of the best fishing occurs during September and October, when the largest fish are taken. Yet a good musky fisherman who can locate the fish, knows which lure or bait to use and how to fish it, and fishes hard, can catch muskies from spring to fall. In some of our southern states, muskies are even caught during the winter.

Though muskies have been caught at almost every hour of the day, the optimum time will vary with the season and the waters. Most anglers fish from early morning to late afternoon or evening. But when the days are sunny and bright and the lake is flat and calm, especially during the summer, you'll usually do better if you fish around daybreak and toward dusk. Fishing can be very good in some waters soon after the sun sets and later at night.

Most expert musky fishermen and guides agree that the best fishing is usually on overcast or rainy days when the surface of the water is rippled or choppy. Fishing can be excellent before or after a storm, but a cold front, while it lasts, will often kill the fishing. A wind from the south, southwest, or west is favored over an east wind, which can also hurt the fishing. Watch for sudden changes in the weather pattern. After several days of fine weather, the onset of rain can make the muskies hit.

The main secret in musky fishing is to locate the fish, then concentrate on making them strike. Your chances are increased if you can locate several good musky spots and spend the day giving each one a good workout. That is why a professional guide is a big help to the beginner or even to an experienced angler fishing a strange lake for the first time. The guide knows his waters and the habits of the fish in varying weather and water conditions. He can take you straight to the good spots.

For many years it was believed that muskies were all loners, shunning the company of their own kind. But this has been disproved recently, and it is now known that muskies often gather in schools of two or three fish to a dozen or more. Homer LeBlanc, a great musky guide on Lake St. Clair, Michigan, has caught as many as eleven muskies in one day from a patch of underwater weeds no larger than a room. Of course, muskies do separate and often feed alone; the biggest ones, especially, do not tolerate intruders in their favorite hangouts. They'll eat the smaller fish and chase away the bigger ones. While some muskies stay put in one spot for long periods of time, others migrate daily from one spot to another, usually from deep to shallow water and back again. Muskies often spend a lot of time in deep water near shallower feeding areas. In fact, in recent years, muskies have been caught in water up to 40 feet deep. However, most anglers fish in water from 4 to 20 feet deep.

Favorite musky hangouts in a lake include coves, sunken trees, brushpiles, logs, stumps, rock bars, sandbars, sloping points of land, underwater islands and humps, dropoffs, lily pads, and overhanging trees. One of the most productive spots is an underwater weedbed in water from 6 to 20 feet deep. Most muskies are caught over the weeds or along the edges, especially those bordering deeper water. Weeds attract and hide small fish, salamanders, frogs, and other aquatic creatures that muskies eat. The presence of prey is also the reason muskies gather at inlets or outlets to a lake.

Muskies migrate with the seasons in pursuit of food. In spring, they stay close to their spawning grounds near bays, coves, channels, backwaters, rivers, and shallow, muddy bottoms. Then in summer, they often move to deep water where ciscoes, whitefish, yellow perch, and walleyes are plentiful. In the fall, muskies often return to feed in shallow water, again following the smaller fish that move into the shallows when the water cools.

Locating muskies in rivers or streams is

somewhat easier because you have less water to cover. Fish the quiet pools, and obstructions that slow the current. Heavy rains raise the water level, muddy the water, and spoil the fishing. Wait until the water starts to clear and muskies start hitting again. When the water is high, muskies often are found close to shore cover, but when the water level drops they move to the middle of the deeper pools.

Sometimes a musky breaks water while feeding on the surface—often to catch a fish, frog, rat, mouse, muskrat, chipmunk, squirrel, duckling, gosling or other small animal. (All of these creatures have been found from time to time in musky stomachs.) Try casting a surface plug at random and watch for swirls or follow-ups behind the lure. Muskies have the exasperating habit of following a lure, only to refuse it near the boat. But at least you'll know they are present and can keep returning to the same spot in the hope they'll grab the lure or bait on another occasion.

Casting is a productive method of catching muskies in lakes and rivers. This is usually done from a drifting boat moving with the wind or current. Fish the weedbeds, rock bars, lily pads, sunken trees, logs, sloping points, underwater islands, and reefs. It is best to cast ahead of the boat or well to one side, spacing your casts about 6 feet apart. If you raise a musky or see one following the bait or lure, drop anchor and work that spot thoroughly.

Spinner-bucktails and spinnerbaits can be retrieved just below the surface in shallow water by holding the rod high and reeling fairly fast. In deeper water, hold the rod down, reel more slowly, and try different depths. Surface lures and plugs are most effective during the summer and early fall, when the water is warm and muskies are most active. One good way to fish a surface plug is to whip your rod up and down in short, fast jerks, reeling all the while so that the plug splashes, weaves, and sways on top. Then reel faster and jerk it so it dips below the surface. Usually a musky will hit the plug soon after it submerges. Jerk baits can be worked in a similar fashion, with 3-foot

sweeps of the rod, to make the plug submerge and dart forward or move from side to side. Let the plug rise to the surface before you jerk it under again. Or you can use the heavier or weighted jerk baits and work them below the surface for most of the retrieve. Surface plugs are especially good when used at dusk and at night.

Crankbaits in the larger sizes are excellent when muskies are lying near the bottom over weedbeds, along dropoffs, bars, submerged islands, and other structure. You make a long cast and reel in fairly fast so the plug travels deep along the bottom. When the plug is directly below the boat, quickly lift the rod tip high overhead, causing the lure to shoot upward; any musky following it will often hit before it escapes.

Another good lure for casting to muskies is a jig weighing from ¼ to ¾ ounce. Add a big plastic curlytail worm or grub to the hook. This can be reeled fairly fast in shallow water with an up-and-down jigging motion. In deeper water, let the jig sink and bounce it along the bottom, especially along the edges of weedbeds. If the worm doesn't produce, try a minnow about 4 to 6 inches long on the hook.

As a general rule, it is best to retrieve a lure fast for muskellunge, especially during the summer and early fall. Later on, when the water gets cold, slow down the retrieve. Surface plugs should be worked fast so that they throw plenty of splash and make a big commotion. But you have to experiment since there are times when a medium or even slow retrieve is better. At other times, an erratic retrieve interests the fish. But whether your retrieve is fast, medium or slow, the lure should look alive and be moving at all times.

Muskies often follow a lure up to the boat, then turn around or sink without striking. Or you may get a swirl behind the lure as it travels on top or just below the surface. When this happens, speed up your retrieve, and when the lure is near the boat, swish it in a circle or figure-eight pattern. Or when the lure is about 12 feet from the boat, swing your rod quickly to one side so that it changes direction. This will often trigger a strike. If muskies continue to follow your lure without striking, try changing lures to find one that interests them.

When artificial lures don't work, try a natural bait such as a dead sucker. Hook this small baitfish once through the head or harness it around the head with line. Since the sucker is dead, it must be given some action with the rod tip so it spurts, dives, darts, and even surfaces. You can also try letting it sink to the bottom, then retrieve it toward the surface with short jerks to make it look alive. Dead suckers can also be trolled slowly behind the boat with similar rod movement.

Live suckers up to 12 inches long make a good bait for big muskies. If you can't get suckers, use a big chub, shiner, or other baitfish. Hook it through the back and let it swim around with or without a float until a musky grabs it. But no matter how you fish suckers or other small fish, you must give a musky plenty of time to swallow the bait. A musky will grab the small fish in the middle, then swim off to swallow it. You must give slack line so the musky doesn't feel the pull. Keep feeding line and wait until the musky makes up its mind to swallow the baitfish. This might take a few minutes or much longer.

When you set the hook, come back hard with your rod tip. Some anglers even set the hook two or three times. Muskies clamp down on a bait and hold it firmly. They also have tough jaws. All of this means that you have to move the lure or bait and penetrate the jaws for the hooks to sink in and hold.

Trolling is often more effective than casting for muskies. In shallow water, with 50 to 150 feet of line out, troll large spoons, spinners, spinner-bucktails, underwater plugs, or jigs. Work your boat over and along the edges of weedbeds or lily pads, around islands, over sunken points, and along the edges of channels, coves, or rivermouths. In shallow water, use a regular mono or braided line without a weight.

In deeper water, troll the same lures as in shallow water but with lead-core line, Monel wire line, or downriggers. Trolling along the weedbeds at the edges where the water drops off from 6 to 20 feet is a good way to take muskies during the summer months. Although lines without a weight can be trolled up to 150 feet behind a boat, muskies are not boat-shy in deeper water and often hit a lure trolled only a few feet behind the boat. Here you can use lead weights or trolling weights from 4 to 6 ounces between the line and leader to get the lure down and keep it there. In some lakes, muskies have been caught as deep as 40 feet. Trolling fast is usually more effective than slow-trolling.

Although rods can be left in rod holders on the boat while trolling, you will usually get more strikes if you work your lure by raising your rod slowly, then letting it drop back quickly. This can be done as you let out line, or as you reel it in, or every minute or two

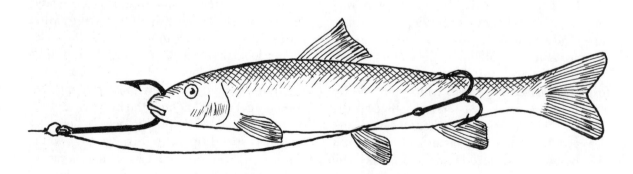

Tandem hook rig to harness sucker for muskies

while trolling. The lure worked in this manner often triggers a strike, whereas a lure moving in a straight line or always at the same depth does not. Rod movement is especially effective with spoons or jigs.

A musky puts up a spectacular fight at times, leaping, lunging, rolling, and splashing around on top of the water. At other times, it sulks and makes short runs below the surface. A big musky has plenty of endurance, staying power, and weight, and a fight may last a half hour or more, depending on your tackle. The fish often heads for a sunken log, rocks, trees, or other obstructions. Many a big musky is lost near the boat when the fish makes a last, sudden surge or thrashes around wildly on the surface.

A musky should be played until it gives up and turns over on its side. Then you can use a wide-mouthed net to scoop up the fish. If the fish is large, it is better to gaff it through the lower jaw. Some expert anglers and guides grab a musky in the eye sockets or under the gill cover. But this should be done only with fish that will not be released. A big musky can also be beached on a sloping shore.

It is believed that muskies reach over 100 pounds in weight, but the largest taken on rod and reel weighed 69 pounds 15 ounces. This fish was caught in the St. Lawrence River, in New York, by Art Lawton on September 22, 1957. Through the years, many other muskies 40 to 60 pounds have been caught. But in most waters, you're lucky to catch a musky in the 15- to 30-pound class. Some outstanding catches of big muskies have been made by Len Hartman, the holder of many records. His big-

Catching a musky this big requires a lot of time, patience, know-how, and a bit of luck. (Wisconsin Natural Resources Dept. Photo)

gest fish was a 67-pound 15-ounce musky caught in the St. Lawrence River on 11-pound-test line!

In addition to the true muskellunge, there is also the so-called tiger musky, which is a hybrid, being a cross between a male northern pike and a female musky. These are being raised in hatcheries and are being stocked in some waters. They are easier to raise and grow faster than true muskellunge. They are also heavy feeders, less wary and easier to catch than purebred muskies. They reach 50 pounds or more in weight.

Where to Go

Some of the best muskellunge fishing is found in Canada, particularly in Ontario, in the Lake of the Woods, Vermillion Lake, Eagle Lake, Kawartha Lake, Pigeon River, Pigeon Lake, Red Lake, and Lake Nipissing. Muskies are also found in Quebec and Manitoba.

In the United States, Wisconsin has more than five hundred lakes and rivers containing muskies. Some of the most productive are Chippewa Flowage, Wisconsin River, Eagle River, Eagle Lake, Pelican Lake, Lac Vieux Desert, Lac du Flambeau, Grindstone Lake, Hayward Lake, Lac Court Oreilles, Moose Lake, Ghost Lake, Deer Lake, and Big Arbor Vitae Lake. In Michigan, Lake St. Clair, Gun Lake, Thunder Bay, Munusconong Bay, the Tahquamenon and Detroit rivers are noted for musky fishing. Minnesota's Leech Lake, Cass Lake, Rainy Lake, Battle Lake, Belle Taine, Mantrap, and Winnibigoshish lakes all have muskies. In New York, Chautauqua Lake, the

St. Lawrence River, the Niagara River, and the Finger Lakes chain are fished for muskies. In Pennsylvania you can try Pymatuning Lake, Tionesta Dam, Allegheny River, Susquehanna River, Delaware River, Juniata River, Conneaut Lake, Lake LeBoeuf, and Lake Edinboro. In West Virginia, the Little Kanawha River, Elk River, Big Coal River, Mill Creek, West Fork, Middle Island Creek, Salt Lick Creek, Cedar Creek, Hughes River, Leading Creek, and East Lynn Lake contain muskies. Virginia has Smith Mountain Lake, Clayton Lake, and the Shenandoah, Clinch, and James rivers. In Kentucky, the Licking, Red, Kentucky, Green, Barren, and Obed rivers, and Kinniconick Creek can be fished. In Ohio, muskies are found in Jackson Lake, Leesville Lake, Pymatuning Lake, Lake White, Clear Fork, Piedmont, Seneca, Clendening, Salt Fork, West Branch, Dillon, Knox, Sunfish Creek, Rocky Fork Creek, and Paint Creek. In North Carolina, you can fish for muskies in the French Broad River, Little Tennessee River, Hiwassee River, Hiwassee Lake, Fontana Lake, and Santeelah Lake. In Tennessee, muskies have been found in Dale Hollow Reservoir, Norris Reservoir, Woods Reservoir, Fort Patrick Henry Reservoir, and Rock Island Lake. Other states with some muskie waters include Vermont, New Jersey, Missouri, Indiana, Iowa, and North Dakota.

But no matter where you seek them, muskies offer a challenge and require plenty of skill and know-how and patience to catch them consistently. Even if you catch only one big musky or a few good-sized ones, you have accomplished one of the more difficult feats in freshwater fishing.

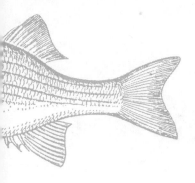

Chapter 15

Pike

At one time, very few anglers in this country or in Canada fished for pike deliberately. In earlier days there was such an abundance of other game fishes that the pike was overlooked or scorned in favor of these supposedly more desirable species. Even today, there are still a few diehards who consider the pike unworthy to be called a game fish. And in Canada and Alaska, where pike are very plentiful, they are still looked down on or ignored by many native anglers.

Some anglers who despise the pike point to the fact that it destroys other fish and young waterfowl. They claim that many good trout and bass waters have been ruined by the introduction of pike. These greedy fish are supposed to have eaten up most of the trout and bass in those waters. In Saskatchewan and Manitoba, pike do devour hundreds of thousands, if not millions, of ducklings.

But a look at the other side of the picture shows that in many waters, trout, bass, walleyes, and pike have lived together for ages and each species is plentiful. In certain waters, trout and bass may decline in numbers when pike first appear. But biologists claim that in many other waters, pike actually improve the fishing by keeping down the numbers of yellow perch, sunfish, and other panfish. True, they'll also eat trout and bass, but the fish that are left grow larger in lakes or rivers where pike are present. In waters lacking pike, panfish and even bass often become plentiful but are stunted.

But whether you admire the pike or hate it, you are missing some good fishing and sport if you don't try to catch this slim, toothy predator. Except for coloring, the pike looks like a smaller replica of its close cousin, the muskellunge. However, pike are more numerous and are found in more waters than the musky. They are also less temperamental and not so fussy about taking a lure or bait. In recent years, more and more anglers have started fishing for pike and are enjoying fine sport.

The pike also goes by other names, such as the great northern pike, northern pike, jackfish, jack, grass pike, and snake. It is sometimes called pickerel, a misnomer, since the two fish are not identical.

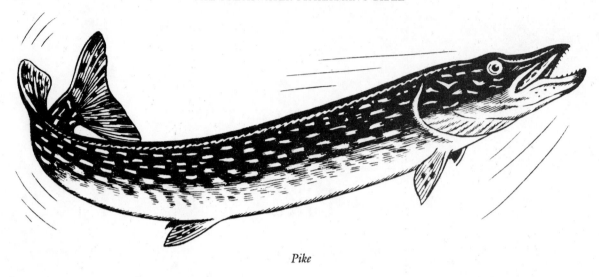

Pike

The pike has a long, slim body with the dorsal fin set back near the tail. The mouth looks like a big duck's bill or an alligator's snout. Most pike are olive or greenish in color, occasionally with a bluish cast. The color becomes lighter toward the belly, which is yellowish or white. Most pike have many yellow-white, bean-shaped spots along the sides of the body. However, there is also a silver pike which is bluish-gray and lacks the lighter spots. This variant is found in some waters in Minnesota and Wisconsin.

The pike is widely distributed, being found in the United States, Canada, Alaska, Europe, and Asia. Although in this country the pike has been introduced into many waters as far south as North Carolina and Texas, it is mainly a fish of the colder, northern waters.

Tackle

For small pike in open waters, regular bass or walleye tackle is adequate—a light or medium baitcasting, spinning, spincasting, or fly outfit. For larger, northern pike, the same tackle used for muskellunge (see preceding chapter) will be most practical. This is especially true when fishing around obstructions.

In recent years, more anglers have been using a fly rod for the utmost in thrills when fishing for pike. Choose a rod 8½ or 9 feet long designed to handle a No. 8 or 9 fly line. Floating or sinktip fly lines are best for fishing near the surface in shallow water. Most of the big streamer and bucktail flies used for big trout, bass, and saltwater fish will also catch pike. Effective patterns include Lefty's Deceiver, Dahlberg Diver, McNally Magnum, Zonker, Bunny Fly, and Aztec. Streamers dressed with Mylar and marabou are also good. And pike will also hit bass bugs, popper flies, and minnow-type bugs on the surface. Most flies are tied on Nos. 1/0 to 3/0 hooks.

Other lures for pike include topwater poppers, crippled minnows, swimmers, and stick baits, as well as minnow-type plugs on top or underwater, and deep divers or crankbaits at various depths. Jerk baits used for muskies will also catch big pike. Spoons are an old-time favorite for pike and are still good in silver, nickel, chrome, gold, copper, and red-and-white or black-and-white. Big spinners with feathers or bucktail and weighted spinners are also productive.

In recent years, pike anglers have discovered that spinnerbaits originally designed for bass, are deadly for pike, especially around weeds and cover near shore. Buzzbaits also catch pike in shallow, weedy water.

The plastic worm, another bass lure, has proven effective for pike. You can rig a plain

Big pike put up a good fight and have to be played carefully until they give up. (Mercury Marine Photo)

Seasonal Tactics

The top months for catching pike in most waters are May, June, September, and October. Pike are most active when the water temperature near shore or on the surface is under 65 degrees F. When it rises to 70 degrees F. or higher, pike seek cooler, deeper water. Although they can be caught throughout the day, the best fishing is usually early in the morning and late afternoon. Pike have been caught at night in some waters, but not in any great numbers. Stormy, dark, rainy days are usually more productive than bright, sunny ones.

The early spring is a good time to go pike fishing because at this time the fish are spawning in shallow water (anywhere from 2 to 15 feet deep). Even before ice-out, pike get ready to spawn by entering streams, shallow bays, coves with weeds and marshes. When feeding or hiding in shallow water, pike love to lie in or near weedbeds, around stumps, lily pads, sunken trees, logs, rocks, and other cover. In lakes, look for them around marshy coves, weeds, reeds, points of land, submerged islands, sandbars, rock bars, gravel bars, or inlets. In rivers, they are found in the quieter pools, eddies, backwaters, pockets of slack water, below falls or rapids, and on the downstream side of stumps, driftwood, logjams, rocks, boulders, and islands. Pike prefer sluggish rivers and the slower-moving sections of fast rivers rather than fast, strong currents.

When summer comes, pike, especially the big ones, move into deeper waters (from 20 to 50 feet deep), where they remain most of the day, returning to shallow waters toward dusk. (Many small pike, on the other hand, remain in shallow water throughout the summer months.) Pike seek deeper waters during the summer not only to escape the warm water and heat, but also to feed on alewives, ciscoes, whitefish, and tullibees, which also move into deeper water at this time. In these deeper waters, pike are usually found over or along some kind of structure—over submerged is-

worm from 7 to 10 inches long weedless-style and fish it on top or just below the surface, but most anglers prefer smaller worms or plastic grubs or curlytails on a jig head. Or they add a plastic frog, lizard, or minnow on a jig head weighing from ½ to ¾ ounce.

Pike can also be caught on various natural baits—frogs, minnows, chubs, alewives, suckers, yellow perch, whitefish, ciscoes, and other small fish.

Whether you fish artificial lures or natural baits, it's a good idea to use a wire or heavy monofilament leader (30- or 40-pound test). For casting, the leader can be from 6 to 10 inches long, but for trolling it should be at least 3 feet. Pike, like muskies, have sharp teeth and strong jaws and can cut a light leader. For the same reason, it's a good idea to carry plenty of lures and baits when fishing for pike. They can mangle a lure or bait in a hurry, and you need plenty of replacements.

lands or humps, or off a long point or dropoff. Though the summer is a slow time for pike fishing, you can still catch good-sized pike by fishing deep.

In the fall, pike return to their spring haunts in shallow waters, and the best fishing of the year is right after Labor Day.

Not too long ago it was believed that pike were mostly solitary fish, spending much of their time in one spot. But this has been disproved in recent years when it was found that pike often move great distances in search of food. In the spring when spawning, they often gather in large numbers (up to three hundred) in a bay or cove, and big catches can then be made in a small area. Later on, even when they move into deeper water, pike may form small schools, traveling from deep water to feed in shallow water. Pike usually move early in the morning or in late afternoon and evening on bright days; on overcast or rainy days, often at midday.

It is often easy to catch pike, even big ones, in northern wilderness waters where they are plentiful and unsophisticated and where competition for food makes them more aggressive. In some of these waters in Canada, anglers fishing in a single cove or bay have caught anywhere from fifty to one hundred pike in one day. Most of them, of course, are released and only one or two big ones are kept. But in more heavily fished lakes near the larger population centers, pike soon learn to avoid most lures and baits. Then you have to locate the fish and know how to work your lures or present the bait properly to get strikes. You also have to spend plenty of time casting or trolling to land a big pike or two.

One of the best methods is to cast a spoon from an anchored or drifting boat toward weedbeds, lily pads, or logs, driftwood, or sunken trees. In shallow water, cast the spoon out and start reeling it back fast as soon as it hits the water. Let it skitter on top for several feet, then let it sink and flutter down. When casting over a weedbed, let the spoon sink, then retrieve it just fast enough to clear the weeds. In somewhat deeper water outside the edges of weedbeds or lily pads, or along dropoffs, let your spoon sink to the bottom, wait a few seconds, and quickly lift your rod tip high so the spoon jumps off the bottom. Then let it settle back again and repeat the lift. Since pike often hit a spoon that is sinking, you have to watch your line carefully to detect a hit and set the hook. You can also catch pike in deep water by letting the spoon down to the bottom and then jigging it up and down.

Pike are caught on large weighted spinners, spinner-bucktails, and spinnerbaits. Spinnerbaits should be retrieved on the surface fast so they buzz and sputter and create a commotion. A tandem or double-bladed spinnerbait is deadly cast into thick weeds. You can also retrieve a spinnerbait just below the surface or even deeper. Buzzbaits can be fished the same way.

Great sport can be had with pike in shallow water when they are in the mood to hit surface plugs. Poppers, chuggers, swimmers, and crippled minnows worked on top to kick up a fuss often arouse pike to hit hard, but they often fail to get hooked. Nonetheless, it is exciting fishing and can provide a lot of action, especially when the water is calm and flat.

Instead of spinning or baitcasting tackle, try using a fly rod with a streamer up to 6 inches long. White, yellow, or combinations of red or blue and Mylar strips are productive flies. Big bass bugs or deer-hair bugs with thick bodies on No. 4/0 or 5/0 long-shanked hooks are also effective. Or you can try some of the saltwater flies and poppers designed for striped bass and tarpon. When fishing a bug or popper, cast it out and let it lie there a few seconds, twitch it to make it quiver, then give it a hard, sudden pop, and retrieve it fast for a few feet. A stop-and-go action or erratic retrieve with a variety of speeds works best.

When pike are in deep water, try a bucktail or marabou jig of ⅜ to 1 ounce with a strip of pork rind or a plastic worm added to the hook. An even better combination is a jig and a minnow. Small suckers, shiners, alewives, chubs, and smelt from 4 to 6 inches long are effective. In the spring, fish this minnow-jig along the edges of weedbeds in water from 6 to 18 feet deep. Work the jig pretty fast in long sweeps of the rod, letting it drop back toward the bottom at regular intervals. Later on, in the summer when pike are in deep water, drift in a boat or back troll very slowly, letting the jig and minnow sink to the bottom. Then raise it off the bottom about 3 or 4 feet in a series of quick, short jerks, let it drop back toward the bottom, and repeat the up and down series of jigging motions. Most strikes will come as the jig and minnow are sinking, so you have to keep an eye on the line at all times. Any sudden movement, slack, or strange action of the line that occurs is a signal to set the hook hard.

Trolling is a good way to locate and catch pike when casting doesn't produce. You can use the same lures mentioned above for trolling. In the spring and fall when pike are in shallow water, you should troll close to shore. Early in the morning and in late afternoon, troll over weedbeds. During the middle of the day, troll along the edges of the weeds and along dropoffs and points of land. Pike are not too boat-shy and are often attracted by the wash of a propeller, so you can let out one or two lines from 30 to 50 feet behind the boat.

During the summer months when pike are in water from 20 to 50 feet, troll with weighted lines, wire lines, or downriggers. Spoons, underwater plugs, spoonplugs, spinners, and crankbaits should be trolled so they travel close to the bottom.

Natural baits also catch pike, especially in deep water during the hot summer months. In the morning and evening, in shallow water near shore, frogs are good cast around weeds and lily pads. Minnows and suckers from 6 to 10 inches long also make good bait. These can be hooked through the back and allowed to swim around under a float in shallow water. In deeper water, use a sinker or bottom rig to take the minnow down to the bottom. Minnows can also be hooked through the lips, cast out, and then reeled in slowly.

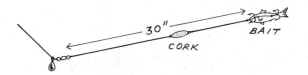

Rig with two treble hooks for fishing a dead baitfish

Instead of anchoring and fishing in one spot, try drifting with the wind and fishing a minnow over weedbeds, reefs, shoals, bars, and points with a free line or with a float. To keep the minnow down, you may have to add a split-shot sinker or two or a small clincher sinker on the leader above the bait. Dead baitfish can also be fished on a free line or under a float European style, with two treble hooks. One hook is imbedded in the side or back of the bait, the other impaled near the tail. Dead baitfish can also be fished on or near the bottom with a sliding sinker or bait-walker rig.

Pike bite well during the winter and are caught in many lakes and rivers where there is some open water near shore. Late winter, when pike are schooling up at the mouths of rivers prior to spawning, is the best time to catch them. Pike are also caught through the ice during the winter. Live minnows are the best bait, but dead minnows jigged on the bottom also catch fish. Jigging a dead minnow on two treble hooks, head down, is a good way to fish through the ice.

A pike usually smashes a lure hard and often hooks itself, but it's a good idea to set the hook with the rod to make sure. A big pike, like a musky, has tough jaws, and large or dull hooks require force to set them properly.

On light tackle, pike will put up a good fight, with the smaller fish, up to 10 or 12 pounds, often jumping out of the water. These smaller fish are also faster and more active. Larger pike are slower and do most of their battling below the surface. Pike also have the habit of allowing themselves to be brought up to the boat without too much fuss—then suddenly going into a frenzy, leaping or thrashing around on top or making a short run. This will often take the

Larry Dahlberg holds a big pike he caught on a fly rod. His popular Dahlberg flies are used for pike and other big freshwater fish. (In-Fisherman Photo)

angler by surprise, and the sudden strain may break the line or straighten the hook.

Pike should be played until they give up completely and turn over on their side before attempting to boat them. A large, wide-mouthed net can be used for smaller fish. Larger fish should be gaffed through the lower jaw. Expert anglers and guides sometimes grab the pike in the gills or by placing a thumb and forefinger into the eye sockets, but this shouldn't be done with fish you plan to release.

It's also a good idea to have a club handy so you can bop the pike on the head and stun it

if you plan to keep the fish. Otherwise keep it in the water and try to remove the hook. A pair of long-nosed pliers are useful for safely removing a hook from a pike's mouth.

The world-record pike caught on rod and reel at present is a 55-pound 1-ounce fish caught in Lake of Grefeern in West Germany on October 16, 1986. The former world record caught in this country in the Sacandaga Reservoir, New York, in 1940, was a 46-pound 2-ounce pike caught by Peter Dubuc. Pike over 30 pounds have been caught in many states. In Canada, where pike from 30 to 49 pounds have been caught, fish in the 20-pound class are fairly common. Some big pike have also been caught in Alaska. But the biggest pike are found in European waters and Siberia. Some pike there run up to 90 pounds.

Although pike are somewhat bony, they make good eating if you fillet the smaller ones and fry them. They can also be baked or smoked.

Where to Go

The best pike fishing is found in Canada, especially in Manitoba, Saskatchewan, and Ontario. In Ontario, Lake Nipissing, Lac Seul, Eagle Lake, Lake Abitibi, Lake of the Woods, Lake Huron, and the Nipigon River are all productive. In Saskatchewan, Lake Athabasca, Reindeer, Cree, Black, Middle lakes, and the Fond du Lac and Churchill rivers have some big pike. In Manitoba, the Little Churchill River, Gods Lake, Island Lake and South Knife, Nueltin, Tadoule, Nejanilini, Kississing, and Reed lakes have pike. Of course, there are hundreds of other lakes and rivers in Canada that contain pike.

In the United States, you'll find some good pike waters in Michigan's Lake Superior, St. Clair River, Diamond Lake, and Paw Paw Lake. In Wisconsin, you can fish the Mississippi River, Grinstone Lake, Big Twin Lake, Forest Lake, Couderay Lake, and Megontonga Lake. Minnesota's pike waters are Minnetonka, Gull, and Pelican lakes. In Nebraska, pike were originally found in the Missouri, Niobrara, Loup, Elkhorn, and Platte rivers, but have also been stocked in many reservoirs such as Lewis and Clark. In North Dakota, you can try Lake Metigoshe, Lake Darling, Garrison Reservoir, and Oahe Reservoir. Oahe Reservoir also extends into South Dakota, where you can also fish for pike in Randall Reservoir, Lake Sharpe, and Lake Francis Case. In New York State, pike are found in the Thousand Islands area, St. Lawrence River, Lake Oneida, Seneca Lake, Finger Lakes, and Sacandaga Reservoir. In recent years, pike have also been stocked in many other states throughout the country as far south as New Mexico, Arizona, and Texas. They acclimate easily in the larger lakes and reservoirs and grow faster in the warmer waters. In Alaska, pike are plentiful in many lakes and rivers in the heart of the state.

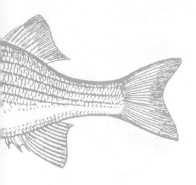

Chapter 16

Pickerel

On days when black bass aren't hitting, many anglers in our eastern states settle for pickerel. This smallest member of the pike family fills a niche somewhere between the black basses and the panfishes. It's not quite as desirable as the black bass, yet it's bigger and more of a true game fish than most of the panfishes. But to a surprising number of anglers, the pickerel is more than just a fill-in fish. Thousands of anglers go fishing for pickerel on purpose throughout the year. In New Jersey, when a vote was taken to determine the most popular fish in the state, the pickerel came out ahead. One reason for this popularity is the pickerel's ability to withstand a wide range of water temperatures. It's found in warm, sluggish streams and ponds and in the colder lakes and rivers. So if you live in one of the eastern states, you'll probably find a pickerel pond, lake, or river nearby that you can fish. And the pickerel is a willing striker—almost always ready to hit a lure or take a bait.

There are actually three species of pickerels found in the United States: the chain pickerel, the redfin or barred pickerel, and the grass or mud pickerel. As far as anglers are concerned, the chain pickerel is the only worthwhile species because the redfin and grass pickerels rarely grow over 12 inches in length.

The chain pickerel has many names: banded pickerel, common pickerel, eastern pickerel, reticulated pickerel, eastern pike, grass pike, green pike, chain pike, jack, jackfish, swamp jack, and snake.

Once you've seen a pickerel you can't mistake it for a young musky or pike. It has a dark-green or brownish-green back shading into lighter green and yellow on the sides. The belly is white, and the chainlike dark markings cover the sides of the fish from gill cover to tail.

The pickerel is found in Canada in Nova Scotia, New Brunswick, and southeastern Quebec. In the United States, its range extends from Maine south to Florida and Alabama and west to the Mississippi Valley, Texas, Missouri, and the Tennessee River system. However, pickerel have been introduced widely and are now found in at least thirty-six states.

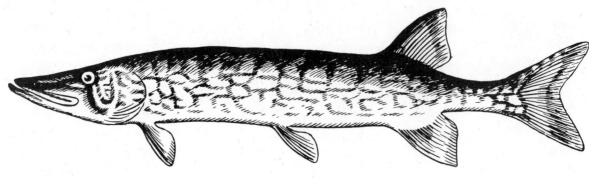

Pickerel

Tackle

Pickerel can be caught with a variety of tackle. Cane or glass poles are used for fishing with minnows or other baits and for skittering a lure or bait on top of the water among lily pads and weeds. Baitcasting and spincasting tackle are also suitable for casting or trolling. Many anglers, however, are turning to fly rods both for bait fishing and fly fishing, since they find that this light tackle provides the most fun and sport. But the most popular pickerel outfit these days is a light spinning rod and reel with 4- to 6-pound-test line. A somewhat heavier spinning outfit, with 8-pound-test line, is needed for fishing in heavy weeds.

Small spoons in red-and-white, silver, nickel, chrome, gold, brass, or copper finishes are old-time favorites that are still effective. Weedless spoons are best for casting into heavy growth or open pockets among the weeds. Weighted spinners such as the Mepps with treble hooks and hair or feathers on them are also productive, as are the smaller spinnerbaits. Unweighted spinners can be fished with minnows, worms, or pork rind for trolling.

Small surface plugs such as poppers, swimmers, gurglers, stickbaits, and crippled minnows all catch pickerel. Slim minnow-type plugs such as the Rapala and Rebel can be fished on the surface by reeling slowly and twitching so they create a wake, or reeled fast to travel just below the surface. Underwater plugs and crankbaits are also effective. Vibrating or rattle plugs such as the Super Sonic or Rat-L-Trap, with their silvery shad finishes, are also good. Tail-spinner lures such as Little George are also effective in deeper water.

Short plastic worms, grubs, or curlytails rigged on a weedless hook are productive lures for pickerel. These can be weighted a bit and reeled on top or underwater. For deeper water, jigs with bucktail, feather, or plastic tails or grubs have proven effective. Flyrodders find that pickerel take most streamers or bucktails designed for trout or bass. A few of the more popular patterns include the Gray Ghost, Mickey Finn, Dahlberg Diver, and the various Matukas, marabous, and Muddlers. For surface fishing with a fly rod, bass bugs, hair frogs, and minnow-type bugs all elicit strikes.

The top natural bait for pickerel is a minnow or other baitfish from about 2½ to 3½ inches long. In coastal tidal or brackish waters, the saltwater killifish often makes a good bait. Big pickerel also take small frogs, earthworms, or nightcrawlers, especially if they are given some action in the water.

Seasonal Tactics

Pickerel start biting early in the year and continue to do so well into the fall. The top months are usually April, May, June, September, and October. But in many cold, northern lakes

This angler is holding a nice string of average-sized pickerel caught in New Hampshire. (Bob Harris Photo)

Pickerel prefer shallow, quiet waters and heavily weeded areas of lakes and rivers. Look for shallow bays and coves with heavy growths of reeds, lily pads, hyacinths, and other vegetation. Look also for logs, stumps, sunken trees, rocks, boulders, brush, and any other cover and obstructions. Pickerel prefer to lie alone in such cover, waiting to ambush a small fish or frog. They often come into extremely shallow water a few inches deep, with their dorsal fins protruding above the surface. However, when the water warms or cools, pickerel often move into the deeper holes, channels, and underwater weedbeds in water from 8 to 12 feet deep.

In rivers, you'll find pickerel in quieter, slower pools, eddies, backwaters, shallow coves, bays, off points, and along weedy shorelines. Small, sluggish, winding streams attract them more than fast rivers. There is good fishing in some of the tidal rivers and estuaries along the Atlantic Coast. Here you usually find them in fresh and brackish water with vegetation.

In a shallow cove or bay with heavy weeds, pickerel are usually scattered, each fish choosing a certain spot and lying there to ambush any prey that enters its area. Any commotion nearby will attract them. In some waters and at certain times of the year, pickerel cruise deep in small groups or schools.

Thousands of pickerel are caught by still-fishing with a bobber and minnow. But you'll have more fun and sport if you use light spinning gear or fly tackle when fishing with minnows. Hook the minnow through back or lips with a No. 1 or 1/0 hook, cast it into likely spots and allow it to remain there a few minutes. Usually, a pickerel will swim over soon after the bait is cast and grab it. If not, wait a while, then reel in and cast to a new spot. Or you can drift along the edges of lily pads or weeds, or along the shoreline, letting your minnow swim around about 40 feet behind the boat. In still-fishing with minnows it is important to give the pickerel plenty of time to swallow the bait. They usually grab the min-

there is often good fishing during the summer months too. Winter fishing through the ice is excellent in many lakes in our northern and New England states. Actually, the pickerel is really a year-round fish in most waters and can be caught in warm and cold weather.

In the spring and fall, you can usually catch pickerel throughout the day. But during the bright, sunny days of summer, early morning or late afternoon and evening are best. However, if the day is cloudy or rainy, you can often have good fishing during the middle of the day even in the summer. Windy days are particularly good for fishing with live baits or underwater lures. But for topwater plugs or bass bugs, the calm water toward evening provides faster action.

now crosswise in their mouths, swim away a short distance, and then stop to swallow it. When they start moving once more, set the hook.

You can also cast a minnow or frog on a weedless hook into thick cover, then retrieve it slowly on top, letting it sink slightly into pockets.

Skittering is still a popular and effective way to catch pickerel. You need a cane or glass pole about 16 feet long baited with a minnow, frog, strip of pork rind, or the belly and two fins of a yellow perch or sunfish. Flip out the bait and skitter or jerk it along the surface in short spurts. It is most effective in open pockets in vegetation.

Pickerel also hit worms, but some movement should be imparted to them by sinking or retrieving them in short jerks. A still worm hanging on a bobber or lying on the bottom doesn't interest pickerel, but if the bait is moving they often hit it.

Casting small spoons, spinners, plastic worms, or plugs can be very effective. Pickerel will hit surface lures that make a commotion. They often streak after such a lure from quite a distance and hit it hard. Underwater plugs that travel just below the surface also work well. Along weedy shores, cast into any narrow openings or pockets or coves that you see; also next to logs, stumps, and rocks. From shore or from a boat positioned next to the weeds or a bank, cast your lure so that it travels parallel to the shoreline.

Pickerel are usually scattered along a shoreline, so it is best to walk along shore and try different spots. If you are in a boat, move along the shore quietly casting into likely spots. In very shallow water, don't get too close but make long casts well beyond the fish, and reel in the lure a few feet in front of it. Pickerel are very skittish in shallow water and easily frightened by noise or movement.

Pickerel often miss a fast-moving lure, so retrieve a lure slowly. A retrieve with plenty of movement and an erratic stop-and-go action brings more strikes and hooks more fish than

Two popular and effective lures for pickerel

a fast, steady retrieve. Pickerel often follow a lure for a short distance, then suddenly decide to strike just as it breaks the surface and leaves the water.

If a pickerel makes a pass at a lure and misses, you'll rarely get it to hit the same lure a second time—at least not very soon. When this happens, rest the spot and change to a different lure. This often provokes another strike. If you get no response, move to another spot where a different fish is lying.

Flyrodders can catch pickerel on bright streamers, bucktails, or bass bugs. The first two should be retrieved with long, fast pulls, while poppers or bass bugs can be worked on top with plenty of splash and commotion.

Trolling also accounts for many pickerel when they are in open, deep water. You can also troll along a shoreline where the water drops off sharply and along the edges of vegetation. Some of the biggest pickerel are caught by trolling in deep water. Spinners, spoons, or underwater plugs can be used for trolling, sometimes with a worm or minnow. In shallow water near shore, let out plenty of line and let your lure travel just below the surface. In deeper water, let the lure travel a few feet down, even along the bottom, on a shorter line.

Winter fishing through the ice, popular with many anglers, often accounts for more and bigger pickerel than are taken during the summer. Most anglers use tip-ups and wait for a bite in a shanty, behind a windbreak, or around a fire on shore. But you can also use a short, stiff rod to lower the bait into the hole. Live minnows make the best bait, but pickerel will also hit spoons, spinners, and jigs worked up and down in short jerks. Though the best

Many pickerel are caught through the ice during the winter. Minnows usually make the best bait. (Pennsylvania Fish Commission Photo)

fishing is usually over submerged weedbeds not too far from shore, it pays to drill several holes in different spots until you locate the fish.

A pickerel on the end of a line puts up a good fight if given a chance on light tackle. Sometimes it comes in with little resistance, but usually when the fish sees the boat it suddenly breaks loose in a series of wild leaps, twists, and surface acrobatics that will surprise and delight you. But since a pickerel doesn't have much endurance, it soon quits and can be netted. The hook tears out of its tender mouth easily, so don't horse the fish or try to lift it out of the water.

Most pickerel run from about 1 to 3 pounds in weight. In some waters, they may reach 5 or 6 pounds, but such big ones are not caught very often. Several pickerel over 9 pounds have been recorded. The present rod-and-reel record fish, 9 pounds 6 ounces, was caught in 1961 by Baxley McQuaig, Jr., in Georgia. Pickerel have a longer growing season in Georgia and Florida and reach a bigger average size than in most of the other states.

Pickerel have a sweet, white, tasty meat but are quite bony. They should be cleaned and scaled and kept on ice soon after being caught or the flesh gets soft. The big ones can be baked or cut into steaks or fillets and fried. Smaller ones can be split open and fried. Some anglers find that if they fillet a pickerel and leave the skin on, then make many small cuts or slashes close together along the entire fillet, it chops the bones into little pieces and helps soften them when the fillet is cooked.

If you live in one of the states where pickerel are found, you'll probably know of or can locate waters containing these fish near your home.

They are especially plentiful in New England, New York, New Jersey, Pennsylvania, Delaware, Maryland, Virginia, North Carolina, South Carolina, Alabama, Louisiana, and Georgia.

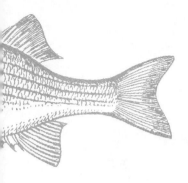

Chapter 17

Walleye

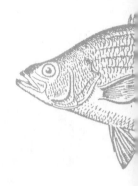

In some northern states, the walleye is the most popular game fish, primarily because it reaches a good size and makes delicious eating. In addition, it is often easier to catch than trout, bass, pike, or muskies. But don't get the idea that walleye fishing is simple, merely a matter of dropping your bait in the water or casting your lure and just reeling it back. Walleyes are often difficult to locate at certain times of the year, and you have to present the bait or lure at the right level and give it the right action to get strikes.

The two subspecies of walleyes found in North America are the yellow walleye and the blue walleye. The yellow walleye is known as the pike-perch, yellow pike, jack salmon, golden pike, yellow pickerel, Susquehanna salmon, opal eye, and dore. (The last name is used in Canada.) The blue walleye is known as the blue pike, blue walleye, and blue pickerel. Another fish, called the sauger (or sand pike or gray pike), is smaller but similar to the walleye.

Walleyes vary in color depending on the waters where they are found. The yellow wall-

eye has a dark, olive-green back, gold or yellow sides, and a white belly. The fins may be yellowish or pinkish with a dark spot at the rear of the big dorsal fin. The blue walleye has a steel-blue back and silvery sides. All walleyes have large mouths with strong canine teeth, and large, whitish, glassy eyes.

Walleyes are found from Canada southward and eastward to North Carolina, Georgia, Alabama, Arkansas, and Tennessee. They are especially plentiful throughout the Great Lakes region, in Wisconsin, Minnesota, Michigan, and in many Canadian waters. Today they are found in at least forty-one states due to intensive stocking programs. They are even found in some southern waters outside their original range.

Tackle

You don't need special tackle to catch walleyes. Almost any baitcasting, spincasting, or spinning outfit suitable for black bass will do for walleyes. Light tackle provides the most sport

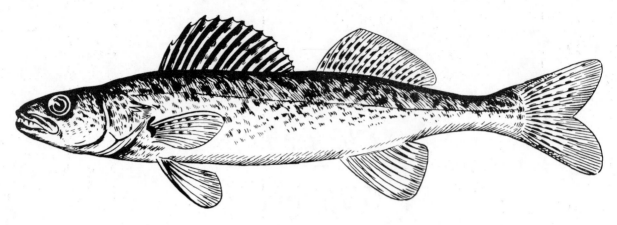

Walleye

and fun, and only when fishing in certain waters and depths for extremely big walleyes do you need somewhat heavier tackle. However, if you fish from shore below dams and in big rivers where long casts may be needed, you need a heavier outfit, such as a light surf-fishing rod 8 to 9 feet long. Fly rods can also be used when the fish are in shallow water near shore.

Not too long ago, most walleyes were caught on spinners such as the June-bug type with a double hook and a minnow, nightcrawler, or lamprey behind it. But today most anglers use such lures as jigs, weighted spinners, spoons, and plugs. Walleyes also take plastic worms, grubs, and curlytails fished deep on jig heads.

Natural baits such as minnows and chubs from 3 to 6 inches long are fished alive or dead behind a spinner or on a jig. In the past, big nightcrawlers were often hooked behind a spinner, but now they are usually fished alone along the bottom with a sliding-sinker rig. Leeches, fished deep on a bottom rig, have become popular in recent years. Walleyes also take soft-shelled crayfish, lampreys, salamanders, and frogs.

Seasonal Tactics

The walleye is mostly a cold-water fish, active during the spring, fall, and winter. In southern waters, the fish move up rivers to spawn as early as February, and good fishing continues into March. Farther north, the spawning run occurs in April and May. There is generally good fishing in most areas in May, June, September, October, and November. In northern lakes, walleyes are caught during the summer. There is often good ice fishing for walleyes in many northern lakes.

In the spring and fall, you can catch walleyes during the day, but during the summer the best times are early morning, evening, and night. In fact, walleyes do a lot of feeding at

Walleyes such as these, and bigger, are caught in many rivers, lakes and reservoirs. These were caught in South Dakota's Missouri River reservoir. (South Dakota Dept. of Tourism Photo)

night from spring to fall, and you stand a good chance of catching them in the dark. If you want to fish during the day in summer, wait for cloudy, rainy weather. Windy days are usually better than windless days. Walleyes are extremely sensitive to light and stay in deeper water on sunny days.

Walleyes are great wanderers, moving about in schools to different sections of a lake or river. In the spring, when the walleyes move up rivers to spawn, they are concentrated in smaller areas and are easier to locate. They tend to move into shallow water during the spring and fall or at night. In Canada, walleye fishing is often good from spring to fall in streams connecting lakes.

In rivers, look for walleyes below dams, falls, rapids or riffles, around rocks, in quiet pools and eddies, and along shoreline rocks and riprap. The tailwaters below dams are especially productive. Toward evening and at night, the fish often move into shallow water around reefs, rock ledges, sandbars, gravel bars, points of land, and mouths of tributary streams. Look for concentrations of minnows in the late afternoon and evening in shallow water or coves. Walleyes often come in to feed on them, and great sport can be had.

In lakes, fish around rocky points, dropoffs, rock bars, gravel bars, shoals, ledges, reefs, weedbeds, mud flats, and deep water bordering rocky shores or cliffs. The mouths of streams entering a lake are often hotspots. Underwater islands and humps or shoals in deep water are good structure to fish during the summer months. Rocky bottoms are especially productive if there is deep water around them. In lakes that are fairly shallow, you'll often find walleyes spending much of the season feeding over weedbeds in water from 5 to 12 feet deep. Also, look for shorelines with visible or submerged brush, stumps, or trees.

One important point to remember is that walleyes are primarily fish eaters, so they are found where baitfish are present. A brisk wind can improve walleye fishing by pushing warm water and plankton into the shallows. Baitfish

follow, and walleyes then move in to feed on the smaller fish. So fish the windward side of submerged weedbeds, reefs, shoals, and points.

As a general rule, fish the shallows early in the morning from around daybreak, in the evening, at dusk, and during the night. Fish deeper waters in the middle of the day. Though walleyes are usually found in water from 4 to 20 feet deep, in some lakes, especially during the summer, they may be found in depths from 20 to 60 feet. In such deep water, they are often found suspended in schools. A depth finder or fish finder is a great aid in locating these schools. Otherwise, try various depths until you locate the fish.

A good way to locate walleyes if you have no electronic gear is by slow-trolling. The most popular rig for this is made by tying a three-way swivel on the end of the line, then tying an 18-inch dropper to one eye, with a sinker on the end, and a 3-foot leader with the hook or lure to the remaining eye. You can use a spinner and minnow or a spinner with worm or a leech for such trolling. Weighted spinners, spoons, or underwater plugs are also effective. To reach bottom in clear, shallow water and keep the rig away from the boat, let out about 100 to 150 feet of line. In deeper water, you can troll the rig closer to the boat. Try to feel the weight moving or bumping bottom at all times.

Anglers have also been making great catches of walleyes on the so-called Lindy Rig. The hook is baited with a big nightcrawler hooked through the tip of the head, or with a leech hooked through the head, or a minnow through the lips. The rig is slow-trolled along the bottom.

When you use a spinning reel with a Lindy Rig, fish with an open bail. (If you are using a baitcasting reel, keep it in free-spool.) In either case, hold your finger or thumb on the line to prevent it from running out. When you feel a bite, release the line and let it slide freely through the hole in the slip sinker. When you feel the walleye has the bait well back in its mouth, set the hook. You have to develop a sense of "feel" to know when the sinker is bouncing bottom or sliding along the bottom. After some experience, you'll be able to tell when a walleye grabs the bait.

Other rigs used for slow-trolling or drifting include the Gapen Bait-Walker, Lindy Bottom Cruiser, and Bottom Walker. These rigs can be fished with leeches, nightcrawlers, minnows, or salamanders, or with floating minnow-type plugs, spinners, or floating jigs. Anglers often add a cork or plastic float on the leader to keep the bait off the bottom.

In recent years, more and more anglers fishing the Great Lakes and other big lakes and reservoirs for walleyes have started using diving planers, planer boards, and outriggers. These are used in much the same ways as when trolling for salmon and lake trout (see chapters on these fish). Once you locate a school of walleyes, set the depth so that the lures travel a bit higher than the fish. The most effective lures for such deep trolling are lively, minnow-type plugs, flutterspoons, or other light spoons and spinners. You can also use a nightcrawler, leech, or minnow behind a spinner.

Most trolling for walleyes is done very slowly, especially when using baits. But some anglers have also had good results by trolling fairly fast to very fast with lures that bump bottom. Crankbaits are good for this and so are metal Spoon plugs. Extra rod action often brings strikes.

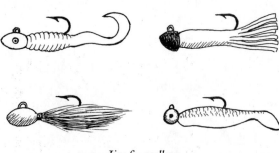

Jigs for walleyes

Once you locate a school of walleyes by trolling, you can drop anchor and cast to them. One of the best lures is a leadhead jig dressed with hair or feathers. Or you can use a plastic tail or curlytail grub. Jigs with hair or feathers are more effective if you add a bait on the hook. Some anglers prefer a plain jig head and add a minnow on the hook. To hook the short strikers, a short snell is tied to the eye of the jig with a treble hook on the end. The jig hook goes through the lips of the minnow and the trailing hook is impaled near the tail.

Any jig you use should be fished deep and slow along the bottom. From a boat you can cast over structure and let the jig sink and settle on the bottom. Walleyes often pick up a jig with a minnow or plastic tail when it is lying still on the bottom. After hitting bottom wait a few seconds and start reeling in slowly in a series of short jerks, bouncing bottom every so often to know you are deep enough. When the jig is directly under the boat, work it up and down, lifting and lowering the rod tip so that it has some action. You have to try to detect a bite and watch the line closely when using jigs, especially in deep water. Walleyes usually hit the lure lightly, so it is hard to notice when it has been taken.

Vertical jigging can also be done from an anchored, drifting or slow-trolled boat. Here you can use such heavy spoons as the Krocodile, Hopkins, Kastmaster, Little Cleo or Mann-O-Lure. Lower it to the bottom and let out enough line so that the lure hangs just above the bottom. Then raise the rod sharply a foot or two and let the spoon drop, lift it a few inches, pause, and let it drop back again. Keep repeating this as long as you are over fish or structure.

When fishing a river you'll also find the jig one of the best lures to use for getting down into the holes, pockets, eddies or channels where walleyes are lying. The jig can be cast upstream and across to get down deep enough and then allowed to swing from the fast current into the slower spots. The strike usually comes as the jig reaches the hole or spot where the walleye is waiting. Spoons and weighted spinners can be fished in the same manner by letting them sink deep and then retrieving them slowly along the bottom.

In recent years, walleye anglers have started using crankbaits for trolling or casting. When cast, crankbaits are most effective in depths up to around 20 feet. An erratic retrieve is best. The plug should act like a disabled minnow. Reel in and then stop, jerk, stop, reel, jerk, stop and continue doing this all the way in. Walleyes are not fast-moving fish and rarely chase a minnow or small fish any distance. Instead, they prefer to lie in or over cover and then ambush a baitfish that is swimming by. That is why it is important to retrieve a lure or bait close to the fish.

Walleyes will sometimes hit surface plugs, such as the Jitterbug and Hula Popper, or floating minnow-type plugs, at daybreak, dusk, or at night when the fish come into shallow water to feed on minnows.

Many walleyes are also caught by still-fishing with live minnows. In fast rivers, use a bottom rig with sinker and a 2-foot leader with hook to hold the minnow. The rig is cast into the river and allowed to drift down with the current into pools and holes. When the sinker hits bottom, let it rest for a few minutes, then lift the rod tip and let the minnow drift to a new spot farther downstream. Let it rest again in the new location, before repeating the procedure. By doing this, you cover more area and keep the bait moving to attract the fish. A big nightcrawler can also be fished in a river

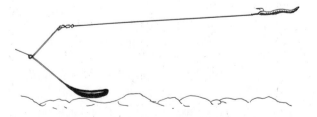

The Gapen Bait-Walker can be rigged with either a bait or lure.

by hooking it through the head once and turning the hook around and burying the barb in the body of the worm to make it weedless.

From a boat on a lake, you can also still-fish with a live minnow on the bottom. If the water is fairly shallow, just add a split shot or two to the line. In deeper water, use a bottom rig with a light sinker. The minnow should be moved up and down every so often to activate it and prevent it from hiding in the weeds.

Walleyes are easily spooked fish, so try to avoid all unnecessary noise. Troll with an electric motor, drift quietly, or anchor for best results. When you fish at night, avoid shining lights on the water. And when you fish in shallow water, troll with long lines or use side planers. If you are casting, stay away from the spot being fished and make long casts. Big walleyes in schools tend to leave when a fish is hooked and runs around.

Walleyes are caught through the ice in many northern lakes. Drill several holes and fish them with tip-ups. Live minnows from 3 to 5 inches long, hooked through the lips or the back, make the best bait. While fishing close to the bottom is usually best, there are times when the walleyes are suspended at a higher level. Vertical jigging with jigs or heavy spoons is also effective.

Once you hook a walleye on a lure or bait, you'll have some sport and action, but don't expect the speed and flash of a trout or bass. Walleyes don't jump or make long or fast runs, nor do they have much endurance. But a good-sized fish, especially if hooked in a fast-moving river, will give you a tough fight on light tackle.

A wide-mouthed net is best for boating a big walleye. Watch out for their sharp teeth when removing hooks from their mouths.

Most walleyes range from 2 to 10 pounds, and any fish over that size is considered a big one. However, in some areas and during certain seasons, big walleyes are commonly taken. Rivers in Arkansas, Kentucky, and Tennessee often yield fish from 8 to 15 pounds during the spawning runs. Fish over 20 pounds have been caught from time to time in these southern

Not all walleyes are caught from boats. Many are caught from shore or by wading. This is especially true toward dusk or in the spring when they are spawning (South Dakota Dept. of Tourism Photo)

waters. The world record on rod and reel is a 25-pound walleye caught in Old Hickory Lake, Tennessee, by Mabry Harper.

Most anglers agree that, no matter what their size, walleyes are among the best freshwater fish for the table. They have a firm, sweet, tasty flesh that can be fried, baked, broiled, or boiled.

Where to Go

The walleye is widely distributed in North America, but some spots are more outstanding than others for the size or number of fish caught. You can't beat Canada, where they are found in Lake Athabasca, on the Alberta-Saskatchewan border, and across both provinces, down into the Hudson Bay basin, through the Great Lakes drainage basin, and over into Quebec, Ontario, and Labrador.

In the United States, walleyes are found in the Great Lakes and are especially plentiful in Lake Erie. In Wisconsin, they are found in Lake Winnebago, Red Cedar and Yellow rivers, Wapogasset Lake, Balsam Lake, Half Moon Lake, St. Croix Lake, Eau Claire Lakes, Whitefish Lake, and Lac Court Oreilles. In Minnesota, over eight hundred lakes have been stocked, the best of which are Fish Hook Lake, Mille Lacs, and Upper and Lower Red lakes. In Michigan, the Menominee, Michigan, and Muskegon rivers are good, as are Gratiot Lake, Lake Bellaire, and Hubbard Lake. In Illinois, the Mississippi and Kankakee rivers are noted for walleyes. In Ohio, Lake Erie, and the Sandusky, Maumee, and Portage rivers contain walleyes. In Pennsylvania, the Susquehanna and Delaware rivers are popular. In New York, the St. Lawrence River, Lake Champlain, and the Delaware River (also in New Jersey) have produced many walleyes. In Tennessee, Center Hill Lake, Dale Hollow Lake, Norris Lake, Old Hickory Lake, Watts Bar Lake, and the Tennessee River are popular walleye waters. In Kentucky, you can fish Lake Cumberland, the Cumberland River, Rockcastle River, Laurel River, Green River, Kentucky Lake, Rough River Lake, and Nolin Lake.

Virginia has good fishing in Smith Mountain Lake, the New River, and Claytor, Leesville, and Philpott lakes. In North Carolina, you can fish such lakes as Chatuge, Fontana, Santeetlah, Hiwassee, and Thorpe. In Texas, walleyes have been stocked in Green Belt Reservoir, Lake Meredith, Diversion Lake, and are also present in White River Lake, Fisher Lake, and Canyon Reservoir. South Dakota has walleye fishing in the reservoirs on the Missouri River in Lake Lewis and Clark, Lake Sharpe, and Lake Oahe. They are also present in South Dakota in Lake Poinsett and Lake Madison. In North Dakota, walleyes are found in the Missouri River, Devils Lake, and Oahe Reservoir. They are even found as far west as the states of Washington and Oregon, in the Columbia River and a few lakes and reservoirs.

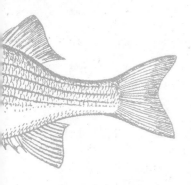

Chapter 18

Yellow Perch

The yellow perch is one of the most popular panfish in the United States. It lives in ponds and lakes, and in large, slow-moving rivers, and may even descend to brackish water in coastal rivers. Usually abundant in most waters, the yellow perch travels in large schools and is a willing biter. All this makes it a favorite with many fishermen. You'll be convinced of this if you ever go down to a lake or river in the early spring when the perch are running and see thousands of anglers fishing from shore or from boats. Such scenes are especially common on our Great Lakes when the yellow perch move in to spawn early in the spring.

Yellow perch are found in the Hudson Bay drainage of eastern Canada, south to Kansas and northern Missouri, in Illinois, Indiana, and Pennsylvania. Along the Atlantic Coast, they range from Nova Scotia to the Carolinas. Yellow perch have also been introduced into many other states in the Midwest and along the Pacific Coast, and are now found in forty-two states.

The yellow perch is sometimes called the red perch, raccoon perch, ringed perch, zebra perch, lake perch, striped perch, and convict. It is easily identified by its six or eight broad, dark stripes over a yellow body. The back is an olive or drab-green color. The ventral and anal fins are a reddish orange.

Tackle

You can catch yellow perch on most tackle—a cane or glass pole, a spinning, spincasting, baitcasting, or fly outfit. A cane pole or fly rod is good for fishing from shore or boat in shallow water. For deep-water casting, still-fishing, or trolling, spinning or baitcasting tackle is more practical.

With any of these outfits, you can cast or troll weighted spinners, small spoons, spinner-and-worm combinations, spinner-and-fly combinations, jigs, or tiny plugs.

Flyrodders fish wet flies such as the Silver Doctor, Yellow Sally, Parmachene Belle,

Yellow Perch

Western Bee, McGinty, Red Ibis, Montreal, and Professor, alone or, preferably, behind a tiny spinner. Streamers and bucktails such as the Gray Ghost, Mickey Finn, Blacknose Dace, White Marabou or Yellow Marabou have proven successful in the small sizes.

However, most anglers seeking yellow perch use natural baits, and among these the live minnow is tops. Small minnows, no bigger than 2 inches in length, are best, and these should be used on small hooks (No. 6 or 8). Millions of perch have also been caught on worms (small garden worms or cut-up night-crawlers). Almost any kind of fish cut into small strips makes good bait. Other baits include the tail of a small crayfish, beetles, grasshoppers, crickets, grubs, nymphs, and most other land and water insects, even small grass shrimp that live in bays and tidal creeks near salt water. Two or three of these tiny shrimp on a hook are offered to perch.

Seasonal Tactics

Yellow perch begin to bite early in spring, soon after ice-out, when they run up rivers and into shallow bays to spawn. This usually occurs in March, April, or early May, depending on the weather, water temperature, and latitude. They move into these spawning areas when the water temperature reaches 45 degrees F. and remain and spawn until the temperature reaches the low 50s. But perch are caught throughout the year.

There is really no special time of day to go perch fishing. You'll catch them all day long in the spring and fall in shallow water near shore. During the summer months, when the perch are in deeper water, the fishing may be better early in the morning and in the evening. They often go on a feeding spree toward dusk and bite right up until dark. Though some perch are caught at night,

When yellow perch are running well and biting it is not unusual to catch big strings of the tasty panfish, especially in the spring. (Michigan Travel Commission Photo)

they usually stop biting when it gets dark.

Since yellow perch are school fish, once you locate them you can usually catch them quickly one after another as long as they remain in the area. They tend to move in toward shore in the evening and remain on the bottom all night; then at daybreak they rise off the bottom, gather in schools, and move toward deeper water. Sometimes you can see them near the surface in large schools in the morning or the late afternoon. Most of the time, however, you have to try different depths until you find them.

One good way to locate yellow perch is to drift with the wind in a boat, slowly towing a hook baited with a minnow or worm down deep near the bottom. Or you can troll very slowly (from a rowed boat, or one propelled by an electric motor) with a spinner, spoon, or spinner and worm or minnow. When you catch the first perch, drop anchor and fish that spot.

Still-fishing with bait is the most popular way to catch yellow perch. A light, sensitive bobber is attached to the line, at the end of which a No. 6 or 8 hook is baited with a tiny minnow, crayfish tail, worm, cricket, grasshopper, grub, or nymph. The bobber should be high enough on the line so the bait almost reaches bottom or the top of the weeds. A slip, or sliding bobber can also be used in deeper water. The bait should be lively to attract the perch. It also helps to keep moving the bait up and down or back and forth to catch the attention of the fish. The yellow perch is a great bait stealer, or else it swallows the bait deep, so don't give it too much time when you get the first nibbles. Wait a few seconds and then set the hook.

One of the best baits for big perch is a belly strip cut from a perch or from another small fish. This should be cut in a narrow triangle about 1½ inches long and ½ inch wide at the base. Insert the hook into the widest part, and add a split-shot sinker to the leader. Fish this bait from a slowly drifting boat with enough line so it moves just above the bottom. Twitch the rod tip up and down slightly to make the bait dart and flutter and look alive. You'll catch big perch this way if you drift over vegetation and structure.

Yellow perch also hit tiny spoons, spinners, jigs, plastic worms and grubs, and plugs. When they are deep, let the lure sink almost to the bottom and then reel it in as slowly as possible.

With a fly rod, use small wet flies, nymphs, tiny streamers and bucktails. Cast these out, let them settle just below the surface, and retrieve them slowly in short pulls. If you get no strikes, let the flies sink deeper and work them at that level. If the fish are still deeper, you have to add a split shot or two on the leader to get the flies down. Of course, you can also use a sinking fly line to get them down when fishing deep.

When trolling, you usually have to let out a lot of line and add a small weight on the leader to get the bait or lure deep enough. When yellow perch won't hit a plain lure, try adding a thin sliver of pork rind or a worm. The main thing to remember when fishing lures for yellow perch is that they are slow and lazy, and cannot catch a fast-moving lure. So work the lure as slowly as possible, with short jerks, twitches, and alternate pauses to give the perch time to grab it.

For drifting or slow-trolling, try a bottom-walking rig such as the Gapen Bait-Walker or the Lindy Bottom Cruiser with about a 24-inch leader and a hook on the end. If you wish, add a small spinner in front of the hook and then add the bait. As the boat moves along slowly, raise and lower the rod and bump bottom every so often to make sure you are deep enough.

Where legal, try chumming to attract yellow perch. Cut up meat, poultry, or fish into tiny chunks and scatter them around an anchored boat. Or bring a can or two of cat or dog food, puncture some holes in the can, and lower it

to the bottom on a string. Another trick is to lower your anchor or a concrete block and then raise and drop it so it hits the bottom. This will stir up food from sandy and muddy bottoms, and even if the weight hits rocks the vibrations caused will also attract yellow perch. Some anglers attach bright-colored flags to the anchor rope to attract perch.

Yellow perch are great winter fish, and many are caught by fishing through the ice. On some lakes, catches of fifty to two hundred perch by a single fisherman in one day are common. For ice fishing, a rod from 20 to 40 inches long is adequate. The line should be 20 or 25-pound-test monofilament for easy handling in the cold weather. Or fish with a line on a spool attached to a tip-up. To the end of the line attach a No. 6 or 8 hook baited with a live minnow about 2 inches long. Other productive baits include goldenrod grubs, mousies, waxworms, nymphs, corn borers, salmon eggs, or a strip cut from a perch, or the eye of a perch. Some anglers obtain minnows early in the season and then either freeze them or keep them in heavy brine for winter fishing.

Anglers ice-fishing for yellow perch during the winter months. (Vermont Travel Division Photo)

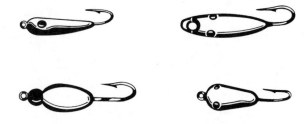

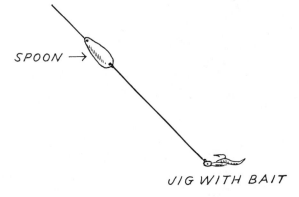

SPOON →

JIG WITH BAIT

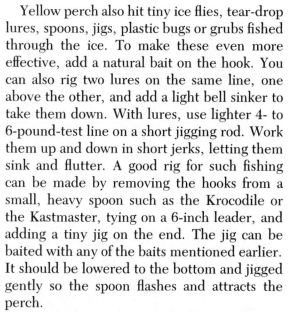

These tiny lures, called (clockwise from left) the rocker, willow spoon, demon, and spot, can be used for jigging and ice-fishing with or without bait for yellow perch.

Rig used in deep water for yellow perch

Yellow perch also hit tiny ice flies, tear-drop lures, spoons, jigs, plastic bugs or grubs fished through the ice. To make these even more effective, add a natural bait on the hook. You can also rig two lures on the same line, one above the other, and add a light bell sinker to take them down. With lures, use lighter 4- to 6-pound-test line on a short jigging rod. Work them up and down in short jerks, letting them sink and flutter. A good rig for such fishing can be made by removing the hooks from a small, heavy spoon such as the Krocodile or the Kastmaster, tying on a 6-inch leader, and adding a tiny jig on the end. The jig can be baited with any of the baits mentioned earlier. It should be lowered to the bottom and jigged gently so the spoon flashes and attracts the perch.

The yellow perch is not much of a fighter on the end of a line. It pulls feebly and slowly, and gives up too quickly, compared to other panfish. The big ones—2 or 3 pounds—provide some fun on ultralight spinning tackle or a fly rod. But unfortunately in most lakes perch are on the small side, rarely going over a pound in weight. In some waters, they are so numerous and stunted that they never reach more than a few inches in length and a fraction of a pound in weight. The largest yellow perch caught on rod and reel weighed 4 pounds 3½ ounces and was caught at Bordentown, New Jersey, in May 1865 by Dr. C. C. Abbot.

Even though yellow perch fight poorly, many anglers spend hours fishing for them because they have white, sweet, flaky flesh that is delicious. They are tough to scale, so keep them wet and clean them as soon as possible.

If you live near the Great Lakes, you can fish for yellow perch in lakes Michigan, Erie, Ontario, and Huron. They are also common throughout eastern Canada. The New England states, especially Maine, have them in abundance in most lakes, and in slow, deep rivers. They are also found along the Atlantic Coast to the Carolinas and have been introduced into many western and Pacific Coast states.

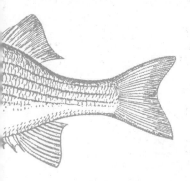

Chapter 19

Bluegill

Every country boy who has fished for sunfish has a warm spot in his heart for these small, colorful fishes. Even in later years, many an older angler turns to sunfish for a day's sport and fine eating afterward, for sunfish are obliging little critters, almost always willing to bite. To add to their appeal, they are widely distributed in this country; chances are that they are present in most waters near your home.

The large sunfish family includes the black basses, crappies, warmouth, rockbass, and the various species of sunfish—the bluegill, pumpkinseed, redbreast sunfish, redear sunfish, longear sunfish, green sunfish, and orange spotted sunfish. Most of the information here concerns the bluegill sunfish, which is the largest and most popular. But all the techniques outlined in this chapter can be applied to other kinds of sunfish.

The bluegill sunfish is also called the bream (pronounced *brim* down South). Its other names are blackear sunfish, blue bream, blue sunfish, blue Joe, bluemouthed sunfish, blue perch, copperhead bream, coppernosed

bream, coppernosed sunfish, dollardee, polladee, and sun perch.

The bluegill has a blue-green to olive-green back, the color becoming lighter on the sides. The breast is orange-yellow or orange-red. The younger specimens usually have vertical bars on the sides, while older and larger bluegills have a dark purplish back, a dull orange breast, and may lack the vertical stripes. The bluegill can usually be distinguished from other sunfish by its dark ear flap on the lower end of the gill cover and a dark blotch on the lower end or rear of the second dorsal fin.

Originally native to the Mississippi River region, the Great Lakes, and the eastern seaboard, bluegills have been widely introduced and are now caught in most of our states. They prefer warm, fertile lakes and ponds rather than clear, deep, cold waters. They are especially big and plentiful in our southern states with their warmer waters and longer growing seasons. And they do well in small farm ponds, where they are commonly stocked along with largemouth bass.

Bluegill

Tackle

More bluegills are probably caught on cane poles than on any other tackle. A light monofilament line testing about 8 or 10 pounds, a small, thin bobber, and a 6, 8, or 10 hook completes the outfit.

Light spinning and spincasting tackle is also suitable for bluegills. For casting small lures and very light baits, an ultralight spinning outfit with 2- or 4-pound test mono is preferred.

Many anglers believe that, for the most fun and sport, a bluegill should only be caught on a fly rod. For baitfishing, the fly reel can be filled with monofilament line testing 6 or 8 pounds. For casting lures or flies, a floating fly line is better. You can also use a sinking fly line when bluegills are deep and you want to reach them in a hurry.

Dry flies for bluegills include the Wulff flies, bivisibles, Gray Hackle, Black Gnat, Light Cahill, and Adams in sizes 8, 10, 12, or 14. Good wet flies are the Coachman, Black Ant, McGinty, Western Bee, Professor, Cowdung, Brown Hackle, and Woolly Worm in sizes 8, 10, and 12. Nymphs of various patterns catch many bluegills, as do tiny streamers and bucktails.

Small bass bugs and panfish bugs are also very good fly-rod lures for bluegills. Sponge-bodied spiders with long rubber legs have also proven effective. These can be made to float by squeezing them to remove any water, or they can be made to sink by submerging them until they absorb water. Sponge-bodied spiders should be tied on No. 8 or 10 hooks.

When it comes to lures, tiny spoons in silver or gold are productive. Small weighted spinners are also good, especially with a treble hook covered with feathers or hair. Tiny jigs weighing from 1/64 to 1/8 ounce are highly effective, especially those with white or yellow heads and hair or feathers. Tiny jigs with white or yellow plastic grubs or curlytails are popular. Small spinners with a strip of pork rind, a wet fly or a sponge spider behind them work well too. Tiny plugs not much longer than 2½ inches also draw strikes. Spinnerbaits can be used for big bluegills, but these should be the smallest ones you can buy. Some of the lures mentioned above are more effective if you add some kind of bait, such as a small worm, to the hook.

Most bluegills are caught on natural baits, the most popular of which is the earthworm. Big nightcrawlers aren't as good as the smaller

Most young anglers start fishing for bluegills and then graduate to other fish. (Arkansas Dept. of Parks Photo)

varieties of worms. Bluegills also take tiny minnows up to 2 inches long. Grasshoppers, crickets, roaches, catalpa worms, mealworms, corn borers, goldenrod grubs, mousies, waxworms, nymphs, and hellgrammites are all used for bait. Freshwater shrimp are excellent bait, especially in our southern states. If you run out of bait, try a tiny strip of pork rind or a thin, small strip cut from the belly of a bluegill or other fish.

Seasonal Tactics

The fastest bluegill fishing occurs in the early spring and summer when the fish are spawning or have just finished guarding their nests. Then they are pugnacious, hungry, and easy to locate near shore. But they also bite well most of the summer and into the late fall. You can catch them all day long with bait or sunken lures. For fly fishing, the early morning, late afternoon, and evening hours are best. Bluegills bite at night at certain times and in certain waters, but for the most part they are daytime fish. Big bluegills also tend to bite best when the skies are cloudy and the water a bit murky.

When bluegills are spawning, they tend to stay close to shore over their nests, which are

circular and light in color and stand out against the rest of the bottom. These nests are usually over clay, sand, or gravel bottoms. If you locate several nests, move from one to the other and catch fish along the way. Most of the nests are in water from 2 to 6 feet deep.

When bluegills are feeding in shallow water, you'll find them around weedbeds, submerged logs, brushpiles, rocks, lily pads, docks, and under overhanging trees. In rivers, look for bluegills in deep, quiet pools and coves, in backwaters and eddies, below dams and falls, and along bushy banks. They tend to stay close to vegetation.

During the hot summer months, bluegills often go into deeper water. The big ones, especially, spend most of their time in deep water, often as far down as 30 feet in the middle of the day. Most of them, however, prefer water anywhere from 10 to 20 feet along some kind of structure or cover.

Most bluegills are caught by still-fishing with or without a bobber. Use the smallest and lightest bobber you can get. To hold the bait deeper in the water, add a small split shot on the leader between the bobber and hook. A slip bobber is also used, especially in deeper water for big bluegills.

One of the best baits for bluegills is a live cricket on a small, thin-wire No. 8 or 10 hook, with a split-shot sinker on the leader. The cricket is also fished on a light (1/64-ounce) jig. You can improvise a jig easily by pinching a split shot onto the hook near the eye.

Large bluegills usually are wary and take off when you get too close. For these fish, a light spinning rod is ideal because you can cast a good distance. The first splash may frighten the bluegills away, but they'll soon return and investigate the bait. It is also a good idea to twitch the bait occasionally to keep it out of the weeds and to attract the fish.

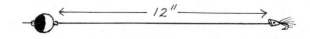

Bobber rigged in front of panfish bug for bluegills

In deep water, you can also fish live bait without a bobber, just add a split shot on the leader and let the bait sink. When it reaches bottom, let it lie there a few minutes, then reel it back slowly along the bottom. Another way to fish baits in deep water is to make up a bottom rig with a light dipsy sinker on the end of the line and a hook on a 10-inch dropper tied about a foot above the sinker. Allow the bait to lie on the bottom for a few moments, then reel in slowly a few feet and allow it to rest again. Or in a boat, drift very slowly with the wind and let the sinker drag along the bottom.

When bluegills are inclined to take flies or panfish bugs on the surface, you can have a lot of fun wading or drifting along the shoreline and casting small dry flies or tiny panfish bugs into likely spots. Drop the fly or bug close to a log, rock, or lily pad, and let it lie there a minute or so. Then twitch it gently so it moves a few inches. Let it lie a few seconds more, then twitch it once again, and again. Dry flies or small bugs are most effective in the evening and when the water is calm. If there are any insects hatching and you see bluegills feeding on them, you can have some fast action with the flies or bugs.

When the water is ruffled or the fish are feeding below the surface, try a wet fly, nymph, tiny streamer, or sponge-bodied spider. Let the fly sink and work it in short jerks below the surface at various depths until you get a strike. Add a split shot to get the fly deeper, or use a sinking fly line. You can fish flies and panfish bugs with a light spinning rod by affixing a clear plastic float or a small surface plug to the end of the line, then tying a dry fly or panfish bug behind the float on a 14-inch leader.

Bluegills are also caught during the winter months through the ice. They take mealworms, waxworms, maggots, corn borers, goldenrod grubs, and nymphs. Small ice flies or tear-drop lures baited with any of these baits are also effective. These are lowered through the ice and kept moving up and down with gentle jigging motions. Bluegills are usually caught at depths of 5 to 30 feet, especially over submerged weedbeds.

A bluegill hooked on light tackle puts up a very satisfactory fight. It is usually of short duration, however, because the bluegill and other sunfish lack the staying power of larger game fish. But the battle is spirited and lively while it lasts.

In most waters where bluegills are found, a half-pound fish is a good one, and a fish around a pound is considered a big one. In some lakes, bluegills and other sunfish may become stunted and never reach a good size. In other lakes, they grow larger than average if conditions are suitable. An example of the latter is Ketona Lake in Alabama, where bluegills weighing over 4 pounds have been caught. The largest on record weighed 4 pounds 12 ounces and was taken by T. S. Hudson on April 9, 1950.

Large or small, bluegills and other sunfish make excellent eating. Their meat is firm, sweet, and delicious. But it takes some time and trouble to clean small bluegills or sunfish, so many anglers save only the larger ones. Fishery biologists frown on this practice, however, and would prefer anglers to catch as many bluegills of all sizes as they can. There are so many bluegills and other sunfish in many lakes and ponds that it is necessary to reduce their number. Those that remain will grow larger, as will any game fish in the lake which need plenty of living space and food.

Bluegills can be caught year-round, even through the ice in winter when these were caught. (Michigan Travel Comm. Photo)

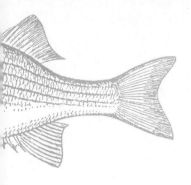

Chapter 20

Crappies

The crappie, a denizen of large lakes and reservoirs, is one of the more popular panfish. Traveling in large schools, they are fairly easy to catch. When crappies are running in large lakes it is not unusual to see hundreds of boats congregated over their beds and other anglers lining the shore.

In recent years there has been a boom in crappie fishing. Many crappie tournaments, or "Crappiethons," are held all over the country. There is even a magazine called *Crappie World*. And many tackle companies are designing special rods and reels for crappie fishing.

There are two kinds of crappies—the black crappie and the white crappie. The deeper-bodied black crappie has a black back, is darkly mottled, and has seven or eight dorsal spines. The white crappie is not as deep-bodied or dark as the black crappie and has only five or six dorsal spines.

Crappies are called by almost sixty different names in various parts of the country, but the more popular ones are calico bass, speckled perch, strawberry bass, silver crappie, and

bachelor. In Florida and other southern states, they are often called specks.

The black crappie is more numerous in northern waters than the white crappie. Its range extends from southern Canada through the Great Lakes and Mississippi River system to Nebraska and south to Texas, Florida, and North Carolina. The white crappie, which is most plentiful in southern waters, is found from Lake Ontario south to the Mississippi River system, Nebraska, Texas, and Alabama. Both crappies have been introduced widely in western states.

Tackle

Tackle for crappies is similar to that used for bluegills and other panfish. Cane poles and glass poles are popular with many anglers. They are particularly useful for fishing around heavy cover where the bait can be lowered into openings. Baitcasting rods are good for casting and trolling. And, of course, light spinning and spincasting tackle is suitable. Fly rods

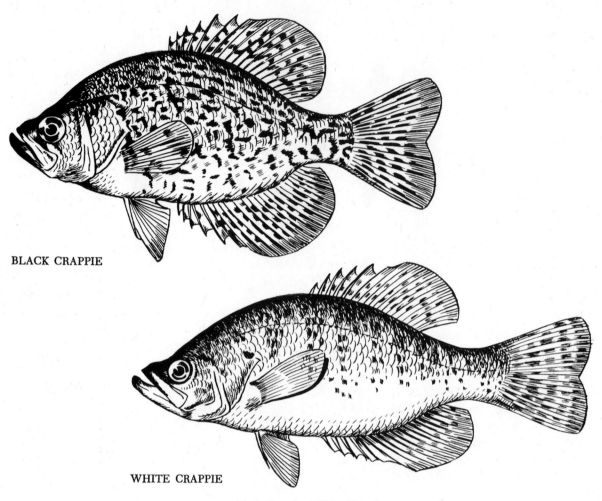

BLACK CRAPPIE

WHITE CRAPPIE

Black Crappie   White Crappie

provide sport when crappies are in fairly shallow water. One of the best all-round outfits is a light 6- to 7-foot spinning rod and a small reel holding 4- or 6-pound-test line for casting light lures and baits. A somewhat heavier spinning rod with stronger (8- or 10-pound-test) line is handy for fishing in very heavy cover or for trolling.

Crappies strike tiny underwater plugs, spoons, weighted spinners, spinner-fly combinations, and jigs. Fly fishermen catch them with small streamers, bucktails, wet flies, nymphs, dry flies, and panfish bugs. One of the most effective and widely used lures is a tiny jig with a chenille body and marabou tail.

Other jigs with hair, feathers, nylon skirts, and especially with plastic curlytails or grubs are good. Small spinnerbaits are also popular with crappie anglers. Jigs and spinnerbaits should weigh from ¹⁄₆₄ to ⅛ ounce.

Natural baits for crappies include minnows, worms, freshwater shrimp, grasshoppers, crickets, mealworms, nymphs, and other land and water insects. But the most dependable bait is a minnow or other baitfish about 1 to 2 inches long.

After you catch the first crappie, cut a strip about ¼ inch wide and 1½ inches long from its belly or side and use it for bait. Similar strips can be cut from other baitfish.

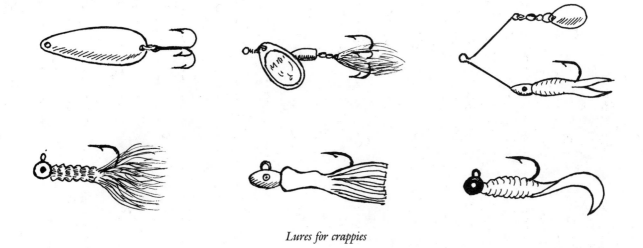

Lures for crappies

Seasonal Tactics

Crappies may start running and biting as early as January and February in Florida and other southern states. March and April are good months in the East and Midwest, May and June in the North and West. These are the months when crappies come close to shore to spawn and are easy to catch, although, they can be caught deep most of the year if you can locate them.

Crappies bite most of the day, but seek shady spots and deeper water to escape bright sunlight. Cloudy, overcast days usually provide better fishing. Many anglers also fish at night, the best period being a few days before and during a full moon.

Crappies become active and start biting soon after ice-out in our northern lakes. They move into shallow water near shore to feed before spawning. Spawning occurs when the water temperature ranges between 63 and 68 degrees F. At this time crappies are found in water from 2 to 8 feet deep. They spawn over sand, gravel, and scattered weed bottoms. Bays, coves, or backwaters with stumps, logs, or brush attract them at this time. They'll stay in this shallow water when the weather and water are warm, but a cold spell often drives

them to deeper water. The spring months offer the fastest fishing, and the biggest catches are made at this time.

Both species of crappies like cover and shade. They hang out in coves and bays around old stumps, logs, brush, sunken trees, lily pads, hyacinths, bullrushes, and other weeds and vegetation. Rivers, streams, and inlets where they enter a lake are usually hotspots. So are the waters below dams. Stumps or brush always attract crappies. They also lurk in shady spots under overhanging branches, bridges, piers, docks, rafts, and anchored boats. During floods, look for them in flooded pastures, coves, and inlets. When the water is muddy, they'll be in the clearer areas near shore. Usually on the more popular lakes and reservoirs locating crappies is easy during the big runs of fish in the spring. At this time, you'll see many other anglers lined up along the shore or fishing from bridges or boats, and you can take your cue from them.

Crappies are also found in many of the bigger, slow-moving rivers. Look for them below dams and in the tailwaters, along riprap or weedy shores, in backwaters, oxbow lakes, and in the deeper pools and eddies, especially near cover. Many canals also contain crappies, usually below spillways and along shorelines with vegetation.

Crappie bag limits are liberal in most states, and big catches like this are common. (Kentucky Dept. of Public Information Photo)

During the hot summer months, when crappies go deep to seek cooler water, fishing for them becomes difficult. They may be on the bottom or suspended at various depths. They may be in schools or scattered. Your best bet is to fish in water from 10 to 30 feet deep. Here again, the crappies hang out over structure of some kind. Look for submerged islands, shoals, rock bars, sloping points, sharp drop-offs, channels, and old creekbeds. A depth finder or fish finder is a big help in locating structure and the fish themselves.

Still-fishing with a cane or glass pole is the most popular way to catch crappies. In shallow water, add a bobber high enough on the line so the bait just clears the bottom. In deeper water, a small dipsy sinker tied on the end of your line and two hooks tied on short droppers about a foot apart make a good rig. Special crappie rigs with two hooks on a wire spreader are sold in tackle shops.

When fishing from a boat, drop one of the rigs and drift slowly so the sinker drags along the bottom. When you get a bite or hook a fish, anchor and fish in that spot. It pays to give the bait some movement by raising and lowering the rod tip or moving the rod back and forth in an arc.

Usually crappies stay at a certain level when feeding. Try different depths until you find the fish. Crappies are school fish, so if you find one, you'll usually catch more.

Crappies migrate to different areas and depths depending on the season and water temperature. They are most active in water temperatures from 65 to 75 degrees F. Water clarity and light are big factors too. The fish will be deeper in clear reservoirs than in dark or murky waters. During the hot summer months, they'll often suspend in depths from 15 to 30 feet during the middle of the day and do little feeding. But toward evening and at night, they'll usually move into shallower water to feed. So the serious crappie angler will have a temperature gauge, flasher, or graph recorder to help locate crappies in deep water.

Crappies tend to bite gently, mouthing the bait, then moving away with it. Don't set the hook too soon, especially when using a big bait such as a minnow, or you'll pull it out of their mouth. Let the bobber disappear, or wait until you feel a strong pull on the line before you set the hook. Do not jerk too hard, since crappies have soft, paper-thin mouths, and a hook tears out easily.

Crappies bite well at night, at which time you can shine a light on the water to draw bugs and insects, which will attract minnows, which will in turn attract crappies. Most night fishermen use minnows.

When fishing small spoons, weighted spinners, small plugs, or jigs, you also have to explore different depths and try different spots. When crappies are in shallow water near shore, retrieve the lures near the surface or a foot or two below. But in deeper water, you have to let the lure sink and work it several feet below the surface, even along the bottom.

When crappies are in heavy cover, try flipping a jig or bait into the vegetation. For this you need a long flipping rod, or a long spinning or baitcasting rod. If you use a jig, you can add a tiny minnow on the hook. Or with the jig alone, you can add some flavoring or scent on the body of the lure. For fishing in heavy cover, many anglers use a weedless jig or make the lure weedless by rigging it so the barb is buried in the plastic body. Also try retrieving a small jig very slowly along the bottom. Work the jig straight or with short up-and-down twitches of the rod tip. Another way to fish a jig is to rig it below a bobber.

In open waters, slow-trolling is often a good way to locate crappies. Follow the shoreline around points of land, along bars, edges of lily pads and other weeds and over sunken rocks, trees, brush, or other cover. Let out anywhere

Crappies bite well at night. A light or two suspended over the water will attract minnows, which will attract crappies.

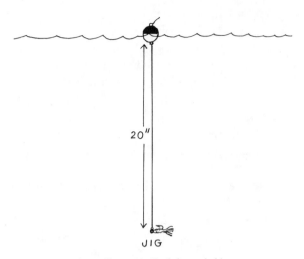

20"

JIG

A small crappie jig below a bobber

from 50 to 150 feet of line, depending on the depth you are trying to reach. Trolling is most effective in depths from 8 to 30 feet with tiny minnows, spoons, spinners, or jigs.

A fly rod can also be used to catch crappies when they are in fairly shallow water. A sinking fly line is best with wet flies or tiny streamers and bucktails. And when crappies come into the shallows in the evening to feed on surface insects, you can sometimes catch them on dry flies, or on small bass or panfish bugs. Work these slowly with plenty of pauses and twitches to bring the crappies to the top and make them hit.

Crappies can often be caught during the winter months. In southern waters, crappies bite well even in open water during the winter, at depths from 10 to 20 feet. But in northern waters, they are often found anywhere from 20 to 40 feet deep. Minnows are the best bait for ice fishing, along with tiny spoons, jigs, and ice flies, perhaps baited with a tiny minnow, grub, mealworm, or strip of fish.

It would be misleading to say that crappies are great fighters on the end of a line. They usually wage a slow, uninteresting, short fight and give up too easily. In addition, they have soft mouths, and a hook often pulls out or drops out readily. So a light rod with a limber tip is

best for getting the most out of them and for saving those fish that are hooked.

Crappies in most waters average about a pound or a bit less, though in some lakes and reservoirs they often grow up to 2 or 3 pounds. Both species of crappies have been known to reach about 5 pounds or slightly more in weight.

The crappies are among the tastiest panfish. They are especially good in the early spring and late fall and winter months, when the flesh is firm. Those taken from muddy waters during the summer may be softer and not so flavorful.

Where to Go

Some of the better crappie waters are found in Wisconsin, Minnesota, Iowa, Idaho, Kansas, North Dakota, South Dakota, Oklahoma, Missouri, Colorado, Illinois, Nebraska, Ohio, and most of the states bordering the Mississippi River. In New York, Chautauqua Lake, Lake Ontario, Croton Reservoir, and other reservoirs near New York City contain crappies. In Pennsylvania, lakes Pymatuning, Glendale, Pinchot, Wallenpaupack, Kinzau, and Erie have crappie fishing. In Mississippi, crappies are found in the Enid, Sardis, and Grenada reservoirs, Moon, Eagle, Rodney, and Mary lakes. In Louisiana, Toledo Bend Reservoir, Lake Bistineau, Bussey Lake, Black Lake, Turkey Creek Lake, and D'Argonne Lake are noted for crappies. In Tennessee, you can try Kentucky Lake, Reelfoot Lake, J. Percy Priest, Woods, and Douglas reservoirs. In Kentucky, you can fish Kentucky, Barkley, and Cumberland lakes. In Texas, Spence, Sam Rayburn, Dam B, Navarro Hills, Toledo Bend, Amistad, and Belton reservoirs have crappies. So do lakes Texarkana, Buchanan, Travis, and Texoma. In Virginia, try Philpott Reservoir, Smith Mountain Lake, Kerr Reservoir, Gaston Reservoir, Buggs Island Lake, and Claytor Lake. Florida has many lakes, rivers, and canals that contain crappies. Some of the more popular ones are Lake Okeechobee, Harris,

Griffin, Eustis, Dora, and Jessup lakes, and the St. Johns River.

On the Pacific Coast, crappies are found in California's West Valley, Black Butte, Comanchee, and Success reservoirs, and Clear Lake. In Oregon, you can fish Owyhee Lake, Siltcoos Lake, Brownless Reservoir, Cold Springs Lake, Fern Ridge Lake, Coffenbury Lake, Smith Lake, and the Columbia and Willamette rivers. In Washington, crappies are found in Coffee Pot Lake, McNary Reservoir, Palmer Lake, Vancouver Lake, Loomis Lake, and Silver Lake.

In these and other states, check with your state fish and game department to find out which waters contain crappies. Crappies are also found in British Columbia, Ontario, and Manitoba.

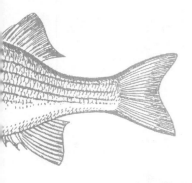

Chapter 21

White Bass

How would you like to catch a freshwater fish that is bigger than the average panfish, fights harder, strikes many kinds of artificial lures, and makes delicious eating? And when these fish are running it's a cinch to catch the limit. Many of you are probably familiar with the fish in question, but those who are not should become acquainted with this silvery little scrapper. It's the white bass, also called sand bass, sandy, silver bass, barfish, gray bass, silversides, striper, and striped bass. But the last two names are better reserved for its relative, the true saltwater striped bass, which is a much larger fish. The white bass is greenish with silvery sides having six or seven dark horizontal stripes.

At one time, white bass had a limited range from the Great Lakes region to the St. Lawrence River and Manitoba, from southern Ontario to New York, and south through the Mississippi Valley to Texas. But in the past forty years, they have been introduced into many waters in the central, eastern, and southern sections of the United States. White bass prefer large rivers, lakes, and reservoirs, and are very plentiful in the man-made impoundments in Texas and in the TVA system in Tennessee. As its range increases, the white bass is becoming very popular with many anglers. Today it occupies a position somewhere between the panfishes and the black bass.

Tackle

For casting light lures to white bass, the ideal outfit is a light spinning outfit. The line should be about 4- or 6-pound test, and the rod should be able to cast lures ranging from ⅛ to ½ ounce. A spincasting outfit is also good and is usually equipped with 8- or 10-pound-test line.

If you prefer a baitcasting outfit, get an ultralight or light model capable of casting the small, light lures used for white bass. Heavier baitcasting or spinning outfits can be used for trolling or bottom fishing.

Fly rods are also popular for catching white bass when they are on or near the surface. A rod from 8½ to 10 feet long capable of handling

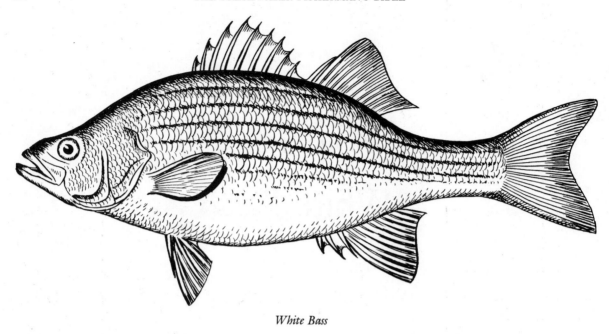

White Bass

a No. 8 or 9 fly line is suitable. For working surface poppers or bugs, a floating weight-forward fly line is recommended. For fishing underwater streamers or bucktails, a sinking fly line is needed to fish these flies deep.

When white bass are actively feeding on top they'll usually hit almost anything that moves through the water and even remotely resembles a shad or other small fish. They'll take small surface and underwater plugs, spoons, spinners, streamers, bucktails, and weighted jigs of all types. The important thing to remember when choosing lures is that they should be small. The big plugs used for black bass and other large fish are not effective. The white bass has a small mouth, and you'll miss too many fish if you use large lures.

If you have no outfit capable of casting very light, small lures you can get around this by making up a "popping" or "chugging" block to add weight. This can be a small section of broomstick or wood dowel from 2 to 3 inches long, with a small screw eye at each end. Tie your fishing line to one screw eye and an 18-inch mono leader to the other. At the end of the leader, attach a tiny spoon, jig, bucktail or streamer fly. Though this rig may be a bit clumsy to cast at first, the wooden dowel provides sufficient weight to cast small lures farther and also attracts fish by creating a surface disturbance. Instead of a wooden dowel, you can use a small surface-popping plug with the tail hook removed.

Seasonal Tactics

The peak season for white bass is usually the spring, when they run up creeks or rivers to spawn. This may start as early as February, March or April in our southern states, or later, in May or June, in our northern states. But white bass can provide good fishing from spring through fall, and even in the winter months in the deep South.

Locating white bass during the spring spawning season is easy in waters where they are plentiful and popular. You'll usually see hundreds of anglers lining the shore or in boats, fishing for white bass. If you join these anglers, you'll have a lot of fun and action pulling in the whites.

During this spring run, look for concentrations of white bass in rivers below dams, falls,

White bass are usually found in big lakes. A good-sized boat and motor, and electronic gear, will enable you to locate and catch more fish. (Outboard Marine Corp. Photo)

riffles, and rapids. They bunch up in the deep runs, quiet pools, eddies, and in the slow water behind rocks. In smaller streams, they can be so thick that their backs protrude above the surface. Feeder streams entering a river are also hotspots.

In lakes or reservoirs that do not have tributary streams for spawning, white bass deposit their eggs on shallow, rocky, or gravel shoals or on sandbars. Though the spawning season is short, lasting only about two to three weeks, white bass remain for some time in fairly shallow water in lakes and reservoirs around the mouths of creeks, under bridges, around islands, along dropoffs, gravel points, sandbars, rock bars, and reefs.

During the summer months, when the water warms, white bass seek deeper water in the middle of the lake. They may be found as deep as 50 feet, especially on bright, sunny days. But even in the summer, they often come to the surface or move into shallow water to feed around daybreak, toward dusk, and during the night. Gizzard shad, threadfin shad, and minnows are the preferred food of white bass; they'll follow these baitfish all over

the lake. The best fishing is around some kind of structure.

In rivers, the sloping points, riprap, wing dams, bends, pools, and eddies attract them. They like moving water but avoid fast currents and stay where obstructions stop or slow the flow of water. The tailraces below dams are good spots in the spring and even in summer when the bass seek cooler water and the forage fish that are trapped or killed there.

Many kinds of lures catch white bass. When they are hitting on top, surface plugs such as the Heddon Tiny Torpedo or Baby Torpedo, small Zara Spook, Zara Pooch or Puppy, and the Cordell Crazy Shad are productive. The smaller floating Rapalas, Rebels, and Redfins are also good topwater lures. Deep-diving plugs, sinking plugs, and small crankbaits can be fished at various depths. Shad-type vibrating or rattling plugs in the smaller sizes are also good lures.

Spinners and spoons are good for casting or trolling. Jigging with heavy spoons such as the Hopkins, Kastmaster, Mann-O-Lure, Krocodile, and Slab Spoon is effective. Small spinnerbaits and tailspinners are also used.

Jigs of various kinds make good white bass lures, either fished just below the surface by reeling fast when the whites are feeding on top or worked deep or jigged vertically. Usually jigs with feathers, bucktail, or plastic tails in white or yellow are the most effective. Fly-rodders can use minnow-type poppers and various streamers and bucktails. The lighter, brighter colors—white, yellow, and silver—are best.

One of the best times to fish for white bass is when they are chasing shad on the surface. Calm days are best for spotting them. Sometimes the best fishing is early in the morning or toward evening. When white bass are chasing small fish on the surface, they often turn the water to a froth, and the commotion can be spotted a long distance away. In large lakes, gulls and terns often congregate over feeding white bass and pinpoint the fish for you.

Fishing for white bass when they are feeding

on top calls for quick action. Anglers cruise around in their boats looking for feeding schools of fish. As soon as they spot a commotion or see birds gathering, they speed toward the spot, cut their motors, and start fishing. Fast reeling usually produces the best results. You have only a short time before the school sounds. Then you have to wait till they reappear or locate another school. This is an exciting sport known as jump-fishing, but it can become hectic when too many boats try to get into the act.

To catch more than one white bass at a time, you can use a double jig rig. Tie a three-way swivel on the end of your line. To one eye of the swivel, tie a 6-inch dropper and a jig on the end. To the remaining eye, tie a 12-inch leader and another jig. When you cast this rig into a school of feeding whites you'll often hook two fish at the same time.

When white bass are not feeding on top, you have to locate them below the surface. They gather at the mouths of streams, over old creek channels, off rocky points, along drop-offs, underwater islands, shoals, and reefs. A depth finder or fish finder is a big help in locating structure, as well as schools of bass or baitfish.

Trolling is a good way to catch submerged white bass. Some anglers prefer to troll even when the fish are surfacing, either at a speed of 5 miles per hour, with the lure a short distance behind the boat, or in a slower-moving boat with a long line deployed. When the whites are very deep, you'll have to troll with weights, lead-core or wire lines, or downriggers to reach them. You can troll over structure with spoons, spinners, small plugs, or jigs.

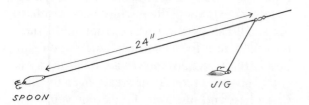

Rig with two lures for white bass in a school.

Try different depths and lures by trolling with two or three rods with varying lengths of line deployed. Keep letting out line with one rod until you get a strike, then mark your line so you can let out the correct length to reach the depth where the fish are. It is also a good idea to mark the spot with a buoy so you can find it again.

When white bass are deep during the summer or winter months, vertical jigging is a good way to catch them. Let a small, heavy spoon or jig down to the bottom and work it up and down in short jerks. Or else, when the lure reaches bottom, reel it back toward the surface with slow jerks.

White bass that are deep can also be caught by still-fishing with live minnows about 2½ inches long. This is often a very productive method at night. To attract the white bass at this time, hang one or two lanterns on the boat so the light shines on the water. This is also a good way to catch fresh bait. The minnows gather below the light and you can scoop them up with a net. Impale a minnow through the back and fish it on a bottom rig with a sinker.

Although in northern waters some white bass are caught through the ice in winter, they are not very active when the water gets too cold. The best winter fishing is found in open water in our southern states, especially below power plants, which discharge warm water. Here they can often be caught on jigs, spoons, and crankbaits.

White bass put up a good scrap for their size and have more zip and endurance than most panfish. They do most of their fighting below the surface and don't leap out of the water. But on light tackle they are a lot of fun and sport.

White bass don't grow too big, averaging from ¾ to 2 pounds in weight, which is still larger than the average panfish. Fish weighing up to 4 or even 5 pounds have been caught from time to time in various waters. The world record on rod and reel is a 5-pound 14-ounce white bass caught by Jim King in Kerr Reservoir, North Carolina, on March 15, 1986.

A string of average-sized white bass. They usually run bigger than most panfish. (Ohio Dept. of Natural Resources)

The white bass is so prolific and has such a short life span that most states have liberal bag limits for them. Most white bass live only three or four years, and if not caught, they die and are wasted. So biologists claim that it's a good idea to catch your limit as often as you can, which is rather easy when white bass are really running and biting. They make good eating, having a firm, tasty flesh.

Where to Go

White bass fishing is best in the deep South where the season is long and the fish are large and plentiful. In Texas, for instance, you'll find them in lakes Texoma, Travis, Buchanan, Mar-

shall, Livingston, Sulphur, Caddo, and Dallas, and in such rivers as the Rio Grande, Colorado, and Pedernales. In Tennessee, most of the man-made reservoirs and lakes have white bass, with Kentucky Lake, Watts Bar Reservoir, Pickwick, Douglas, and Center Hill lakes offering good fishing. Kentucky has Kentucky Lake, Herrington Lake, Lake Cumberland, Dale Hollow Lake, Lake Barkley, Nolin, Dewey, Buckhorn lakes, and such rivers as the Dix and Rockcastle. Lake of the Ozarks and Bull Shoals in Missouri are noted for white bass. In Arkansas, Lake Hamilton and the Ouachita River are fished. Virginia's South Holston Lake, John W. Flannagan Lake, Claytor Lake, and Smith Mountain Lake all contain white bass. In South Carolina, you'll find white bass in Lake Hartwell, Clark Hill Reservoir, Lake Murray, Lake Greenwood, the Savannah and Catawba rivers, and the Santee-Cooper waters. In Wisconsin, Lake Mendota, Lake Winnegago, Lake Monona, Wisconsin River, and Wolf River contain white bass, as do the Illinois River, Quiver Lake, Lake Matanzas, and the Fox Chain o' Lakes in the state of Illinois. Georgia's Lake Hartwell, Clark Hill, and Lake Sidney Lanier are all productive. In Florida, you can fish Lake Seminole and the Apalachicola River. In New York, white bass are found in Oneida Lake and the St. Lawrence River. With the exception of Lake Superior, where they are rare or nonexistent, all the Great Lakes contain white bass.

White bass have also been stocked in at least twenty other states as far west as California. So the above is only a partial list of white bass waters. Write your state fish and game department for further information about white bass lakes and reservoirs in your area. The fishing will vary from year to year, as white-bass populations fluctuate depending on the forage fish and other food present in a certain body of water. So if you have a choice of lakes or reservoirs, choose the one that has a big population of these spunky game fish.

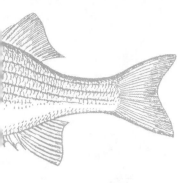

Chapter 22

White Perch

White perch are considered panfish, but few anglers go fishing for them deliberately and they are rarely mentioned in outdoor journals. Yet white perch have many qualities that make some freshwater anglers rate them over most of the other panfishes.

The white perch is not related to the yellow perch, or to any perch, for that matter. It is a member of the same family as the white bass and the striped bass. In fact, it resembles both of these fish in general outline but lacks the stripes. The back varies in color depending on where a white perch is found; usually it is olive, dark grayish-green, or silver-gray. These colors shade into a paler olive or silvery green to silvery white on the belly. Freshwater perch are usually much darker than those found in brackish or salt water.

The white perch is also called the bluenose perch, gray perch, black perch, silver perch, silver bass, and sea perch.

The white perch is found from Nova Scotia down to the Carolinas, mostly in rivers, creeks, saltwater or brackish ponds, and bays on the Atlantic coast. Though they have been introduced into many freshwater lakes and ponds in the eastern states, their natural habitat remains the rivers emptying into the sea, and saltwater and brackish ponds formed by sandbars that cut them off from the ocean. These backwaters usually "salt out" in time and become mostly freshwater. But white perch continue to live and thrive in them.

Tackle

White perch are caught on various kinds of outfits, from cane and glass poles to light saltwater tackle. For fishing in quiet ponds or creeks in shallow water near shore, an ordinary cane pole does the trick nicely, with or without a bobber. When white perch are in shallow water near shore or feeding on the surface, a fly rod makes an excellent outfit. A light, freshwater spinning, spincasting, or baitcasting outfit can be used for casting. In brackish or salt water with strong currents or tides, a heavier freshwater or light saltwater rod with heavy sinkers is needed to hold bottom or to fish among rocks.

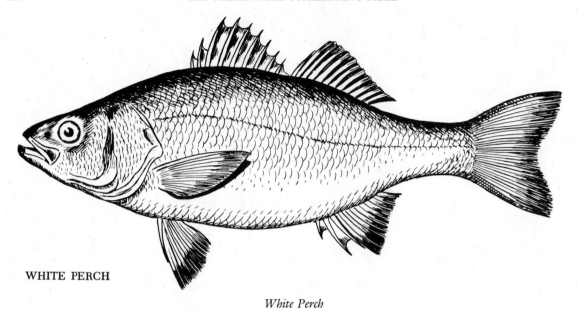

WHITE PERCH

White Perch

White perch often hit wet flies or streamer flies. Those with silver, tinsel, or Mylar bodies are especially good. When feeding on surface insects, white perch also take most of the popular dry-fly patterns used for trout. Also effective are small panfish or bass bugs that imitate crickets, grasshoppers, beetles, or ants.

Other effective lures for white perch include small silver and gold spoons and weighted

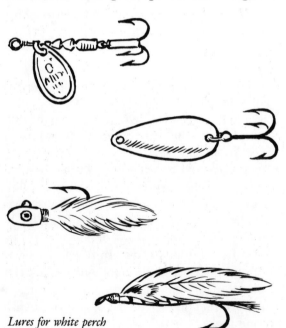

Lures for white perch

spinners. For trolling or casting, a small spinner rigged in front of a wet fly, a streamer, or a worm is a good combination. And in recent years, tiny jigs with bucktail, feather, nylon, or plastic bodies or tails have been used with good results. Tiny plugs of the Rapala, Rebel, and Flatfish type also catch white perch.

White perch take natural baits such as earthworms, nightcrawlers, minnows, baby eels, and small, soft-shelled crayfish. Also good are grasshoppers, crickets, and grubs. In brackish and salt water, white perch are often caught on grass shrimp, bloodworms, clamworms, sandworms, and pieces of clam or shedder crab.

Seasonal Tactics

The white perch season lasts from early spring to late fall and even through the winter months in most waters where the fish are found. They spend the winter in deep water or brackish bays, then move into rivers and creeks to spawn in April, May, or June. The spawning runs often take them up big rivers into fresh waters many miles from the sea. They also spawn in tidal rivers in shallow coves, bays, tributary streams, and estuaries. Those in lakes run up tributary streams in the spring. The peak fishing in most waters is in the spring and fall.

You can catch white perch during the daytime, although they probably will be in deeper water, from 8 to 20 feet, at that time. They move into shallow water, from 2 to 8 feet, near shore toward evening, at dusk, and at night, which are the best times to fish for them there. In some large, deep freshwater lakes, or in large saltwater bays such as Chesapeake Bay, white perch could be anywhere from 30 to 100 feet deep.

The white perch is quite an adaptable, hardy fish, able to live in warm and cold waters, and in fresh, brackish or salt waters. However, they prefer, and are most plentiful in, brackish water over mud, clay, sand, or rocky bottoms. Fishing is usually best about two hours before to two hours after high tide.

White perch may move about in groups of several fish or in big schools numbering hundreds or even thousands. They also tend to travel around quite a bit, which, of course, makes them difficult to locate. When you fish unfamiliar waters, it is wise to consult a fishing guide or an angler who knows the lake about the usual whereabouts of the fish. Or look for anglers fishing from shore or boats; if they are catching white perch, go ahead and join them. If you have a boat equipped with electronic gear, you are ahead of the game.

Early in the morning or toward evening when the lake is calm, you often see schools of white perch close to the surface or breaking water. If they are merely swimming around, you may not be able to entice them to hit a lure or take a bait. But if they are feeding on insects or chasing minnows, you usually get some action.

Still-fishing with a cane or glass pole near shore, in shallow creeks or other shallow waters, is a popular way to catch white perch. Since they start feeding early in the spring, soon after ice-out, they attract many anglers at this time. Use a bobber above a hook baited with worms, minnows, or any of the natural baits mentioned earlier. White perch like a moving bait, so let it sink as deep as it will go, then move it gently to one side or raise it a foot or so and let it sink again. Keep doing this at regular intervals so the bait doesn't just hang motionless. Of course, with live bait this isn't as important as with dead bait.

After you catch your first white perch, cut a thin, tapered strip about 1½ inches long from its belly or side and impale the wide end on a No. 4 or 6 hook. The flip it out, let it sink a few feet, and bring it in with short, gentle twitches.

For still-fishing some distance from shore, a spinning rod is preferred, with a standard bottom rig—a small sinker tied on the end of the line and a hook on a short leader tied a few inches above the weight. This can be baited with a worm or minnow in fresh water or with a bloodworm, clamworm, or grass shrimp in brackish or salt water. Cast the rig out from shore, put your rod in a holder, and wait for a bite. White perch bite with vigor, but because of their small mouths, give them time to mouth the bait before you set the hook. You can fish this bottom rig from a drifting boat. Once you hook a fish, drop anchor and fish that spot as long as the perch keep biting. Some anglers tie a small balloon with a long string around the tail of the first perch they catch and then release it to follow the rest of

This rig with a double-bladed spinner and a trailing hook baited with a worm is highly effective when used in drifting or trolling for white perch. (Bob Harris Photo)

the school. This way they can keep up with the school as it moves around.

At times, white perch take spinners, spoons, jigs, or spinner-and-worm combinations. These are worked near the surface or at different depths. In a stream, cast upstream and across and let the lure sink and travel close to the bottom. White perch like movement and action, but the lure shouldn't move too fast.

Trolling is also a good way to catch white perch. Troll spoons, spinners, jigs, or spinner-bait combinations on a long line so the lure travels close to the bottom. Once you catch a perch, throw out a buoy to mark the spot.

Small streamer or bucktail flies such as the Mickey Finn, Gray Ghost, or Black Ghost tied on No. 6 or 8 hooks are effective for trolling. Late evening, when white perch move into shallow water, is the best time. But the ultimate in sport with white perch is to cast dry flies, wet flies, nymphs, or streamers when the fish are feeding on top in shallow water. Good dry flies include the Light Cahill, March Brown, Wulff patterns, and the bivisibles. Toward evening, try small panfish popping bugs. Twitch dry flies or bugs gently to make them ripple the surface. When casting wet flies, streamers, or bucktails, use a weighted sinking fly line. Then try different depths to find fish.

When white perch are in very deep water, vertical jigging from a boat is one of the best ways to catch them. You can use a leadhead jig, a spoon, or other small metal lure weighing about ¼ or ½ ounce. Such spoons as the smaller Kastmaster, Hopkins, Mann-O-Lure, Slab Spoon, Krocodile, and the Dardevles are all good. Let the spoon down to the bottom, reel in a couple of feet, and then work it up and down in short jerks. Many times, you don't even have to jig the lure, because white perch are usually in thick schools, and some of them will hit the lure as it flutters or sinks. You also can jig for white perch through the ice during the winter.

White perch put up a much better fight than the yellow perch, crappie, or rock bass. The

This angler has hooked a husky white perch in a New Hampshire lake. White perch are plentiful in most of the New England states. (Bob Harris Photo)

big ones, especially when hooked in a river with a strong current or in salt or brackish water where a strong tide is running, often put up a long, spirited battle. However, the tackle must be light for them to show their best, since most white perch will be on the small side.

The average white perch runs from about 6 to 10 inches long and weighs less than a pound, though in some lakes and brackish waters fish going 3 pounds have been caught. One of the largest was a 19½-inch white perch weighing 4 pounds 12 ounces caught in Messalonskee Lake in Maine in June 1949 by Mrs. Earl Small.

The white perch has a firm, flaky, sweet-tasting flesh and is excellent fried. Fillets of white perch cut into chunks make a delicious chowder. In the early spring or late fall when the females have eggs or roe, you can remove these, dip them in flour and egg and fry them.

The bag limits for white perch in most states are very liberal, and you can bring home plenty of fish to be frozen for future use. Many lakes become overpopulated with white perch, which soon eat up most of the food leaving little for themselves or other fish. So the remaining white perch tend to become stunted, and it's often a good idea to keep as many as you can, even if they are small.

Where to Go

White perch abound in Canada, particularly in Nova Scotia and in New Brunswick. Maine is noted for the white perch found in most of its coastal rivers, lakes, and ponds. They have also been introduced into many inland lakes there. New Hampshire, Massachusetts, Rhode Island, and Connecticut all have good white perch fishing. In New York, you'll find white perch in many waters on Long Island and in the reservoirs and large lakes upstate. They are very plentiful in the Hudson, Delaware, Toms, and Mullica rivers, and many lakes in New Jersey. In Virginia and Maryland, the Chesapeake Bay and its many tributaries contain white perch. In North Carolina there is white perch fishing in Lake Waccamaw, and the Albemarle Sound and its tributaries. White perch are also found in Vermont, Michigan, Ohio, Pennsylvania, Delaware, and South Carolina.

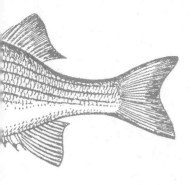

Chapter 23

Striped Bass

The saltwater striped bass has long been a popular food and sport fish in this country. In the early 1600s, New England settlers were catching them on a cod line baited with a piece of lobster tail. Over the years, stripers have been caught in many coastal rivers from Maine to Mississippi during their spring spawning runs. Many of these stripers were caught accidentally by anglers fishing for other game fish. But a few anglers were deliberately catching stripers on flies in some of these rivers as far back as the Civil War.

Then when the Santee and Cooper rivers in South Carolina were blocked by dams in 1941, some stripers were trapped in the two lakes—Marion and Moultrie—that were formed by the blockage. The striped bass thrived and spawned in these lakes and the rivers entering them, and sport fishing for them became popular.

After World War II, attempts were made to stock striped bass in other freshwater lakes and reservoirs. At first these weren't very successful, but gradually, as biologists learned more about striped bass culture, stripers were introduced into many waters and a new fishery was created.

Striped bass were introduced into lakes not only to provide sport fishing but also to control big populations of small fish that were threatening the existence of black bass and other game fish. It was found that the introduced striped bass ate gizzard shad, threadfin shad, glut herring, and alewives in sufficient quantities to keep their numbers down, thereby improving the game fishing. In addition it was found that the stripers feeding on these forage fish grew even faster than they did in their normal saltwater habitats.

Also, biologists developed a hybrid by crossing a striped bass with a white bass. Called the whiterock bass or the sunshine bass, it resembles the striped bass closely but is smaller, less streamlined, and has broken rather than straight stripes. But it has proven to be a hardier fish than the striped bass, and some anglers claim it fights harder on the end of the line; so the hybrid has been stocked in many states and is often found in many of the same waters as the striped bass. It can be

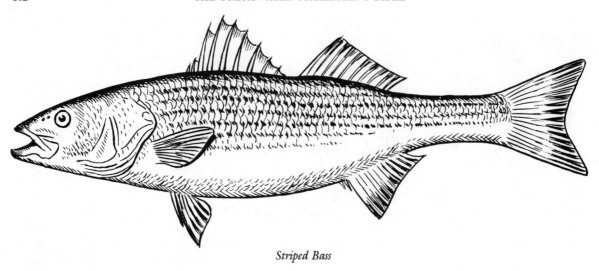

Striped Bass

caught with the same techniques as stripers.

Striped-bass fishing in fresh water is now booming, as more and more anglers discover these fish and learn how to catch them. Like many anglers fishing for saltwater stripers, some freshwater anglers have become striped bass specialists, spending most of their time seeking this highly prized newcomer. So great is its popularity that the freshwater striped bass has been called by many "The Super Fish" and "The Fish of the Future."

In the past, the striped bass was also known as the squidhound, linesides, greenhead, rockfish, and rock. But most anglers today refer to it simply as the striper, owing to the seven or eight longitudinal stripes on its sides. The back of the striped bass varies from a light tan to a dark olive or bluish-green, depending on where it is found and the color and depth of the water from which it is taken. This upper color shades to silver along the sides and to white along the belly.

Tackle

Tackle for freshwater striped bass is similar to that used for other large game fish. A fairly heavy freshwater spinning, spincasting, baitcasting, or trolling outfit is suitable. Some anglers use heavy fly rods. In some areas where you have to make long casts or fish fast tail-

waters below dams from shore, two-handed saltwater spinning rods are needed. Many tackle companies make special striper rods, reels, and lures.

Most of the lures designed for other freshwater fish can be used for striped bass. However, the lures should match the size of the forage fish the stripers are feeding on. Also, hooks should be somewhat larger and stronger than those used on most fresh-water lures. Many anglers find that lures for saltwater stripers are also suited for big freshwater stripers. And, as mentioned, there are now many lures designed especially for freshwater striper fishing. Later on in this chapter we will name specific lures that are good for striped bass.

When it comes to natural baits, striped bass are caught on live and dead gizzard shad, threadfin shad, herring, alewives, smelt, needlefish, waterdogs, small eels, minnows, panfish, and even small trout where it is legal to use them. Some anglers have also used dead small saltwater fish such as anchovies, sardines, and herrings with great success.

Seasonal Tactics

The season for catching freshwater striped bass is a long one, especially in our southern states, where they are often caught year-round. In most states, however, the best fishing starts in the spring, when stripers move up the rivers to spawn. This may be as early as February or March in the South, and as late as May or June in the North. During the summer months, fishing is good in the deeper waters in rivers, lakes, and reservoirs. Then there is usually another surge of fast fishing in most waters during September, October, and November.

Generally you'll find that most striper activity peaks in shallow water during the early morning and evening hours, especially in the summer. In fall and early winter there is often surface action at any time of the day. Stripers are also more apt to feed near the surface and in shallow water on cloudy, rainy, or overcast days. Some of the best striper fishing takes place at night, from dusk to midnight, and then just before daybreak.

Finding stripers in a large lake is more difficult, since they tend to move around quite a bit, following the schools of baitfish and feeding at different times, and places. Look for fallen trees, driftwood, or submerged brush along sloping points and dropoffs bordering deep water. Stripers also hang around pilings, old creeks, and channels. The mouths of rivers entering a lake or reservoir are other productive spots. Stripers like fast currents, rips, and moving water and gather at such spots to feed. They do not like very warm water, so during the hot summer months they go deep or seek cool streams or underwater springs. The cooler water in the tailraces below dams also attracts them during the hot months. Stripers prefer a water temperature between 65 and 70 degrees F.

Early in the morning, at dusk, and during the night, when stripers move into shallow water near shore to feed, they are found at the entrances to coves and along bars and points. During the middle of the day, they are often suspended in deeper water of from 15 to 40 feet. In some deep lakes, they may be in depths up to 70 feet or more. For fishing in deep water, a depth finder or fish finder is a big help.

The most exciting time to fish for stripers is when they are feeding on baitfish on the surface. When you see birds diving or fish breaking, rush to that spot with rods rigged and ready. This is called jump fishing.

It is important not to get too close to the fish and frighten them. Approach the edge of the school on the upwind side, shut off your motor about a hundred feet away, and drift toward the fish. Then cast into the feeding stripers with surface plugs—poppers, chuggers, swimmers, stickbaits or crippled minnows with propellers. Some of the most popular surface plugs include the Striper-Swiper, Striper-Strike, Pencil Popper, Tennessee Popper, Chugger Spook, Pop'n Sam, Zara Spook, Dog Walker, and Devil's Horse. Floating minnow-type plugs such as the Rapala, Rebel, Redfin, and Bang-O-Lure are also effective. Most surface plugs should be reeled fairly fast and given some action to create a commotion.

If stripers are deep, you can catch them on underwater plugs, crankbaits, spoons, or jigs. In fact, the smaller stripers usually feed on top—the bigger ones will be a few feet to 30 feet deep. Here you should try reeling in a lure fast with no rod action. If this fails, try a spoon or jig and make long upward sweeps of the rod, then drop the tip so that the lure rises and sinks in an attractive manner. You have to keep your eye on the line and try to feel a hit. Stripers usually grab the lure while it is dropping, so keep a tight line.

In rivers, surface plugs are effective, especially below dams, in the morning and evening or when the fish are breaking or chasing baitfish. Otherwise, underwater plugs, spoons, spinners, and jigs are called for. Jigs are especially deadly because they get down fast and deep and reach stripers lying near the bottom. In fast currents, cast well upstream and across and let the jig swing, sink, and bounce along the bottom.

When stripers are down deep, vertical jigging is a good way to reach and catch them. Almost any sturdy bait-casting, popping or spinning rod with 8- to 20-pound test line can be used. Heavy spoons such as the Hopkins or jigs can be used to reach suspended stripers or stripers feeding deep on baitfish. The lure is lowered to the school of fish and is worked up and down in a jigging motion to bring strikes.

Freshwater striped bass are also caught by trolling. Trolling is especially effective when stripers are scattered or when concentrations are difficult to locate. But it can also be done effectively even when stripers are feeding on top or when you are over known structure or along dropoffs and channels.

For trolling, you need heavier tackle than that used for casting. A stiff-action spinning rod and 10- to 20-pound-test line will do the trick. But if you plan to do a lot of trolling for stripers, revolving-spool reels and rods to match are better. The reels should be filled with lines testing from 15 to 25 pounds. Lures for trolling include underwater plugs, crankbaits, spoons, spinners, jigs, and plastic lures. Various combinations, such as a plug and a spoon, a spoon and a jig, or two jigs, are often trolled. One of the most effective combos is to remove the front treble hook from a crankbait such as the Magnum Hellbender and tie on a 30-inch leader to the eye. On the end of this leader, attach a small spoon or a plastic-tailed jig. With such a rig you can reach depths of 30 feet or more.

There are days when stripers want the real thing, and then live baits fished on Nos. 1/0 to 6/0 hooks are deadly. Baitfish up to a foot or more in length are used for big stripers.

In some lakes and reservoirs, such as Lake Lanier in Georgia, anglers have found that live trout 6 to 12 inches long are deadly baits. The trout are fished on slip-bobber rigs, anywhere from 4 to 15 feet deep. Check local regulations before using trout for bait.

To fish a live baitfish, add a light clincher or rubber-core sinker on the leader. When fishing in strong currents, you might need a heavier egg-shaped sinker about 2 feet above the bait. A barrel swivel on the line at this

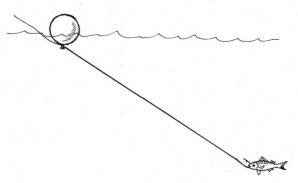

Balloon float affixed to line from 10 to 20 feet above live baitfish drifts bait over fish.

point acts as a stop to keep the weight a proper distance from the bait. Fish this rig slowly along the bottom.

In recent years, anglers have found that attaching a balloon float above a live baitfish is deadly for big striped bass. The balloon is blown up to about 5 inches in diameter and is attached to the line anywhere from 10 to 20 feet above the hook. The angler anchors upwind or upcurrent from the spot he plans to fish and lets the balloon and bait drift toward it. Or he drifts and lets the balloon out some distance behind the boat.

You can also use a bottom rig with a three-way swivel when fishing with live or dead baits. Tie a 3-foot leader with the hook to one eye of the swivel. Then add a shorter dropper line, about a foot long, to another eye of the swivel to hold the sinker. The line attached to the sinker should be weaker than the line holding the hook and bait, so that it breaks off when caught on the bottom. The fishing line, of course, is tied to the remaining eye of the swivel.

Give the fish plenty of time to swallow the bait before setting the hook. The bigger the bait, the more time you should give the fish to swallow it.

A hooked striper puts up a long and determined fight, but rarely on the surface. When first hooked, it makes a long, fast run and heads for deeper water. Do not try to stop or even slow down this first run, but let the fish take

This angler is gaffing a good-sized striper caught on a plug in the Kerr Reservoir on the North Carolina-Virginia border. (Joe Arrington Photo)

line freely. It may make several other runs, but these will be shorter. When fishing a river from shore, you may have to follow a big striper downstream. When a striper gives up, use a big, wide-mouthed net or a gaff to land it.

Most freshwater stripers run between 2 and 20 pounds. But many fish of 30 and 40 pounds are caught, and quite a few fish over 50 pounds have been taken. Gary Helms caught a 60-pound 8-ounce striper in Melton Hill Lake, Tennessee. The present world-record fresh-water striper is a 66-pound fish caught by Theodore H. Furnish in O'Neill Forebay, Los Baños, California, on June 29, 1988. The record for hybrid stripers is a 24-pound 3-ounce fish caught in Leesville Lake, Virginia, on May 12, 1989, by David N. Lambert. But no matter what their size, freshwater stripers or hybrids make good eating.

Today you'll find freshwater stripers and/or hybrids in Alabama, Mississippi, Louisiana, New Mexico, Kansas, Utah, Nevada, Arizona, Colorado, West Virginia, Virginia, Texas, Tennessee, Arkansas, North Carolina, South Carolina, Oklahoma, Kentucky, Georgia, Florida, Indiana, Wisconsin, Illinois, Iowa, Delaware,

Gary Helms holds a giant 60-pound 8-ounce striper caught in Melton Hill Lake, Tennessee. (Allen Ricks Photo)

Maryland, Missouri, Nebraska, New York, New Jersey, Pennsylvania, Connecticut, Rhode Island, Massachusetts, New Hampshire, Maine, California, and Oregon.

The future for the freshwater striped bass and hybrid looks bright. Stripers are reproducing naturally in some of the waters where they are now found. In other waters, they are being stocked annually or at intervals to maintain a fishery. Biologists welcome the stripers and hybrids because they keep the forage-fish populations down, and because in lakes or reservoirs where they cannot reproduce naturally, they can be kept under strict control. Many states now have their own striper hatcheries so that they do not have to depend on other states for a supply of eggs or young stripers. So it looks like freshwater striped bass and hybrid fishing is not only here to stay, but also will increase in the future to provide sport for more and more freshwater anglers.

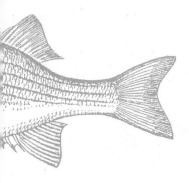

Chapter 24

Catfish

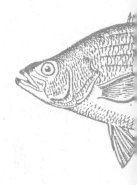

Fishing for catfish is very popular in waters where these dark, smooth, bewhiskered fish are numerous. In the South, for example, you'll often see the banks of large lakes and rivers lined with hundreds of eager catfish anglers. Additional hundreds will be out in small boats, dangling their lines near the bottom, hoping a big catfish will come along and engulf the bait. Even in northern lakes and rivers where channel catfish are present or have been stocked, they have proven more popular than black bass.

The reasons for this popularity are simple: Catfish often come big, and they make delicious eating. Also, they are found in warmer, muddier waters, often near cities, where trout, bass, and other more delicate game fish have tough going. In addition, catfish bite well at night: Many anglers do a bit of catfishing after a day's work.

When we talk about catfish we must mention that at least twenty-four species are found in North America. But of these, we are mainly concerned here with the four usually caught by anglers: the blue catfish, channel catfish,

white catfish, and flathead catfish. The biggest is the blue catfish, also called the chucklehead, great blue catfish, great forktail catfish, and Mississippi blue catfish. This species is gray or dusky blue on the back with a silvery white belly and a deeply forked tail. The blue catfish can weigh 150 pounds or more.

The channel catfish resembles the blue catfish but is smaller and more streamlined. Also known as the squealer, willow catfish, fiddler, forktail catfish, speckled catfish, and silver catfish, this species is usually gray or grayfish-blue on the top, with a silvery tinge and black spots along its sides. Its tail is also deeply forked. Channel catfish may reach 50 pounds or more.

The white catfish is pale olive or blue-gray on top and white on the belly. The tail is forked but not so deeply as in the channel catfish. The white catfish may reach 60 pounds in certain waters but rarely goes over 15 pounds in most areas. It has also been called the Potomac catfish.

The flathead catfish is yellow or olive-brown on the back with brown blotches along the

CATFISH

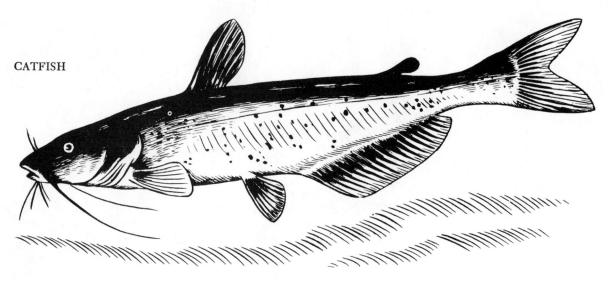

Catfish

sides. It is also called the yellow cat, mud cat, and shovelhead cat. It sometimes reaches over 100 pounds in weight in large rivers.

Originally, catfish were found in the central and eastern parts of Canada, the Great Lakes region, the Mississippi Valley, and the eastern part of the United States. But during this century intensive stocking has spread the catfish's range throughout most of the United States.

Catfish have been caught on all kinds of tackle, from simple handlines to deep-sea rods and reels. The ordinary cane pole is often used when catfish are close to shore or in narrow creeks. For the smaller catfish, up to about 15 pounds, spinning, spincasting, or baitcasting tackle is adequate. But for big catfish in large rivers and where strong currents prevail, you need heavier outfits. For boat fishing, a heavy baitcasting rod and reel or a light saltwater boat rod and reel is needed. If the bottom is rocky or filled with obstructions and the catfish are big, you often need lines testing 40 or 50 pounds. For fishing from shore where long casts may be required, the lighter surf-spinning or surf rods with revolving-spool reels are more practical. Use 20- or 25-pound-test line on a surf-spinning reel, 30- or 40-pound-test on a revolving-spool reel. For fishing with

bobbers in rivers, some anglers prefer 10-foot, European-type rods with large spinning or baitcasting reels.

Various types of rigs are employed in cat-fishing. For fishing in quiet waters, the baited hook is merely tied to the end of the line, cast out, and allowed to sink and lie on the bottom. But when distance is needed or when you are fishing in a strong current, a bottom rig consisting of a sinker on the end of the line and a hook on an 18-inch leader tied a few inches above the sinker is often used. Some anglers like two or three hooks on such a rig.

Another popular rig is the sliding-sinker rig, similar to the one often used for carp fishing. You need an egg-shaped sinker with a hole in it. The line runs through the hole, and the sinker is stopped from sliding down to the hook by a barrel swivel tied about 2 feet above the hook. When drifting in a boat, many anglers

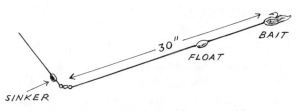

Rig used when drifting in a boat for catfish

like to use a bottom-walking sinker rig, such as the Gapen Bait-Walker, which can move along the bottom without getting hung up too often.

To hold the bait near bottom in deep water or strong currents, heavy sinkers up to 10 ounces or even more may be required. In most catfish waters, however, lighter weights are adequate.

Nos. 1/0 to 4/0 hooks are usually used for smaller catfish. But for big catfish and big baits, you need strong Nos. 5/0, 6/0, or 7/0 hooks. The Eagle Claw and O'Shaughnessy patterns are usually favored. Treble hooks are also used to hold softer baits such as doughballs and cheese baits. Some treble hooks even have a coil spring around the shank to hold soft baits securely.

The list of suitable catfish baits is long and varied. Garden worms and nightcrawlers are tops. Up to a dozen or more small worms or four nightcrawlers may be used on a single hook. Another good bait is a freshwater clam or mussel, opened and allowed to stand for a day or two to ripen. Chunks or strips of beef, pork, lamb, or poultry are used, as are heart, liver, and lungs. The entrails of rabbits, poultry, or fish are also good.

Big catfish have also been caught on small dead birds, mice, chicks, rabbits, and frogs. Smaller catfish take grasshoppers, catalpa worms, locusts, and grubs (usually fished two or three on a single hook). Other excellent baits are a soft-shelled crayfish tied around a hook, or the tail meat of a hard-shelled crayfish.

Various kinds of small fishes make effective catfish baits. In the South, gizzard shad and river herring are commonly used, along with their entrails. Small perch, sunfish, suckers, carp, small catfish, or bullheads are favored for big catfish. Big baitfish are cut into chunks or strips.

Catfish are caught on berries and other fruits, laundry soap, congealed chicken and animal blood, and baits made from strongly scented or flavored combinations of cheese, meat, fish, and flour. Most catfish anglers like to make their own stink- and doughball baits, but these can also be bought in tackle stores already prepared and packaged.

When you go catfishing, it's a good idea to take along several kinds of baits and try them all until you find the ones the fish want. Although catfish eat almost anything, they have their preferences and fussy periods when they want a certain kind of food and ignore all others.

Catfish can also be caught at times on slow-moving underwater plugs, crankbaits, spoons, spinners, and jigs. Various jigs, especially those with plastic grubs or curlytails, are often

Prepared baits for catfish

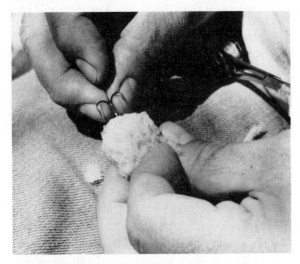

Pieces of sponge or foam, flavored or scented to attract catfish, are popular lures. (Minnesota Dept. of Natural Resources Photo)

effective. Small catfish, especially channel catfish, are more apt to take a lure since they are able to move faster than bigger fish.

Catfish anglers also use various kinds of sponge, foam, plastic, and bait-holder lures, which are less messy than stinkbaits or natural baits. One of the simplest is a flavoring- or scent-soaked piece of sponge or foam on a treble hook. The same thing can be done with short lengths of plastic worms or grubs. There are also hollow plastic bait holders, such as the Gitzit, which are filled with bait squeezed from a tube. Other lures are made to look like catfish foods. In fact, you can fill almost any plastic lure with fish bait, or rub it with some kind of flavoring or scent, and use it to catch catfish.

Seasonal Tactics

The season for catfishing may begin as early as March or April in southern waters and continue through much of the winter. Catfish have been caught in November, December, January, and February in southern states, in deep water and around warm-water discharges from power plants. Farther north, fishing for catfish may start later and end earlier, but usually the months from May to October are best. Catfish are more likely to be congregated in rivers below dams during May, June, and July, when they are spawning. In the northern states, catfishing is often good during the summer months, June usually being a good month in most areas. In Florida, of course, catfish can be caught year-round.

The best time to go catfishing is when a river is rising from a recent rain and becoming discolored. At this time, catfish go on a eating binge, feeding around the clock on foods washed into the river by the rains. After the water has been muddy for a few days, and the catfish have filled their bellies, the fishing may fall off. When the water is clear, the best times to fish are early morning, in the late afternoon, the evening, and at night. In fact, you can't choose a better time to go catfishing than at night. That's when they leave their hideouts and roam the shallows and shorelines looking for food.

Catfish bite better on cloudy, overcast days, especially in deep water. If you fish during the day when the water is clear, you have to locate the holes where catfish lurk. In large rivers, big catfish often stay in water from 30 to 60 feet deep. Look for them along undercut banks, around rocks, brick walls, cement blocks, caves, stumps, logs, sunken trees, brushpiles, and similar cover. The mouths of rivers entering a lake are prime hotspots; these and deep pools, channels, and eddies are best during the daytime. At night, try the rapids, riffles, and shallows near shore.

Big catfish are often found below big dams. In many southern states, the best spots are the "boils"—that is, the tailwaters where catfish feed on baitfish that are stunned, crippled, or chopped up by the turbines.

Some anglers like to head through the boils to fish the quieter water next to the dam. Some run their boats up to the boils, then cut the motor and drift downstream, bouncing bottom with their sinker and bait. Others anchor their boats farther downstream above a hotspot and let the current take their rig toward it. This can be dangerous if a larger volume of water is suddenly released from the turbines.

The most effective bait here is usually a small, whole gizzard shad or herring such as is found in the tailwaters. (A big one can be cut in half.) It is fished on a bottom rig with one or two hooks above a sinker of 4 to 16 ounces or more, depending on the depth and the strength of the current. Most of the catfish lie in the slower currents between the main currents created by the turbines, or below big rocks, or in holes on the bottom.

From shore, a fishermen casts sinker and bait with a long surf rod and lets them go down to the bottom. Then he puts his rod in a holder and waits for a bite. A catfish is usually slow about taking a bait and must be given plenty of time. Don't try to set the hook on the first nibbles but wait until the fish really swallows the bait and starts moving off with it.

Anglers seeking channel catfish in smaller, shallower rivers like to wade and drift the bait into likely spots. In fast water you can drift the bait without a bobber and it will sink deep enough. But in the slower-moving stretches, a bobber keeps the bait moving with the current. The bait should be close to the bottom at all times. Take a position in a rapid or riffle above a pool and let the bait wash down into the deeper water below. Hold the bait for a few minutes in one spot, then lift the rod tip, release some line, and let the bait move downstream to a new spot. Allow it to drift under overhanging trees or bushes, undercut banks, or tree roots. Also, cast above logs, stumps, or rocks.

When catfish are in the mood, you can have a lot of fun trying to hook them on artificial lures. A weighted spinner or jig is good, especially if the hook is tipped with a strip of pork rind, fish, or a worm. Small plastic worms, minnow-type plugs such as the Rapala or Rebel, and crankbaits also produce. Lures should be retrieved slowly and close to the bottom. You can also troll lures very slowly so they travel along the bottom. Jigging for catfish is effective, too. Add some fish scent to the jig, or bait with a worm, small minnow, or strip of fish.

When fishing lakes in the spring, look for catfish spawning along shorelines with ledges, undercut banks, caves or holes, hollow logs, and riprap. Later in the season, look for them in deeper water over old foundations, stone fences, sunken timber, boulders, old river channels, and along dropoffs and the edges of submerged islands. Catfish may suspend in deep water or move to different parts of a lake. A sonar outfit is needed to locate them. Catfish often feed along windswept shores when a strong wind stirs up food or drives baitfish toward shore. Creeks entering a lake are hotspots when a heavy rain muddies the water and sweeps food down.

In states where it is allowed, catfish are caught on handlines. Lines are tied to stakes or trees and the baited hooks left for hours in the water. Trot lines may be stretched across a stream and tied to trees on both banks. Short lines with baited hooks are tied to this main line at regular intervals. The trot lines are usually set in the evening and allowed to remain in the water until morning.

Years ago, an effective and popular way to catch catfish from a boat was by jugging. In those days, people used stone or glass jugs, or metal gallon cans. A strong line with a hook was attached to the handle. The hook was baited with beef liver, beef heart, chicken liver, minnows, or chunks of fish. The containers were released in the current at different spots and were followed by the boat. When the container went down, the anglers hauled in the catfish.

Some people also catch catfish when they are in their spawning holes by wading into the water and probing with their hands until they feel a fish. Then they work their hand into the catfish's mouth or gills and pull it out. Called grabbling, groping, tickling, or noodling, this method is legal only in some states. Before you attempt to catch catfish with your bare hands, check your state and local fish laws.

A catfish, however, is at its best when caught

Big strings of smaller catfish are often caught in many waters. These will provide some tasty meals. (Tennessee Wildlife Resources Photo)

on rod and reel. If you use the lightest tackle that is practical for the waters you are fishing and for the size of the fish running, you can have a lot of fun and sport. Channel catfish, especially, will put up a great scrap, making fast runs and sometimes thrashing around on the surface. But most catfish fight deep, boring toward the bottom for a submerged rock or log. Big catfish, of course, will give you the most trouble, and in some waters heavy tackle is essential.

Catfish make good eating, but must be skinned before you eat them. This is done by cutting the skin around the head and down the back and belly. Then, using pliers, grab the skin and pull it toward the tail. Small catfish can be cooked whole, but the larger ones should be cut into fillets or steaks. Frying and

stewing are the usual methods of cooking the fish, with the former particularly popular in the Midwest and South.

Old-time records in this country show many big catfish going over 100 pounds caught commercially or on handlines and trot lines. One account mentions a blue catfish weighing 315 pounds caught in the Missouri River in 1866. In recent years, a few catfish over 100 pounds have been caught but didn't qualify as rod and reel records. The world record on rod and reel for blue catfish is a 97-pound fish caught in the Missouri River in South Dakota in 1959. The world record for flathead catfish is a 98-pound fish caught in Lewisville Lake, Texas in June 1986. The record channel catfish weighed 58 pounds and was caught in Santee-Cooper Reservoir in South Carolina in 1964. The record white catfish is a 17-pound 7-ounce fish caught in Success Lake, California in 1981.

Where to Go

In the Midwest and South, the Mississippi, Missouri, Ohio, Illinois, White (in Arkansas and Missouri), and Green (in Tennessee) rivers are noted for catfishing. Also notable is the Tennessee River, especially in the tailwaters below dams such as Watts Bar, Wheeler, Chickamauga, Guntersville, Wilson, Pickwick, and Kentucky. White catfish and channel catfish have been planted in many waters throughout the country and have joined the bass and bluegill in many farm ponds. The white catfish has been introduced into the Great Lakes and in California, where they are plentiful in the lower Sacramento and San Joaquin rivers. White catfish are also found in the Connecticut River and in many lakes and ponds throughout the state. In Virginia, they are found in the Potomac River, while in North Carolina they are common in the Cape Fear and Roanoke rivers. White catfish and channel catfish reach a large size in South Carolina, especially in the Santee-Cooper Reservoir. Many rivers and reservoirs in Texas have catfish, with the Rio Grande one of the best. In Florida, the St. Johns River and its bulge, Lake George, as well as Lake Okeechobee are great catfish waters. In recent years, anglers have also discovered the excellent channel catfishing in Canada, especially in Manitoba. This is only a partial listing; many other waters in the states mentioned also contain catfish.

A huge catfish caught in South Carolina's Santee-Cooper system. Even bigger ones have been taken from these waters.

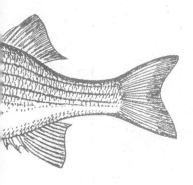

Chapter 25

Bullheads

The bullheads are the smaller members of the catfish family, but what they lack in size they make up in numbers and popularity. This is the fish usually sought by small boys and girls. But don't get the idea that bullheads are only for youngsters. It's common to see adults fishing for bullheads. These fish are able to survive in warm or polluted waters that other fish find uninhabitable, and are available to all anglers, even those near large cities. In fact, the bullhead is the most prevalent species in many park ponds and lakes in big cities.

Three kinds of bullheads are found in the United States. One is the brown bullhead, also called the speckled bullhead, pond catfish, red catfish, marble catfish, brown catfish, and pollywog. Its back ranges from olive to brown; its sides are mottled with light and dark patches. The second species, the yellow bullhead, also called the pond bullhead, has a white chin and whiskers, slightly round tail, and yellow belly. The third one is the black bullhead, also called the creek bullhead, black catfish, and stinger. The body color of this bullhead varies from greenish brown to black shading into a green-

ish bronze. It has a light vertical bar at the base of the tail.

Bullheads, also known as horned pouts in some areas, are now found in many parts of the United States outside of their original range. They are very popular pond fish on farms throughout the country and are beginning to rival the usual inhabitants of these ponds, the black bass and the bluegill.

There is one drawback, however, to stocking bullheads in farm ponds. Though they grow slowly, they breed rapidly and may overpopulate a pond to the detriment of game fish such as trout or bass. If there are too many bullheads in a small body of water, they fail to reach a good size. Because of this, they should be caught as rapidly as possible or taken from the pond with nets at regular intervals to reduce their numbers. In many states there are no closed seasons or bag limits on bullheads. You can fish for them year-round and take as many as you like.

It would be foolish to recommend any specific fishing tackle for bullheads because they can be caught on almost any outfit available.

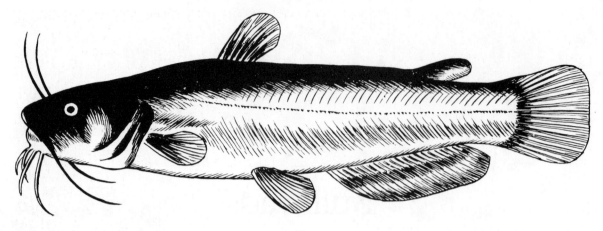

Bullhead

Cane or glass poles are popular with kids and many adults. But you can also catch them on any outfit you may already have—spinning, spincasting, baitcasting, or fly tackle. Of course, if you want to have the most sport and fun you should use the lightest tackle possible. There's a big difference between catching a bullhead on a heavy rod and hooking one on an ultralight spinning rod or a fly rod.

Although bullheads have been known occasionally to strike an artificial lure, they are usually caught on natural baits. The list of such baits is long, but day in and day out the lowly earthworm takes the most bullheads. If you are using big nightcrawlers, one or two worms on a hook are sufficient. But when using smaller garden worms, you can put a half dozen or more on a single hook.

Strips of beef liver, chicken liver, or meat often make good baits. In fact, you can use small pieces of almost any kind of meat (including chicken) to catch bullheads. Small minnows are excellent baits, as are small pieces or strips of almost any fish. Bullheads have also been caught on doughballs, bread, insects, stinkbaits, shrimp, crayfish tails, small frogs and tadpoles, clams, mussels, and most of the other baits used for catfish.

Bullheads bite from spring to fall, but the best fishing usually starts around April in the South and continues from May to September throughout most of their range. When the water warms up past 50 degrees F., they start to become active but bite best when the temperature goes over 60 degrees.

Although bullheads bite during the day, they are not very active in waters that are too clear. The best fishing in rivers is usually when the water is rising and turns murky from a recent rain. Under such circumstances, the bullheads will bite well all day long. In clear lakes and rivers, you'll find the best fishing early in the morning, toward dusk, during the night, and on cloudy or rainy days. As soon as it gets dark, bullheads become active and prowl the shallows and shorelines in search of food.

Consequently, many bullhead fishermen do most of their fishing at night. To get in on the fun and the large catches, bring along a lantern or build a fire on shore, cast out your lines, and wait for a bite. If bullheads are present, it won't be long before your baits will be taken.

Bullheads are gregarious by nature, and where you find one, there will usually be others. They like the slower pools, eddies, and deeper parts of a stream. They prefer mud bottoms in lakes or rivers, but will also be found over gravel, sand, and rocky bottoms in many waters. Look for them under bridges, below dams and riffles or rapids, and along undercut banks and tree roots.

In quieter river waters and in most lakes, you can fish for bullheads without a sinker,

One of the best times to fish for bullheads is at night, soon after sundown. (Oklahoma Dept. of Wildlife Photo)

since the bait will usually go down to the bottom of its own accord. A bobber can be used to indicate bites and also to provide some extra weight for tossing the bait out from shore. But make sure the bait reaches and rests on the bottom.

In faster waters, a sinker is needed. A good rig can be made by tying a bell sinker on the

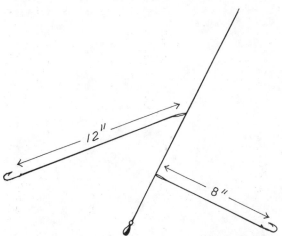

Two different baits can be fished for bullheads on this double rig.

end of your line, then tie a hook on an 8-inch snell about 4 inches above the sinker, and tie a second hook on a 12-inch snell about 4 inches above the first hook. The hooks on this rig can be baited with two different baits, which will lie on or near the bottom where bullheads feed. Since bullheads have large mouths and tend to swallow the bait, long-shanked hooks in size 1 or 1/0 are preferred.

Cast the bottom rig out and allow it to sink, then place the rod in a forked stick or rod holder and wait for a bite. The click should be set on your reel, especially if you are fishing at night. Small dock bells can also be used to indicate bites when you are fishing at night with two, three, or more rods.

When you get the first nibbles, wait a few seconds, until the bullhead swallows the bait, before setting the hook. A large bullhead in a fast river will put up a strong fight on light tackle. But most fishermen using cane or glass poles just yank them out of the water without much ceremony.

You can increase your chances of catching

bullheads by chumming a spot you plan to fish, at dusk, a day or two in advance to give the bullheads a chance to find the food and gather in numbers. For chum, you can use a can or two of cat or dog food, small pieces of worms, meat, fish, clams, or mussels. The same can then be used for bait when you come back later to fish the spot.

When you do catch a bullhead, hold it carefully so that you don't get stuck by the sharp and poisonous spines. They aren't too dangerous, but the wound may be painful and cause the fingers or hand to swell. The best way to remove the hook from a bullhead or small catfish is to grab it so that the spines emerge between your fingers and the fish can be held firmly. Still safer is to pin the fish to the ground with your foot and then remove the hook.

Since bullheads often clamp their jaws on a hook or swallow it deeply, a stick with a notch on one end, a hook disgorger, or longnosed pliers can be a big help in removing it.

Bullheads rarely grow big, averaging between ½ and 1 pound. A few may reach 3 or 4 pounds, but such fish are not caught too often. However, bullheads over 5 pounds have been caught. The rod and reel record for a yellow bullhead is 4 pounds 4 ounces. The record for a brown bullhead is 5 pounds 8 ounces. And the record for a black bullhead is 8 pounds.

Like most catfish, the bullhead makes good eating but must be skinned beforehand. Most anglers cut the skin around the head, grab the edge with gripping pliers, and pull the skin off the body. A quick way to do this without pliers

Bullheads do not grow as big as other catfish, but they make just as good eating. (Ohio Dept. of Natural Resources)

is to cut a slight depression just ahead of the dorsal fin on the fish's back and deep enough to cut through the backbone. Grasp the head of the fish and, cutting away from the head, remove the dorsal fin and spine. Then slit the skin on top of the bullhead's back all the way down to the tail. Finally, grab the fish's body near the tail with one hand, hold onto the head with the other hand, and bend the two sections sharply until the backbone emerges. Grip the end of the backbone between your thumb and a knife blade and pull on the fish's head. This skins the fish and at the same time removes the entrails, which stay attached to the head. This technique sounds difficult, but once you get the knack, it is easy and quick.

Bullheads are found in many parts of the United States. The brown bullhead ranges from Canada throughout the Great Lakes–St. Lawrence region, south to Virginia. A subspecies is found from southern Illinois to Arkansas, the Carolinas, and Florida. The black bullhead is found from Canada to North Dakota, and from the Great Lakes region south to Wyoming, Colorado, Tennessee, and Kansas. A subspecies is found in Alabama, Texas, and Louisiana. The yellow bullhead ranges from North Dakota through the Great Lakes to New York and south to Texas and the Tennessee River system. Another subspecies is found from New Jersey southward.

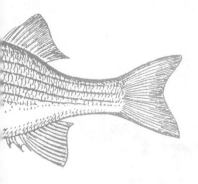

Chapter 26

Shad

There are records of shad being caught on rod and reel in the Connecticut River as early as 1869. But anglers who enjoyed sport fishing for shad remained a handful until after World War II, when spinning tackle came into use and more and more outdoor writers began popularizing shad fishing in their newspaper columns and magazine articles. Now thousands of anglers fish for shad not only along the Atlantic Coast but also along the Pacific Coast, where shad were introduced in 1871.

Shad were so plentiful in the early days of this nation that they choked the rivers and were caught by the colonists in great numbers for use as fertilizer. Since Atlantic salmon were also plentiful in those good old days, the colonists saw little reason to eat the bony shad. Later on, when salmon started to disappear because of pollution, dams, and overfishing, shad became more popular for food. But they too declined in numbers as time went on; by 1900, the runs of shad were small or nonexistent in many rivers. Then steps were taken to eliminate pollution, some of the dams were removed, and permanent fishways were es-

tablished on the remaining dams. Shad have gradually been making a comeback, and good runs have been reestablished in many rivers.

The American shad is also called the common shad, white shad, Atlantic shad, silver herring, and jack. Anglers have also dubbed it the "white lightning" and "poor man's salmon" because of its fast, flashy, fighting qualities on the end of a line. There is also the Alabama shad, which is smaller than the American or white shad. Both are members of the herring family and are sometimes mistaken for the hickory shad, a close relative often found in the same waters. Incidentally, much of the same tackle and techniques described in this chapter can be used for hickory shad, which run up many of the same streams in the spring as the American or white shad. However, they are generally smaller than the American shad, so you can use lighter tackle and smaller lures.

The American shad has a deep, compressed body. Its back is greenish with a metallic luster, and its sides and belly are silvery. There are dark spots on the shoulder, often followed by smaller spots.

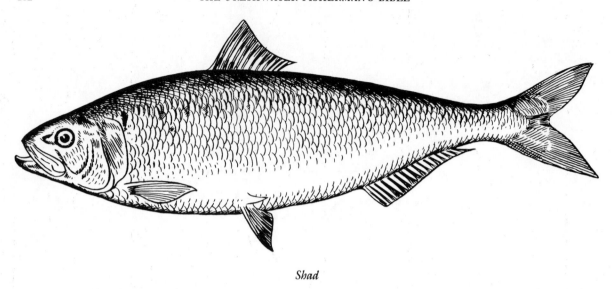

Shad

Shad are found along the Atlantic Coast from the St. Johns River in Florida north to the St. Lawrence River in Canada. The Alabama shad is found in the Gulf of Mexico and ascends some of the rivers there. On the Pacific Coast, they range from Southern California north to Alaska. Shad spend most of their lives in saltwater but return to rivers to spawn. Although they seldom feed during the freshwater run, they will hit lures. Almost all shad are caught on rod and reel in fresh water during the spawning migration.

Tackle

You can use different kinds of freshwater outfits to catch shad: baitcasting, spincasting, spinning, and fly rods are all suitable. Since shad lures are small and light, you should have a rod that can cast lures from 1/16 to 1/2 ounce. The most popular outfit is a light, limber, 6- to 7-foot freshwater spinning rod and a small spinning reel filled with 4- or 6-pound-test line. This is best for casting from shore or a boat. For trolling, a slightly heavier spinning rod with 6- or 8-pound-test line is recommended. Light, limber baitcasting or spincasting rods, with appropriate reels, are

preferred for casting heavier lures or for trolling. Fly rods for trout or bass, from 8½ to 10 feet in length, capable of handling weight-forward No. 8, 9, or 10 fly lines, are suitable. The fly line should be a fast-sinking or extra-fast-sinking or a shooting-head line with monofilament backing on the reel. Light, short rods are best for fishing small streams and the headwaters of rivers. Long, heavy rods are better for big rivers and long casts.

Shad flies are simple lures, often cast with a fly rod or let out in a strong current from a boat with other tackle. These flies are usually tied on Nos. 2, 4, 6, and 8 hooks and consist of a body of silver tinsel and sparse wings of white, red, or yellow feathers. They are equipped with red beads in front of the hook. In fact, a hook wrapped with silver tinsel and two or three silver or red beads in front will often catch shad. Flies with Mylar ribbing or tubing are also good. Some of the old-time favorites include the Connecticut River, Susquehanna River, Tom Loving, Maryland, Western, and California. There are many others tied especially for shad in specific rivers and areas.

You can also use gaudier trout flies such as the Parmachene Belle, Scarlet Ibis, and Yellow Sally. Pacific Coast anglers often use steel-

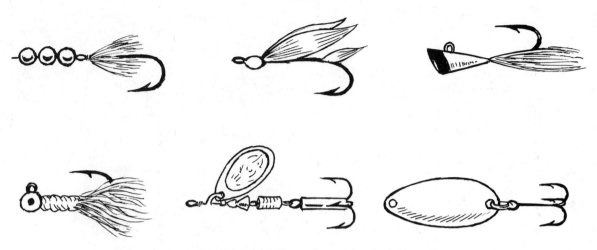

Lures for shad include special flies and conventional spinners and spoons.

head flies with yellow, orange, or red fluorescent yarn bodies and silver or Mylar ribbing. Small streamers and bucktails such as the Black Ghost, Mickey Finn, and White Marabou are also favored. Shad also take many standard dry-fly patterns when they are in the upper reaches or headwaters of rivers in clear, shallow water.

Shad take almost any small, shiny metal lure, such as a spoon or a weighted spinner. Spoons weighing ⅛, ¼, and ⅜ of an ounce, not much longer than 2 inches, in silver, nickel, brass, or gold, are effective. Popular spoons are the smaller Kastmaster, Tony Accetta Pet, Krocodile, Little Cleo, and Dardevle. But the most popular and effective lures are shad darts or other tiny jigs that are fished deep in the swift current where shad are usually found. Jigs from ¹⁄₁₆ to ¼ ounce, with a red head and white body or a red head and a yellow body with white or yellow bucktail hair tied around the hook, are the most popular.

On some rivers, anglers often troll with a tandem rig consisting of a small spoon attached by a swivel to the line and another lure, usually a small jig, attached to a 3-foot leader, which in turn is tied to the swivel. This is trolled, sometimes with a bit of added weight.

Shad have been caught on worms, tiny minnows, and grass shrimp. But few anglers fish for them with baits; most prefer to use flashy and effective artificials.

Seasonal Tactics

The shad fishing season varies according to the location, weather, and water temperature. It may start as early as December, with good fishing during January, February, and March, on the St. Johns River in Florida. Farther north, it usually begins in April or May, with May and early June the peak periods. In California, the season may start in March and continue through May. In Oregon and Washington, May and June are good months, with the fishing often continuing into July.

The time of day to go shad fishing depends on where you fish. On the St. Johns River, some of the best fishing is in the middle of the day. Farther north you can have good fishing early in the morning and in the late afternoon and evening. On the Connecticut River it was found that shad are most active at water temperatures between 62 and 71 degrees F. In northern rivers, they don't hit as well on cold, stormy, windy days as they do on warmer days. Fishing is better on overcast, cloudy days, early in the morning and toward evening, than on sunny days. Sudden rains that raise the water level and muddy the river spoil the fishing.

An important fact to keep in mind is that shad travel in schools at various depths, and their behavior is unpredictable. They may be inactive for hours, then suddenly start hitting. After a few minutes to an hour of furious activity, they may suddenly quit or leave. Then you can cast for hours without getting a strike.

Since shad move upstream to spawn, they follow the main channels and the strongest flow of water. You will therefore find them darting in and out along the edges of such channels. They often flash and turn in the current, or may even roll on top. In shallow, clear water, you can often see them milling around or lying in the current. But more often than not, shad are near the bottom in the deeper pools and eddies. The best fishing is usually in spots where there are obstructions such as falls, dams, or shallow rapids that concentrate the shad in a small area. The bend in a river where the water is deep and the current strong is also a hotspot.

On some rivers it's easy to locate the best shad fishing spots, since you'll find anglers lining the banks or wading shoulder to shoulder and casting to the fish. Or you will see a small fleet of boats trolling or anchored in a spot where shad are present.

When fishing lures, the usual procedure is to cast a spoon or jig slightly upstream and across the current and allow it to swing and sink toward the bottom. Most strikes occur at the end of the arc when the lure starts to rise. Steady reeling brings strikes, but also try retrieving the lure in short jerks. This is especially effective with shad darts or jigs, which have no built-in action. You should feel the lure touch bottom every so often. If you are not getting down deep enough, add some weight to the line or change to a heavier lure.

Flyrodders use either weighted flies, weight added to the leader, or a sinking fly line to get down deep enough. Here again the best results are obtained by casting upstream and across and letting the fly swing downstream

This angler has hooked a shad in the Merrimack River in Massachusetts. Shad put up a great fight on light tackle. (Bob Harris Photo)

close to the bottom. If the current is fast, you usually don't have to give the fly any added action. But in the slower currents or quieter waters, you can give the fly short twitches during the drift or after the swing.

Shad have also been known to hit a No. 12 or 14 dry fly when they are in water not more than a foot or two deep. Best results are obtained by skating the fly on the surface so that it creates a slight ripple. This fishing is most productive late in the season when the shad are in the clear, shallow upper reaches of the river, and especially when caddis flies are hatching.

Casting for shad can also be done from an anchored or drifting boat, but most anglers prefer to troll. Anywhere from 50 to 150 feet of line is let out, and the spoon, spinner, or jig is trolled slowly, close to the bottom. A combination rig with a small spoon on the end of the line and a tiny jig about 2 feet above it on a short dropper is effective. Work the rod up and down in short jerks while trolling, or you can let the current do the work of activating the lures. You'll often catch more shad if you troll across the current at an angle rather than directly upstream or downstream.

Another method is to anchor the boat above a good spot and then let your lure hang suspended in the current just above the bottom. A spoon usually has its own action, but shad

darts or jigs should be twitched at regular intervals. If you have trouble getting the lure down close to the bottom, try a rig with a three-way swivel. Attach a 3-foot leader with the lure to one eye of the swivel; a dropper with a sinker to another eye, and the fishing line to the remaining eye. With this rig, use a small weighted spinner or a spoon.

Shad often hit a lure hard, but at other times you'll feel only a series of light taps.

When you hook a shad, you'll know why it has been called "white lightning." It will make a fast, long run, then often leap out of the water so quickly your eyes can barely follow it. It is a game fish that fights right up to the end;

These shad were caught in the Delaware River—one of the most productive rivers along the Atlantic Coast for this species. (Pennsylvania Fish Commission Photo)

many are lost during the battle. Shad have soft mouths, and a sudden pull will rip the hook out of their jaws. They must be played with extreme care, and even then you'll probably lose more fish than you'll land. A long-handled, wide-mouthed net is needed to land your catch.

Shad can reach 15 pounds in weight, but most range from about 3 to 6 pounds. Nowadays, an 8-pound shad is considered a big one. The record American shad on rod and reel is an 11-pound 4-ounce fish caught in the Connecticut River in Massachusetts on May 19, 1986, by Bob Thibodo. The Alabama shad runs smaller, from 1 to 2 pounds, but has been known to reach 4 pounds. Hickory shad are even smaller, usually ranging from 1 to 2 pounds, or a bit more.

The females, or "roe shad," grow larger than the males, or "bucks." Shad roe is considered a delicacy, and the females command a higher price in the fish market than the males. Shad are very bony and unless properly cleaned and prepared are difficult to eat. Boning a shad to remove the fine bones is an art few anglers have learned. A fillet of shad can be fried, planked, broiled, or baked. Some cooks find that if they make many small cuts or slashes along the fillet, then cook it for a long time over low heat, most of the bones will soften or dissolve.

Where to Go

Starting in Florida, we find shad in the St. Johns River in the northeastern part of the state. On the Gulf of Mexico side of Florida, the smaller Alabama shad run in the Chipola, Appalachicola, and Suwannee rivers. In Georgia, the Ogeechee, Woodbine, Satilla, Altamaha, and Savannah rivers have shad. So do some rivers in Alabama. In South Carolina, the Edisto, Cooper, Santee, Black, and Pee Dee rivers can be fished. North Carolina's shad rivers include the Tar, Cape Fear, Neuse, and Roanoke. In Virginia, you can try the James, York, Mattaponi, Chickahominy, Appomattox, Rappahannock, and Potomac rivers. Maryland's Potomac, Susquehanna, Patuxent, and other rivers and streams entering Chesapeake Bay all contain shad. In New York, Pennsylvania, and New Jersey they are found in the Delaware River. There are also runs up the Hudson River, with some fishing below the Troy Dam in upper New York State. Some of the best fishing spots for shad in the Connecticut River are the Enfield Dam, Windsor Locks Bridge, and Holyoke. The Farmington River and its tributaries in Connecticut also have some shad fishing. In Massachusetts, you can find shad in the Connecticut, Merrimack, Palmer, and North rivers.

On the Pacific Coast, shad are found in California in the American, Russian, Sacramento, Feather, Yuba, and Trinity rivers. In Oregon, the Columbia River, Coos Bay, Coos River, Sandy River, Willamette River, and Umpqua River have shad runs. And in Washington, you can catch shad in the Columbia, Washougal, Chehalis, and Willapa rivers.

On the Pacific Coast, many anglers who formerly were strictly salmon and steelhead fishermen have tried shad fishing and become enthusiasts. Some of them claim that pound for pound the shad will outfight a steelhead or salmon.

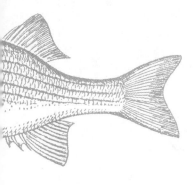

Chapter 27

Carp

No freshwater fishing guide would be complete without mention of the carp. Although the carp still hasn't attained the same popularity in this country as it has in Europe, it is nevertheless sought by thousands of anglers. Carp fishing is a time-honored sport in Europe, and carp fishermen are a highly skilled group who take their sport seriously. They prepare their tackle and baits with utmost care, check the weather, the wind, select their spots, walk carefully and quietly, and fish for many hours and as often as they can. If they catch a really good-sized carp, they consider it a trophy worth mounting. In England, especially, carp are rated very highly as a sport fish, as is evident by the number of carp-fishing clubs and tournaments that have been established there.

At one time there were no carp in the United States and many countries in Europe. Their original range was in Asia and Eastern Europe. They are especially plentiful in China, where they have been raised in ponds for at least 4,000 years. They were introduced to many countries in Europe from their original habitat. Carp were present in England

during the time of Izaak Walton, who wrote about them in his classic, *The Compleat Angler*.

In many European countries, carp were raised in ponds for food and were considered a delicacy. Even to this day, tons of carp are cultivated selectively in ponds for sale to fish markets.

The very first introduction of carp into the United States is hard to pin down, but there are records of carp being brought over from Holland as early as 1832 by a Captain Henry M. Robinson. He kept them in a pond near Newburgh, New York, and it is said that some of the carp escaped into the Hudson River. A Californian, J. A. Poppe, introduced carp into that state in 1872. These fish were brought over from Holstein, Germany, and placed in a private pond in Sonoma County. Of the eighty-three carp only five survived the trip, but these spawned and soon were numerous enough to be sold and stocked in many waters in the West.

But the real march of the carp began in 1877, when the United States Fish Commission imported 345 carp from Germany and placed

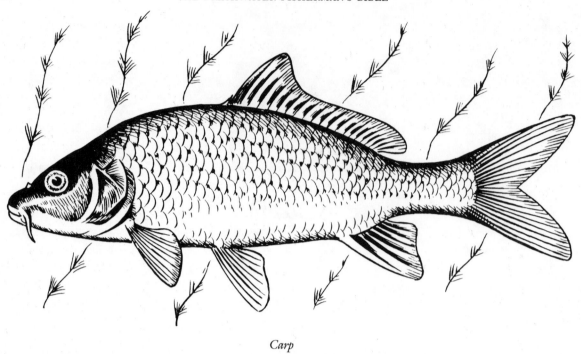

Carp

them in ponds in Druid Hill Park in Baltimore, Maryland. From there, they were transferred to Babcock Lake in Washington, D.C. By 1879, the lake had produced 12,265 carp. Soon there were shipments of young carp going out to twenty-five states and territories.

By 1900, carp had become so plentiful that many freshwater anglers turned against them. Unfortunately for the carp, other game fish began their decline at around this time, and many anglers blamed the carp for this development. They were accused of eating fish and spawn, of muddying the waters, and of not being much of a game or food fish.

We now know that, because of their rooting, feeding, and spawning habits, carp spoil waters for many game fish. They compete for living space and food with the game fish, they roil the waters, and they make them unsuitable for spawning for such fish as black bass and panfish. But it has also been found that carp do not eat the spawn of other fish. In addition, carp have been blamed unfairly for conditions that are really the result of siltation, pollution, fluctuating water levels, and warm water temperatures. There are many waters today in which game fish cannot live or reproduce, but in which the hardy carp often thrives and multiplies. Thus the carp provides fishing in many ponds, rivers, and lakes that would otherwise be barren, at least as far as the angler is concerned.

So while many anglers and some fish and game departments consider the carp a pest in certain waters, it still is a highly regarded sport fish in others. In any case, the carp is here to stay and can provide a lot of fun and sport and good eating.

Although there is only one species of carp in the United States, this species has been divided into three types: Scaled carp are, as the name implies, completely covered with scales; those with patches or large irregular scales are called mirror carp; and those with no scales are called leather carp. Of the three, the completely scaled variety is the most common. Carp are also called German carp, golden carp, silver carp, mud carp, mudhog, waterhog, riverhog, bugle-mouthed bass, and old puckerpuss.

The carp resembles its close relatives, the goldfish and the buffalofish. (See Chapter 28 for information on the buffalofish.) The carp is usually olive-green on the back, with bronze sides and a white or yellowish belly. It has a long dorsal fin with a serrated spine in front. The carp's sucker-type mouth is toothless, but it does have teeth in its throat. It has two barbels, or "whiskers," on each side of its mouth.

Tackle

Carp fishermen use all kinds of tackle, from an ordinary handline to saltwater rods and even fly rods. In waters where the fish aren't too big, a light spinning rod is adequate. But for all-round carp fishing in waters containing big fish, a heavier spinning rod, 6 to 7 feet long, and a reel filled with 8- to 12-pound-test line are better. Another good outfit for all-round carp fishing is a fairly heavy baitcasting rod and reel with 15- to 20-pound-test line. In Europe, many anglers like to use rods up to 12 feet long for carp fishing. Such rods are becoming popular with some anglers in this country, and are now being made by tackle companies.

Carp have been caught by flyrodders on bass bugs, wet flies, nymphs, small streamers and bucktails. This is especially true during the summer months, when carp may be feeding on insects such as Japanese beetles. (Bass bugs and dry flies are particularly effective at this time.) When fishing flies or bugs, wait until you see a fish lying in the water or slowly swimming below the surface. Then cast the fly about 4 feet in front of the carp and let it settle slowly with no added action.

Carp also hit plugs, spoons, spinners, and jigs. One of the top lures is the Ugly Bug, a jig-type lure made by the Gapen Tackle Company. This lure has long rubber legs and resembles a small water insect or even a baby crayfish. The best colors are black or brown, and the 1/16- and 1/8-ounce weights are most effective. Dan Gapen, the manufacturer of this lure, has taken carp up to 24 pounds on the Ugly Bug by working it very slowly along the bottom in river pools where crayfish are abundant. The lure also works in lakes, especially those without weeds or vegetation. Gapen has also caught carp on other lures. He finds that adding a bit of natural bait—a worm or corn kernals—to the lure produces more strikes. You might also try dipping your lure in some kind of scent or flavoring that appeals to fish.

Most anglers fish for carp with natural or prepared baits, and at the top of the list is the time-honored doughball bait. Doughballs are usually prepared from flour or cornmeal mixed with various sweetening or flavoring agents. You can make such a bait quickly and easily by combining 1½ cups of boiling water with 1½ cups of cornmeal. Stir this mixture over a low flame for about five minutes, adding about 2 or 3 tablespoons of sugar, molasses, or honey. When the cornmeal becomes thick and sticks to the sides of the pot, it is ready. Let the mixture cool and then knead it until it becomes thick and smooth. Form a ball and keep it wrapped in aluminum foil or wax paper in a refrigerator until ready to use.

Some anglers also add vanilla flavoring or strawberry gelatin to the mixture. Add the package of gelatin to the boiling water at the same time as the flour or cornmeal, stirring constantly. The gelatin makes the dough softer and more gummy and also gives off a scent that carp evidently like.

Another simple recipe for doughballs calls for cornflakes, to which you add some flour and then water. Knead until the ingredients are well mixed, then form balls.

Doughballs are impaled on either a single hook (such as the Eagle Claw No. 1 or 2 for small fish, or Nos. 1/0 to 3/0 for big fish) or on a small treble hook. Hooks can be covered entirely, right up to the eye, the doughball formed into a large pear shape. This will also provide weight for casting, thereby eliminating the need for sinkers in quiet water. Small carp prefer smaller doughballs.

Another good bait for carp is fresh white bread. Just break off a chunk from the inside

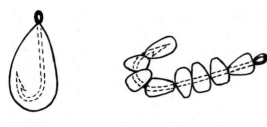

Doughball (left) and corn kernels are popular carp baits.

of a loaf, knead it to form a ball, and put it on the hook. Carp also take bread crust floating on top of the water or suspended just off the bottom. Some anglers use bobbers. Others fish the bait plain or on a bottom rig. Since carp are suspicious and cautious and often refuse a bait if they feel the weight, many anglers prefer to use a sliding egg-shaped sinker slipped on the line above a barrel swivel. This enables the carp to pull the line through the sinker without feeling the weight. A 20-inch leader and a hook complete the rig.

Carp have also been caught on fresh, cooked, or canned corn kernels, peas, lima beans, parboiled potatoes and parsnips, mulberries, freshwater clams and mussels, soft-shelled crayfish, and worms.

No expert carp fisherman in Europe would go carp fishing without first "baiting" the waters to attract carp to the area. They scatter boiled potatoes, oatmeal, bread, crackers, or canned corn on the water two or three days before they plan to fish. This attracts the carp and shortens the wait for a bite. However, baiting, or chumming, is illegal in many states or waters, so check your state and local laws before doing this.

Seasonal Tactics

The best carp fishing is usually in May and June, when the fish start to feed after a long winter fast. At this time, they also come into shallow water to spawn very near the shoreline. Carp like warm water and move about a lake in search of it. They feed in the shallows

if the temperature of the water is between 50 and 70 degrees F. When the shallows cool, they head for deeper water, and do not feed much in water below 50 degrees. As mentioned earlier, carp are extremely hardy fish and can tolerate temperatures in the 90s, but they are not as active at such temperatures.

In the spring and fall, carp fishing can be good throughout the day. But in the middle of the day during the summer months, carp will be in the shallows, either lying just below the surface or slowly cruising back and forth on top, but usually not biting. Then the best times to fish are early in the morning, in the evening, and at night. On cloudy, rainy, or windy days, however, carp often feed even in the middle of the day. If there is a fairly strong wind blowing food toward shore, fishing improves.

Though carp can adapt themselves to many different kinds of water, they prefer and thrive best in waters with muddy bottoms and lots of vegetation. They are less abundant in cool lakes or rivers with hard or rocky bottoms. Productive spots are quiet pools and coves, and swampy or marshy waters. Carp are also found in many tidal rivers, right down to brackish water. Here, the fishing is governed by the tides, with good fishing in the shallows, marshes, and swamps at high tide and in the deeper channels, holes, and pools at low tide.

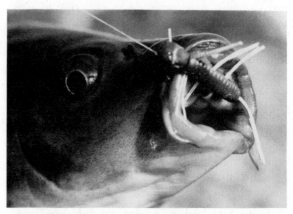

Carp are caught at times on artificial lures such as this Ugly Bug, which has a jig head, soft body, and many rubber legs. (Dan Gapen Photo)

Carp often form schools. In the spring, when they come very close to shore to spawn, you can see and hear them splashing loudly. One large female will be surrounded by several smaller males crowding against her. But after spawning, the carp become smart, wary, and cautious, and the only way to catch them is with a quiet approach. Keep a low profile so that the carp won't see you or your shadow. Walk softly. You need a lot of patience to be a good carp fisherman and often have to sit quietly for hours waiting for a bite.

Carp do not rush a bait, as do trout, bass, or even panfish, but rather feed very slowly and deliberately, grubbing in the mud and vegetation along the bottom for their food. They may pick up a bait and drop it several times before they finally take it for good. Most carp fishermen use two or three rods, which they place in forked sticks or rod holders along the bank. They let the baits sink to the bottom, then set the clicks on their reels, especially when fishing in rivers where a strong current would take out slack line. Other anglers fishing quiet waters in lakes prefer to leave the bail open on a spinning reel or put a baitcasting reel into free-spool. Or they coil some line on the ground to allow plenty of slack so a carp can pick up a bait and move off with it without feeling any tension.

The first indication of a bite will be a slight movement of the line where it enters the water. Don't try to set the hook when you see these first nibbles. Keep waiting; if the carp decides to take the bait, the line will suddenly straighten out fast and rise from the water. That's the time to grab the rod and set the hook.

If you are using light tackle, you'll probably be surprised at the speed and strength of a carp. The small ones are fast and are often mistaken for bass or other game fish when they make their runs back and forth. A big carp is slower but often takes off on a long, powerful run. They also have plenty of endurance, which means that you can't rush or horse them when using light tackle. The best procedure is to play the carp until it's exhausted and can be beached, netted, or gaffed.

Carp are not protected in most waters, and fishing for them by various methods is permitted in many states most of the year. They are shot with bow and arrow when they come into shallow water near shore to spawn or feed. They are also speared, mostly at night from a boat equipped with a powerful light. Carp are also snagged with single or treble hooks on the end of a strong line and pole as they run up narrow brooks, or whenever they gather in numbers. In the winter, they are snagged through the ice. Skin divers have taken many carp with spear guns in waters where such underwater hunting is allowed.

Though most of the carp you catch on rod and reel will weigh from about 3 to 10 pounds, carp weighing from 10 to 30 pounds are not rare. Carp in the 40- to 50-pound class are sometimes taken in nets by commercial fishermen and from lakes being cleared by fish and game departments. There is also a report of a carp weighing 74 pounds caught by an angler in Mississippi. But it wasn't recognized as a record because the rod was handed to another angler when the reel froze, and the first angler waded into the water to grab the fish. The present official rod and reel record is a 75-pound 11-ounce carp caught in Lac de St.-Cassien, France, on May 21, 1987. Every so often, a carp in the 80- or 90-pound class is taken by commercial fishermen.

What do you do with carp, after you catch them? Eat them, of course; properly prepared, they make a fine meal. In Europe and some of the larger cities in the United States, carp are relished by gourmets. They can be fried, broiled, steamed, baked, pickled, or made into fish cakes. Smoked carp is considered a delicacy and is expensive. Any good fish cookbook will have recipes for preparing and cooking carp.

Some of the best carp fishing is found in big rivers, lakes, and reservoirs such as the Hudson, Connecticut, Delaware, Potomac, and Mississippi rivers, and Lake Ontario. The Patuxent River in Maryland has produced many carp from 20 to 40 pounds. There are so many other waters where carp are found that there is no space here to list them all. Write your state fish and game department for a list of the waters containing carp in your area.

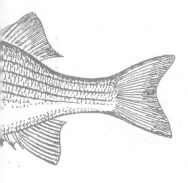

Chapter 28

Other Fishes

This chapter includes fishes taken on rod and reel that deserve mention even though they are not as common or popular as the others covered in this book.

Rock Bass

Rock bass are found in almost two thirds of the United States, from the Great Lakes to the St. Lawrence River west to Wyoming, Colorado, and Arizona and south to the Gulf of Mexico and Florida. They have been introduced widely, especially in the East, where formerly there were none. They are also called the goggle-eye, redeye, sun perch, lake bass, sunfish bass, frogmouth perch, redeye sunfish, redeye bream, redeye perch, rock sunfish, and just plain rock.

Most rock bass are caught by anglers fishing for other species. Yet the rock bass can provide some excellent sport and fine eating. It is a very willing biter and, once located, is usually easy to catch.

As the name implies, the rock bass loves to hang around rocks. In fact, it prefers the same rocky areas as the smallmouth bass in most waters. However, rock bass like the slower, quieter spots rather than the fast, turbulent currents. In rivers, look for rock bass in the rocky stretches and over gravel bottoms. They are found along undercut banks and rock ledges, under overhanging trees or branches or bushes, around logs, and anywhere else they can find shade and cover. Rock bass in rivers stay out of the main currents and fast-water, preferring instead the quiet pools, eddies, and backwaters. Big rock bass in rivers are often found in the tails of pools, below dams, and around bridge supports and sunken trees. Look for them on the upstream side of obstructions, waiting for the slow current to bring them food. They are usually in shallow water in the morning, evening, and at night. In the daytime, they stay hidden in shady spots or in deeper water.

Many rock bass are caught by youngsters with cane or glass poles, fishing with or without a bobber. A light or ultralight spinning outfit is good for baitfishing or casting light lures. And, as always, a fly rod will provide the maximum in fun and sport.

Rock Bass

Most rock bass are caught on worms, hellgrammites, grasshoppers, crickets, catalpa worms, mealworms, crayfish, or minnows. Small crayfish, about 2 inches long, make an excellent bait, if you break off the claws and run the hook through the tail. With larger crayfish, break off the tail, peel off the shell, and just use the meat.

Rock bass can also be caught on spinner-and-fly and spinner-and-bait combinations. They also take weighted spinners, small spoons, and jigs. Flyrodders can catch rock bass on dry flies such as the Royal Coachman, the Wulffs, bivisibles, Irresistible, Goofus Bug, and Muddler Minnow. Wet flies such as the Black Gnat, Western Bee, Red Ibis, Coachman, Colonel Fuller, Woolly Worm, and various nymph patterns are also productive. Small streamers and bucktails work well, since rock bass often feed on small minnows. Bass bugs and panfish bugs can also be used.

Small rock bass often travel in small schools and are usually easy to catch. The bigger rock bass are more wary, more solitary, and more likely to be found in deeper water or hiding in the shade. To catch them, you have to approach their hiding spots carefully and make fairly long casts, especially when the water is clear.

Although rock bass aren't great fighters on the end of a line, they are often day-savers when other fish refuse to bite or are hard to locate. And they make pretty good eating if taken early or late in the year from cold, clean waters. The flesh of those taken from waters with muddy bottoms, especially during the summer months, may be soft and have a muddy flavor.

Eels

This snakelike fish has no doubt repelled many anglers who do their best to avoid catching them. But many others, having discovered that this unique fish can provide fun and is a table delicacy second to none, fish for eels often.

The eel, of course, is a true fish, despite its appearance. It breathes in the water by means of gills like any other fish, whereas a snake breathes out of the water by means of lungs. Eels vary from gray to greenish-brown to black along the back, these colors gradually blending with the whitish belly.

The American eel is found along the East

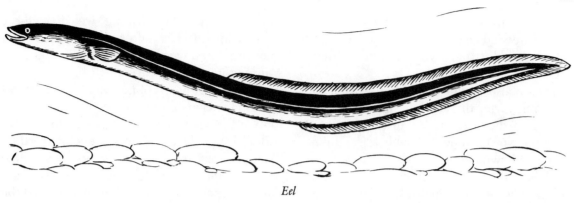

Eel

Coast from Labrador to the Gulf of Mexico. Eels migrate up the Mississippi River and its tributaries and are found in many states east of the Rocky Mountains. The American eel is similar to the European eel, which is highly prized for food. Both the American and European eels travel to the Sargasso Sea region near Bermuda to spawn. The female eels spend six to eight years in freshwater lakes and rivers. Then they descend the rivers in the autumn to meet the male eels, which have been living in brackish and saltwater bays. Together, they slowly move toward their spawning areas in the Sargasso Sea. Here in the deep water the females lay their eggs and die.

When the eggs hatch, the larvae of the eels are shaped like tiny willow leaves. For a while, they remain in deep water, but then slowly rise to the surface and start a slow drift toward land, which they reach in about a year. Here they change into the cylindrical form of the adult eel, but are still transparent and only about 2 or 3 inches long. At this stage, they are known as glass eels, or elvers. Soon they lose their transparency and take on the dark colors of their parents. Then the females ascend the freshwater rivers, while the males remain in the brackish and saltwater bays and estuaries.

To catch eels, you can use handlines, cane or glass poles, spinning, spincasting, baitcasting, or fly rods. Most eels run pretty small (rarely more than a pound or two in weight), so light tackle will provide the most fun and sport.

Eels feed mostly on or near the bottom, poking their pointed snouts into every crevice or hole in search of food. They feed on a wide variety of animal matter, including crayfish, frogs, worms, insects, and small fish. Worms and small minnows usually make the best eel baits.

When fishing for eels, use a rather thick line and a No. 1 or 1/0 long-shanked hook such as the Carlisle. Eels will wrap themselves around a line and often swallow a hook deep. A long-shanked hook is easier to remove and is less likely to be swallowed all the way down. And a heavy, thick line is easier to untangle if an eel gets wrapped up in it. Also, bring along a dry rag to hold the eel when removing the hook, since they are slippery and hard to hold. A potato sack or burlap bag is handy for carrying any eels you keep.

Eels can be caught from April to November in most waters, but spring and fall are the best times. If you can find a river where the eels are migrating to the sea in the autumn, you'll have some great fishing at this time, particularly in September and October.

The best eel fishing is at dusk and throughout the night. Usually the darker the night, the better the fishing. Eels can also be caught during the daytime, especially in rivers that are muddy from recent rains.

Most eels are caught by still-fishing from shore, with the angler casting out his line and bait and letting it lie on the bottom. In lakes or quiet pools and eddies, no sinker is needed to take the bait down and hold it close to the bottom. But in rivers with fast currents, a small sinker is needed on a bottom rig. And a weight is also needed if you have to cast to a distant spot.

Eels are also caught by bobbing with a gob of several worms threaded on fine thread and lowered to the bottom. When the eels start eating the worms, they are slowly raised to the surface and swung into a basket or net.

Eels can be speared at night while wading in shallow water or from a boat while shining a powerful light. A special spear with several tines is needed.

You can also catch eels for food or bait by using eel pots, similar to minnow traps with funnel entrances, which are baited with dead fish or meat and allowed to remain on the bottom overnight.

Any small eels you catch can be used live as baits for black bass and striped bass. Larger eels can be cut up into sections and used to catch catfish. And, of course, eels make good eating and have a firm, sweet flesh that can be fried, boiled, or pickled. Smoked eels are considered a delicacy and bring a fancy price in gourmet shops and fish markets.

Suckers

Suckers are popular. They are usually the first fish to run in any numbers early in the spring, soon after the ice is out. Many anglers who can't wait to start fishing welcome these rubber-lipped fish after the long winter months, when word gets around that they are running in a nearby stream.

There are nearly one hundred different kinds of suckers found in North America. But only a few species are big enough to be considered sport fish, and only a few bite readily. Among these are the white sucker (also called the common sucker); the redhorse sucker (also known as the redfin or redfin sucker); and the longnose, or northern sucker. These are the three main species of suckers caught by anglers.

Suckers are caught on all kinds of fishing tackle, from ordinary handlines to fancy casting outfits. The cane or glass pole probably catches more suckers in small streams than any other gear. A fly rod provides a lot of sport on these narrow, confined waters. On larger, wider rivers and lakes, a light baitcasting, spincasting, or spinning outfit is more suitable.

Most suckers are taken on small worms. Other baits include the tail meat of a crayfish, the soft meat of freshwater clams or mussels, grubs, insects, small pieces of meat, and doughballs. All of these should be fished on Nos. 2 to 8 hooks.

The best time to catch suckers is early in the spring, as soon as possible after ice-out, when the warm rains swell the streams and the suckers move up narrow creeks to spawn. This may occur as early as February and March

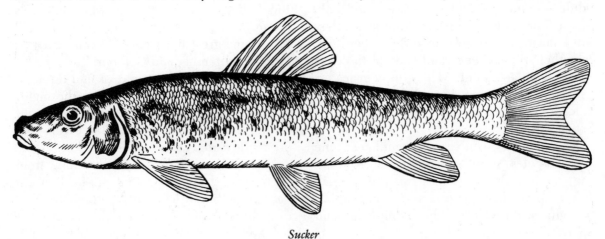

Sucker

along their southern range and as late as May or June farther north. April is usually a good month in many waters.

Later on during the summer months, suckers are harder to catch because they scatter widely and do less feeding. You'll often see them gathered in small schools suspended midway between the surface and the bottom. They aren't interested in baits and do not take baited hooks. Some anglers then resort to snagging, if this is allowed in their area. They tie three or four treble hooks above a small sinker, cast this into the school of suckers, and jerk violently to hook a fish in the body.

The most productive method of sucker fishing when they are on the bottom and feeding is to flip out your baited hook and let it sink. If the current is strong you may have to use a bottom rig or add a small weight above the hook. Then you let the bait lie on the bottom and wait for a bite. Suckers, like carp, feed slowly along the bottom, sucking up the mud or sand to find food. They'll come across your bait sooner or later, but they rarely take it in a hurry. Give them plenty of time to mouth the bait, and don't try to set the hook at the first nibbles. Wait until the line starts to move away fast before you set the hook.

Suckers are not too popular as food fish because of their numerous small bones. But they have a sweet, tasty flesh, which is at its firmest and best early in the spring. They aren't as good during the summer months, when they turn soft and may also have a muddy flavor from certain waters. The bones can be removed from the larger fish. Cut the smaller fish crosswise and fry the pieces in deep fat or oil; this will usually soften the bones. Suckers can also be baked or broiled.

Whitefish

One group of fishes neglected by most anglers are the whitefishes. These silvery fish with large, smooth scales and forked tails are fairly numerous and are being discovered as sport fish by more and more anglers. Although there are many species of whitefishes found in North America, only three are highly prized as sport fish at the present time.

One of the largest and most numerous is the lake whitefish, whose range extends from New York to New England, Canada, Newfoundland, Labrador, and Alaska. It is very common in the Great Lakes region, where millions are caught commercially.

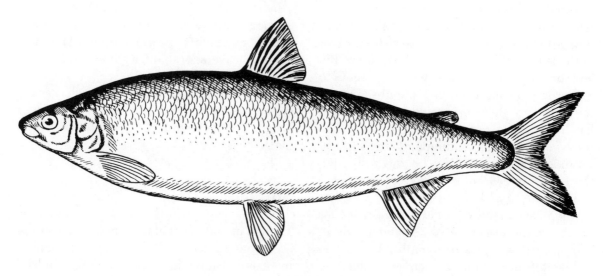

Whitefish

The second popular whitefish species is the cisco, or lake herring. It resembles in habits and appearance the lake whitefish and is found in many lakes and some rivers in the Great Lakes region, in Canada, and in Alaska.

The third member of this group is the mountain whitefish, also called the Rocky Mountain whitefish. Found mostly in lakes and streams from the Rocky Mountains west to the Pacific and in British Columbia, it is most plentiful in Montana, Wyoming, Utah, Idaho, Oregon, and Washington.

Most of the tackle used for other game fish can be utilized for whitefish. For deep fishing, the spinning rod and baitcasting rod are best. For shallow water and surface fishing, the fly rod has proven effective. The lighter, limber rods are preferable because whitefish don't run too big and have tender mouths.

Whitefish often hit wet flies, dry flies, nymphs, tiny streamers or bucktails, spoons, spinners, or jigs. They'll also take worms, small minnows, cubes cut from larger fish, salmon eggs, nymphs, or mature insects.

It's a common practice when fishing for whitefish to chum, or bait, the area ahead of time for several days, since whitefish tend to gather in spots where they get a free handout. (Canned sweet corn, boiled rice, or tiny pieces of fish or meat can all be used as chum.)

You'll find lake whitefish at various depths, depending on the season. In spring and fall, they may be in depths from 10 to 60 feet, while in the summer they may go down as far as 150 feet or even more. Lake whitefish tend to gather around shoals or river mouths. During the summer, they may come up to feed on hatching insects, especially mayflies, at which time you'll see them dimpling the surface. During the winter, they can be caught through the ice in water from 20 to 50 feet deep.

The time to bring out your dry or wet flies is when lake whitefish or ciscoes are rising for insects on the surface. Rocky Mountain whitefish also hit wet flies or nymphs. When you see whitefish dimpling the surface to feed on insects, cast your fly right to the spot. Since

whitefish hit fast, you have to be alert to set the hook. The best time for this sort of fishing is usually from late afternoon until dark.

Casting or trolling very slowly with tiny spinners and spoons will often take whitefish and ciscoes. Tiny jigs are also effective, but have to be retrieved at various depths until you locate the fish. The same is true of any other lure. Unless you reach the level where whitefish are suspended or feeding, you won't get any strikes.

Baitfishing can be done near the bottom in spring, summer, fall, and winter for lake whitefish and ciscoes. No. 6, 8, or 10 hooks, baited with tiny live or dead minnows or cubes cut from larger fish, can be used with or without a sinker, depending on the depth.

A hooked whitefish often puts up a surprising fight, somewhat like a trout's struggle. It may thrash on the surface, roll, twist, then bore deep. Stream-dwelling whitefish such as the Rocky Mountain species are exceptionally lively and strong, especially with the help of a strong current. Whitefish must be handled carefully on the end of the line because they have tender mouths from which hooks pull out easily.

Most lake whitefish will range from 1 to 5 pounds in weight, though some specimens weighing from 15 to 20 pounds have been caught commercially. Ciscoes are smaller, averaging from ½ to 1 pound, but have been known to reach 8 pounds. Rocky Mountain whitefish average about a pound and sometimes reach 4 pounds.

Highly prized as food, whitefish have a sweet, delicious flesh that can be fried or baked. Smoked whitefish is a delicacy sold in many stores.

Sturgeon

Though not often caught by anglers on rod and reel, the sturgeon offers the nearest thing to big-game fishing in North American inland fresh waters. There are several species of stur-

Sturgeon

geon, but the one usually caught on rod and reel is the white sturgeon. This is the largest of the sturgeons in our waters, sometimes reaching 12 feet in length and over 1,000 pounds in weight. The white sturgeon is found in rivers from California to Alaska, and penetrates far inland during its spawning run. Anglers fishing for striped bass, salmon, and steelhead in Pacific Coast rivers sometimes hook sturgeon by accident, but only the smaller ones are landed on the light tackle used.

Sturgeon were once plentiful in most rivers along the Pacific coast. The Snake River in Idaho formerly produced many each year, but now the fishing has fallen off drastically, and big sturgeon are scarce. A few still run up the Columbia and Willamette rivers in Oregon, but since dams have blocked their runs, they are also becoming scarce in these rivers. Your best bet is to fish the Fraser River in British Columbia, where sturgeon going over 700 pounds have been caught on rod and reel in recent years. Some sturgeon are also caught in California bays and rivers, and there is also some sturgeon fishing in Florida's Apalachicola River below the Woodruff Dam.

If you want to catch big sturgeon you have to equip yourself with heavy tackle. Although many fish up to 360 pounds have been taken on heavy saltwater surf-spinning tackle, a conventional saltwater rod and reel with revolving spool is much better. For this type of fishing, big saltwater reels loaded with lines testing anywhere from 50 to 80 pounds are used.

Large hooks—Nos. 6/0 to 9/0—are attached to short leaders and tied above a sinker weighing from 3 to more than 16 ounces to anchor the bait in a strong river current.

Various baits are used for sturgeon, depending on the area and river being fished. Anglers in Washington and Oregon often use several lampreys on a big hook. Others like to use smelt, sardines, herring, or other small fish. Pieces of meat can also be tried, as well as several big nightcrawlers on a hook. Anglers fishing in the Apalachicola River in Florida find that a large clump of river moss or green algae gathered from the rocks in the water makes a good bait.

Sturgeon in rivers are usually found in the deeper pools and fairly fast-flowing water along the edges of the main current. The deep water below dams or high falls blocking their spawning runs upriver are also hotspots. Most of the fishing for big sturgeon is done from boats, although they have also been caught from shore. You have to give a sturgeon plenty of time to find and take the bait. A sturgeon swims along the bottom slowly, sucking up food. It usually takes the bait gently at first and plays with it for quite a while. But when it does swallow the bait, the line will move off steadily, at which time you can set the hook.

A hooked sturgeon is not a spectacular fighter, but it is powerful and has plenty of endurance. The fight may last an hour or two or even longer, depending on the size of the fish, the strength of the current, and the tackle used. In a boat, you can follow a big fish downriver and stand a better chance of landing it than when fishing from shore.

Along the Pacific coast, sturgeon are caught year-round, but the spring, early summer, and winter months are usually most productive. In the Apalachicola River in Florida, the best months are from April to September.

The lake or rock sturgeon is a species sometimes caught on rod and reel in the Great Lakes region. They are also speared through the ice in Wisconsin.

Sturgeon, as almost everyone knows, is the main source of genuine caviar, and smoked sturgeon is an expensive delicacy. But the flesh can also be eaten fresh, either fried, broiled, or baked. Smoked sturgeon is sold in many delis in large cities.

Freshwater Drum

Another relatively unknown but, at times, worthwhile fish is the freshwater drum. Also known as the drum, sheepshead, gray bass, silver bass, white perch, grunt, grunter, croaker, ginder, gou, and gaspergou, it is a member of the Family Sciaenidae, which includes many species of saltwater drums and croakers. Most of these fish, including the freshwater drum, are capable of making a croaking or drumming sound, hence the names.

The freshwater drum is found from the Hudson Bay drainage south to Lake Champlain and the Great Lakes drainage through the Mississippi River region south to the Gulf of Mexico.

It lives in lakes and rivers and usually prefers shallow water near shore. It can be caught on almost any freshwater tackle. Most of the freshwater drum hooked on artificial lures are caught by anglers casting for other fish.

To catch them deliberately, the best baits are a soft-shelled crayfish, shrimp, worm, or piece of fish. The bait should be fished on the bottom, since the drum feeds on clams, mussels, snails, and crayfish.

Freshwater drum average from 2 to 5 pounds. A 15- to 20-pounder is taken from time to time, and there are records of this fish reaching 50 or 60 pounds. It is not considered a particularly good food fish, though it is eaten quite a bit in the South.

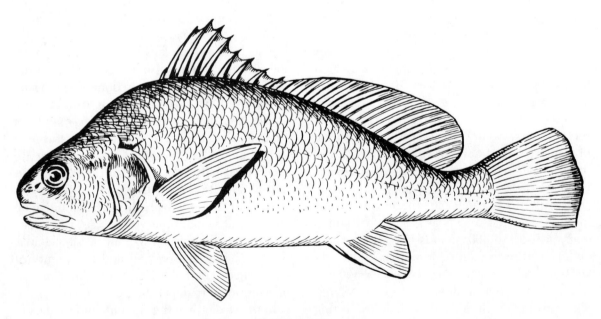

Freshwater Drum

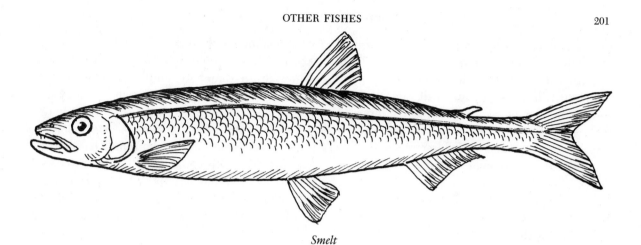

Smelt

Smelt

A more popular fish is the American smelt, also known as the saltwater smelt, freshwater smelt, frostfish, and icefish. This small, slender, silvery fish with a translucent green back is found from Labrador south to New York and in Newfoundland, New Brunswick, Nova Scotia, Ontario, Quebec, the Great Lakes region, and in many New England rivers and lakes.

In the spring, soon after the ice is out, smelt run up rivers from brackish or saltwater bays and estuaries to spawn. They also enter rivers emptying into large lakes. This may occur in March, April, or May, depending on the area and water temperatures.

During these spawning runs, millions of smelt are caught at night with dip nets. The congregation of men, women, and kids all engaged in smelt dipping on some of the rivers emptying into the Great Lakes is a sight to see. Equipped with hip boots or waders, a flashlight or headlight, and a long-handled dip net, they wade in shallow water and draw the wide-mouthed net to scoop up the silvery fish.

Smelt can also be caught on tiny hooks baited with small minnows, pieces of fish, small shrimp, or bits of worm. The best fishing is usually during the fall, winter, and spring in brackish and salt waters. Occasionally smelt also hit a fly or a tiny, bright lure. And on large lakes, such as New York's Lake Champlain, they can be caught through the ice during the winter months, usually on a tiny minnow or a

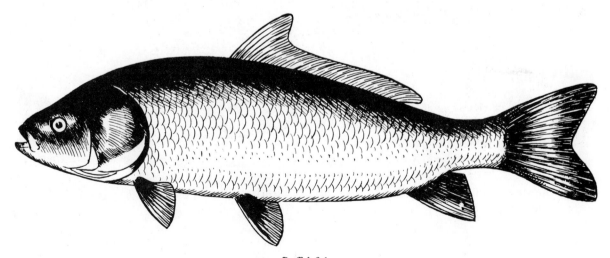

Buffalofish

slice of fish on a hook lowered near the bottom. The bait should be raised and lowered at regular intervals to attract the smelt.

Most of the smelt caught will range from 6 to 8 inches in length, with some reaching 12 inches. Fried, they make delicious eating. During the commercial fishing seasons, tons of smelt are caught to be served in restaurants or sold in fish markets.

Buffalofish

Another of the lesser freshwater fish sometimes caught by anglers is the buffalofish. There are three species: the bigmouth buffalo, the black buffalo, and the smallmouth buffalo. They belong to the sucker family and resemble the carp. They also have the same habits as the carp, preferring sluggish waters and feeding on many of the same foods. Buffalofish, which are not too common in our northern waters, are found mostly in the Mississippi River region. However, some turn up as far north as the lakes and rivers of Minnesota.

Most of the buffalofish that are caught on rod and reel are taken in southern waters on doughball baits. They come big at times; some specimens 4 feet in length and 60 pounds in weight have been reported. Those taken from clean waters have good flavor and make good eating. But buffalofish caught in muddy, weedy waters may have a muddy taste.

Fallfish or Chub

Not many anglers realize that the minnow family can provide great sport on rod and reel. Of course, the carp, which belongs to this family, is well known and popular with many anglers (see Chapter 27). But there are other members of the minnow family that can also be caught on rod and reel. One of the largest is the squawfish, of which there are several species. They attain 2 feet in length and a weight of several pounds. They'll grab a lure or bait and put up a spirited fight in fast water. The squawfishes are found mostly in our western states.

Another member of the minnow family that can provide good sport is the fallfish. It is also called the Mohawk chub, Delaware chub, white chub, silver chub, or just plain chub. It is found from Canada south to Virginia along the East Coast.

Many fallfish are taken by trout or bass fishermen on flies, lures, or natural baits—worms, minnows, crayfish, hellgrammites, and various insects.

Fallfish are often found in the larger rivers and streams in many of the same spots inhabited by trout or smallmouth bass. They are caught by casting or trolling. When first hooked, they put up a fast, lively fight, which has often led anglers to mistake them for trout or small bass. But fallfish lack the endurance of these fish, and after the first few short runs and some thrashing around they soon give up.

Fallfish run from 6 to 10 inches, with a few reaching 20 inches. When caught, they should be cleaned as soon as possible and kept on ice, or else their flesh will turn soft and become unfit for the table. Those taken from cold, clean waters make the best eating. Their flesh is sweet and delicious, despite the presence of some fine bones that must be removed.

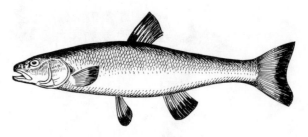

Fallfish or Chub